PRISON POLICY IN IRELAND

This book is the first examination of the history of prison policy in Ireland. Despite sharing a legal and penal heritage with the United Kingdom, Ireland's prison policy has taken a different path. This book examines how penal-welfarism was experienced in Ireland, shedding further light on the nature of this concept as developed by David Garland. While the book has an Irish focus, it has a theoretical resonance far beyond Ireland.

This book investigates and describes prison policy in Ireland since the foundation of the state in 1922, analyses and assesses the factors influencing policy during this period and explores and examines the links between prison policy and the wider social, economic, political and cultural development of the Irish state.

It also explores how Irish prison policy has come to take on its particular character, with comparatively low prison numbers, significant reliance on short sentences and a policy-making climate in which long periods of neglect are interspersed with bursts of political activity all prominent features.

Drawing on the emerging scholarship of policy analysis, the book argues that it is only through close attention to the way in which policy is formed that we will fully understand the nature of prison policy. In addition, the book examines the effect of political imprisonment in the Republic of Ireland, which, until now, has remained relatively unexplored.

This book will be of special interest to students of criminology within Ireland, but also of relevance to students of comparative criminal justice, criminology and criminal justice policy making in the UK and beyond.

Mary Rogan is Lecturer in Socio-Legal Studies at Dublin Institute of Technology. Her research interests include prison policy, criminal justice policy-making, penal reform, prison law, penal politics and the history of punishment. She is a qualified barrister and current Chairperson of the Irish Penal Reform Trust.

PRISON POLICY IN IRELAND

Politics, penal-welfarism and political imprisonment

Mary Rogan

Routledge
Taylor & Francis Group

LONDON AND NEW YORK

First published 2011 by Routledge
2 Park Square, Milton Park, Abingdon, Oxon, OX14 4RN

Simultaneously published in the USA and Canada
by Routledge
711 Third Avenue, New York, NY 10017

Routledge is an imprint of the Taylor & Francis Group

© 2011 MARY ROGAN

Typeset in Bembo
by GCS, Leighton Buzzard, Bedfordshire

British Library Cataloguing in Publication Data
A catalogue record for this book is available from the British Library

Library of Congress Cataloguing in Publication Data
Rogan, Mary.
Prison policy in Ireland: politics, penal-welfarism and political imprisonment/Mary Rogan.
p. cm.
Includes bibliographical references and index.
1. Prisons--Ireland. 2. Prison administration--Ireland. 3. Punishment--Ireland. I. Title.
HV9650.3.R64 2011
365′.9417--dc22
2010038947

ISBN 13: 978-0-415-61618-8 hbk
ISBN 13: 978-0-415-61619-5 ppr
ISBN 13: 978-0-203-82888-5 ebook

To my parents, Anne and Séamus

CONTENTS

LIST OF FIGURES

ACKNOWLEDGEMENTS

I wish to express my sincerest gratitude to a number of people whose expertise, help, encouragement and patience have been invaluable in the completion of this work. I am grateful to Professor Ivana Bacik for her guidance and encouragement and to Professor Ian O'Donnell for his assistance and expertise. I thank the staff of the of the National Archives of Ireland, Dublin, the National Library Archive Collections, Dublin, the Dublin Diocesan Archives, the Kilmainham Jail Archives, the University College Dublin Archives, the Central Statistics Office, the RTÉ Archive the Irish Film Archive, the library staff of Trinity College Dublin, Dublin Institute of Technology, University College Dublin, the Central Catholic Library, Dublin, the British Library and the National Library of Ireland.

A very special word of thanks must go to Professor Mick Ryan for his kindness and encouragement in seeing this book to completion.

Many others have been supportive, understanding and provided friendship and humour along the way. I am grateful to you all.

My deepest thanks are due to my parents. Selfless assistance and encouragement such as theirs can never be repaid but merely acknowledged and I do so here with sincerest gratitude.

INTRODUCTION

This book has a number of interconnected aims. It seeks to investigate and describe prison policy in Ireland since the foundation of the state in 1922, to analyse and assess the factors influencing policy during this period and to explore and examine the links between prison policy and the wider social, economic, political and cultural development of the Irish state. In doing so, it argues that the tools of policy analysis have an important contribution to make to our understanding of penal change and prison policy.

The case of Ireland provides significant explanatory potential, given its historic links close proximity to the United Kingdom, along with a shared language, similar legal system and an inherited set of administrative structures and institutions as well as legislation. However, as will be seen, the course of Irish prison policy after independence shows a different trajectory from that of its nearest neighbour. The reasons for these differences are themselves theoretically significant.

The book discerns three central motifs in this story of Ireland's prisons. The first is that of politics. Irish politics is characterised by centrism, with a lack of ideology apparent. Instead, pragmatic politics, as well as individual reforming Ministers and civil servants, have had a particular impact on the creation of change across prison and other policies. Political crises and upheavals have led to significant penal developments, but in the absence of such catalysts penal change has been slow with a significant degree of inertia evident.

Politics has had another impact on prison policy. Political pressure occasioned by perceived crises in the prison system, particularly overcrowding and a high use of temporary release, has resulted, over time, in expansion of the prison system. The combination of these factors has been more influential than any particular penal ideology or agenda.

The manner of the development of penal-welfarism in Ireland is also of wider importance. Much attention has been focused on the applicability or otherwise of the influential *Culture of Control* (Garland 2001). However, far less engagement with Garland's earlier and arguably more compelling work *Punishment and Welfare* (Garland 1985) is evident. This book examines the 'conditions' in which penal-welfarism may or may not be propagated, providing further insight as to why those conditions may endure or the foundations eroded. The book also shows that penal-welfarism in the form it took in Ireland was influenced greatly by the actions of a small group of influential policy actors. Though the nature of Irish social provision may be especially unusual, the book argues that closer attention to the mechanics of policy-making and the autonomy of those actors would enrich penological scholarship.

The final theme identified is that of political imprisonment. While the question of the penal policies in relation to those considering themselves to be involved in a political conflict with the state has received much attention elsewhere, most notably in Northern Ireland (McEvoy 2001), there has been no comparable analysis of such policies in the Republic of Ireland, particularly during the tumultuous periods during the Civil War after Independence. This book aims to address that absence and contains assessment of the reaction, and resistance, of prisoners in the Republic to such policies. It also explores the manner in which the recurrent presence of a threat of 'subversion' has affected ordinary prison policy. It is the first such book to do so.

Ireland has recently become known for its hidden and dark history in the treatment of those incarcerated in a host of institutions outside prison. While the prison population was low for several decades, there was a network of coercive establishments dealing with those whom society considered to be deviant in some way, particularly regarding sexual morality. This book does not examine that history. The presence of these institutions did have an effect on Irish prison policy, as the prison system was not required to deal with these populations, and the conditions that created those institutions were also influential on the direction of the prison system. However, those seeking to explore the most shameful aspects of the history of Irish confinement will have to look elsewhere (Kilcommins *et al.* 2004; O'Sullivan and O'Donnell 2007). This book deals largely with the adult prison population, and particularly policies as they applied to male prisoners. Other stories are crying out to be written and undoubtedly will be, as more exposure of these matters, such as this book seeks to achieve, will lead to the development of that understanding.

Many areas of Irish crime control and criminal justice need further exploration. It is hoped that this book, along with the growing criminological academy in Ireland, will contribute to the creation of an increased awareness of the factors leading to penal change and the manner in which those changes are felt within prisons. More than this, however, it is hoped that comparative penology will be thereby enriched and the theoretical standpoints used to analyse historical and contemporary prison systems will be tested more closely.

Finally, it should be noted that the term 'Ireland' is used throughout this book to refer to the Republic of Ireland.

The book commences with an analysis of the literature on the sociology of punishment and policy-making. The chapters that follow tell the story of Irish prison policy, its formation and the context in which it was created. Chapter 2 looks at prison policy from Independence (1922) until the end of the 1930s. Chapter 3 examines prison policy during and in the immediate aftermath of World War Two, known in Ireland as 'the Emergency'. Chapter 4 looks at the post-war years while Chapter 5 examines the crucial decade of change – the 1960s. Stagnation in prison policy was followed by an impatience of action and a number of important developments, spearheaded by then Minister for Justice Charles Haughey along with a number of high-ranking civil servants. An analysis of the 1970s follows in Chapter 6, when threats of subversion reappeared and prison populations increased, though elements of a rehabilitationist philosophy were maintained. The 1980s, a decade of crisis involving high levels of overcrowding, the use of temporary release to relieve pressure on accommodation and 'making do' as a form of policy was pursued, are dealt with in Chapter 7. Chapter 8 looks at the 1990s, 'the crucial decade', in which penal expansion was contemplated and commenced on a significant scale. The reasons for this are also explored in Chapter 9, and it is found that politics and practical considerations drove this approach. Chapter 10 concludes with an analysis of the nature of prison policy in Ireland and the manner in which that policy is formed.

1

UNDERSTANDING PRISON POLICY
The sociology of punishment and policy-making

Introduction

This book has three key aims: to investigate and describe prison policy in Ireland since Independence (1922), to analyse and assess the factors influencing policy during this period, and to explore and examine the links between prison policy and the wider social, economic, political and cultural development of the Irish state in these years.

These aims place this work at the intersection of two theoretical and methodological schools within penology: the sociology of punishment and the more recently established area of policy analysis. As well as drawing on the perspectives of both positions to inform this work, this book seeks to show that the best and fullest understandings of prison and broader penal policy in any jurisdiction can be created through an application of the methods and insights provided by penologists and scholars of policy analysis. This chapter explores and critiques the theoretical literature on the sociology of punishment and policy-making, placing the Irish situation within it.

The sociology of punishment

A large body of work has been accumulated within what is termed the sociology of punishment. A number of disparate theories can be identified within this school of thought. However, they have a unifying central feature: that is, the aim to 'explore the means by which society, at any given point, governs itself and maintains order' (Zedner 2004: 76).

A variety of theoretical perspectives have assessed the functions of the prison outside that of the control of crime. These have linked the operation of penal forms to particular ends, including the formation of a 'disciplinary society' in the Foucauldian sense (Foucault 1977), regulation of economic or labour markets, in the Marxist tradition (Melossi 1981; Rusche and Kirchheimer 1968), ideological dominance (Mathiesen 2000), increasing 'social control' (Cohen 1985) or social solidarity following Durkheim (1997). Other theorists, notably Elias (Elias and Jephcott 1994) and Spierenburg (1984) have linked penal changes to underlying social impulses and trends, particularly the increasing 'civilisation' and democratisation of society.

In recent years, another body of theory has developed within the sociology of punishment which has as its aim a multi-variate analysis of punishment and its forms.

Cultural accounts and the prison

A theoretical perspective most associated with the last two decades, 'cultural accounts' of punishment focus less on the function of punishment, or its role in social order. Instead, these interrogate and explore punishment, in the words of Zedner, 'as the product of cultural mentalities and prevailing sensibilities and as contributing to the larger formation of culture' (Zedner 2004: 82). This project has the venerable aim of providing a broad-ranging account of punishment and penal institutions and endeavours to fulfil it by looking at punishment and penal forms from a variety of perspectives.

A number of works in the sociology of punishment utilise the concept of culture and the tools of cultural analysis and a rich body of work has developed tackling a wide variety of topics within the rubric of studies of punishment from a cultural perspective. Cultural accounts have become the latest growth industry in criminology, being utilised in the exploration of many forms of crime, the links between culture 'industries' and crime, as well as methods of crime control and responses to crime. It is the latter type of investigation that most concerns this work.

Garland and 'culture'

One of the most influential theorists working in the field of cultural assessments of punishment is David Garland. His works, most notably *Punishment and Modern Society* (Garland 1990) and, particularly, *The Culture of Control* (Garland 2001), have employed explicitly cultural methods, with *Punishment and Welfare* (Garland 1985) also arguably exhibiting elements of such a methodology. Garland has become, to some degree, the 'straw man' or flag-ship of this approach, depending on one's view of the enterprise. As such, an interrogation of his methods and influences illuminates many of the pertinent issues surrounding cultural studies of punishment and the prison.

Garland posits that punishment is a complex cultural artefact that is informed and influenced by broader conceptions, values, ideas, beliefs that constitute the nature of wider social mentalities and sensibilities.

In his earliest explicit analysis of cultural accounts of punishment, *Punishment and Modern Society*, Garland argued that cultural patterns shape the manner in which we think about crime and punishment, providing intellectual frameworks by which we determine what is considered acceptable as forms of punishment and, more specifically, what the particular distinctions, categories and types within that range should be.

In this assessment, Garland's hypothesis is that his kind of sociology of punishment takes account of cultural forces to provide further illumination as to why our penal responses have developed in the way they have. Overall, for Garland, 'the specific culture of punishment in any society will always have its roots in the broader context of prevailing (or recently prevailing) social attitudes and traditions' (Garland 1990: 210).

The manner in which punishment communicates meaning and is a constituent of culture is also ambitiously explored by Garland. To investigate these mechanisms, Garland employs the anthropological terminology of 'mentalities' and 'sensibilities'. 'Mentalities' refers to the phenomena of cognition – the conceptions, values, categories, distinctions, systems of belief and frameworks of ideas that operate within the penal system, normative schemes or guides to conduct such as justice, morality or manners. 'Sensibilities' refers to ways of feeling, or emotional configurations. When applied specifically to punishment, 'sensibilities' delimit the extent to which and manner in which punishment can be deployed. They provide the parameters of emotional tolerance for degrees and types of punishment. Tonry (2001a, 2001b, 2004) also uses the concept of 'sensibilities' in both his analysis of American penal culture and his argument that there are many important 'unthought thoughts' or insights that have been forgotten or overlooked in contemporary US and UK penal policy.

The idea of investigating the linkages between punishment and prevailing social attitudes or normative positions is so uncontentious that, in Garland's own words, it is 'hopelessly banal' (Garland 1990: 200). However, the way in which this idea is actually executed is the subject of debate and argument.

Interrogating 'culture'

Garland's analysis of cultural accounts of punishment and its methods and functions was already well developed in *Punishment and Modern Society.* However, as rigorous as his original assessment was, it did not have a significant impact upon the penological academy in the way that his later work stimulated such enormous discussion and debate (Young 2002b), though arguably, the picture of prison policy in the post-war era has been shaped largely by his assessment.

Garland returns to the conception of culture in his much quoted and highly influential *The Culture of Control: Crime and Social Order in Contemporary Society* (Garland 2001). In this he takes an overtly cultural approach towards what he sees as a convergence in criminal justice cultures in the USA and UK since the

1970s, a convergence that he argues involves increasing punitivism and a new 'culture' of control.

However, as Zedner elucidates ably, Garland's work in *The Culture of Control* makes little reference to his original account of culture and its use in studies of punishment put forward in his 1990 writings (Zedner 2002: 255).

Perhaps prompted by the criticisms regarding the use of cultural methodologies and the claims of *The Culture of Control* and to clarify the manner in which he employs the concept of 'culture' in a number of other pieces (Garland 2002, 2005a, 2005b), Garland reappraises the use of culture in sociological analyses of punishment and the value of integrating cultural analysis into 'the explanatory project of a multi-dimensional sociology of punishment' (Garland 2006: 419). Garland reiterates, correctly it is submitted, that cultural investigations are vital to a proper understanding of the context in which penal practices exist, but, again, it is submitted wisely, that such investigations must be integrated into 'multi-dimensional' accounts of such practices, in order to ensure that social explanation remains the focus in sociologies of punishment.

Multi-dimensional social theory

Garland seeks to avoid the difficulty presented by the lack of clarity about what 'culture' means. Such uncertainty is over whether it refers to a 'cultural' sphere, independent of other forces that shape penal institutions such as social, political or economic, or whether it means something that encompasses all traditions and values within a social group or society, in essence the whole social world.

Garland presents a remedy to this dilemma, arguing that culture should be studied as part of a multi-dimensional social theory, utilised as an integral component of sociological or historical explanation, but not as an alternative. He states that his own work has always, in fact, been conducted along these lines.

There is no doubt that the influence on punishment of matters such as styles of thought, structures of feeling, values, sensibilities, motivations, and the public representations of these is part of the cultural dimension of penality. This, it is argued, presents the theorist with the opportunity of examining why symbols, values or ideas come to motivate conduct. However, these conceptual phenomena are one dimension of punishment to be studied among others. The actual practices of punishment, the manner in which policy is implemented and the way in which people talk about penal reform and change must remain in the foreground of discussion. These investigations must, concomitantly, be framed within wider discussions of alterations in sensibilities and mentalities that they display. A multi-dimensional social theory must explore them all and Garland is correct to clarify what may have been a confusion of his own making.

Garland's conclusions and recommendations can be read as being prompted by a desire to re-tie the sociology of punishment to a firm historical and sociological base. Garland's assessment, it is submitted, views 'culture' not as a separate form of analysis or method, but rather another name for 'multi-disciplinarity'. As Ryan states, 'the best academic writing in criminology has always drawn on a number of established (and related) disciplines, history, politics and sociology, to name but three' (Ryan 2007: 438).

This is vital to ensure both precision in analyses of prison policy, and also that all matters impinging upon the creation of that policy are taken seriously. The fact that policy is at the centre of this study means that such a synthesised analysis is particularly necessary to take account of the political factors involved in the creation of that policy, with the economic constraints these also imply, as well as social transformations and cultural elements. This is uncontentious. However, while multi-disciplinarity may be the most satisfying approach to the investigation of punishment and prison policy, we are no further on in unpicking what exactly that entails. This book argues that policy analysis can provide the missing link in understanding the nature of crime control and penal policies.

One of the concerns that appeared to motivate Garland's restatement of the use of cultural analysis in the sociology of punishment is that of ensuring that such sociology is fully explanatory and, by implication, historically accurate, and that 'feelings' and 'sensibilities' identified are done so correctly. This is patently a direct response to the criticisms made of the type of analysis employed in *The Culture of Control*: that of the 'grand narrative' which ignores the particular, and essentially glosses over elements of the penal story that do not fit in with an overarching assessment.

These difficulties bedevil much of the cultural enterprise, and arguably are not remedied by substituting 'multi-disciplinary' assessments in the stead of cultural investigations. The investigation of long periods of time by reference to single categories of assessment, such as 'penal-welfarist', or 'late modern', will inescapably mean that subtle variations are overlooked and individual events are bundled together in an attempt to evince a coherence to what may have been piecemeal incidents without any such intended linkage, though this is a challenge that sociological accounts of imprisonment share with all historical narrative.

This has been the most penetrating and significant criticism of Garland's work, particularly *The Culture of Control*; that it suffers from over-breadth and generalisation, glossing over localisms, peculiarities and in-depth analysis.

Convergence and conflict: explaining change

Related to this are the criticisms of influential works that have identified a form of 'convergence' in policy, or a 'common' criminal justice culture, particularly between the US and the UK and that in such accounts local peculiarities and discordant trends are erased in the pursuit of analytical 'neatness' and the presentation of a coherence and programmatic development that is unwarranted. A further criticism that can be levelled at such analysis, and also that of Foucault, is that it denies or erases the impact and importance of individual actors and agency in the creation and formation of policy and 'movements' in the dispensation of punishment.

Punishment in prisons is a judicially sanctioned action, carried out by various administrators and actors within prison sites. The regimes are created by officials in these sites and within the civil service more broadly, under the general direction of a minister responsible to a Cabinet and to the electorate. Prison policy, while undoubtedly rooted in the social, political and cultural make-up of a state, is very clearly and pointedly based in administrative and legislative decisions, which are all subject to the particular processes, influences and constraints of the political arena.

Jones and Newburn in particular warn that cultural accounts such as those of Garland, when taken to extremes, can diminish the role of political agency in the creation of policy (Jones and Newburn 2002, 2005b). O'Donnell also advocates the adoption of a narrower focus in discussions on penal change, noting the differences and nuances both between and within jurisdictions, to 'give impetus to the "scholarly dialetic" between the general and the particular' (O'Donnell 2004b: 205).

There is another body of work identified by Jones and Newburn that carries out a very close and detailed analysis of individual penal cultures or instances of penal change. Such accounts of criminal justice policy and its transformation tend to have as their central concern the role of political choice and the 'politics' of crime control, with less of an emphasis on structural-cultural factors. One example of this is the towering four-volume work of Windlesham: *Responses to Crime* (Windlesham 1987, 1993, 1996, 2001), which combined extensive documentary analysis and reading of policy development and political negotiations in various areas with an assessment of the 'mood' of government at various times in relation to criminal justice matters, though the particular interpretation by Windlesham of some events has been questioned (Ryan 2003).

Historical sociology and recovery

On the face of them, these projects involve entirely polarised intellectual endeavours, methods, questions and even zones of analysis, both geographically and intellectually. One deals with the rough and tumble of politics, while the other employs the ostensibly loftier tools of structural and cultural analyses.

A good contrast between the two is offered by Loader and Sparks when they compare Windlesham's work with that of Garland in *The Culture of Control*, arguing that the former represents 'a painstaking contemporary history of political debates, policy formations and legislative battles … an internal, Westminster-centric treatment of political events and processes', but which, unlike that of Garland, gives 'scant reference to either the economic, social or cultural contexts within which they are played out, or the criminological and political ideas that relevant actors implicitly or expressly mobilise and tussle over' (Loader and Sparks 2004: 11).

Though preferring the latter approach overall, believing it to provide the more compelling assessment, Loader and Sparks note a number of problems with Garland's methodology, and suggest that what they describe as a 'historical sociology' of crime policy is ultimately the most illuminating mode of assessment as it takes on board both the actions of those who affect penal policy and the social context in which those actors operate.

Loader and Sparks, advocating a methodology they describe as 'historical recovery', insist that the actual political choices, conflicts, influences, and self-conceptions of penal agents and actors are as important to an accurate understanding of penal change as the broad cultural shifts and structural movements. Garland's work in *Punishment and Welfare* (Garland 1985) in particular, was arguably an early example of an attempt to take real account of the political discourse, influences and motivations of penal reformers and policy-makers at the time which he studied, as well as tracing these against the backdrop of broader societal change. Cohen's *Visions of Social Control* also predates these criticisms, appearing in 1985. In this book, Cohen criticised what he saw as a sociological tendency towards overgeneralisation, of being 'often quite insensitive to variations, differences and exceptions' (Cohen 1985: 240), a point that could be taken directly from a critique of *The Culture of Control*.

It is often overlooked at this remove that Garland's 1985 work involved a close reading of political documents, policy positions and penal practices as well as the investigation of wider social and cultural changes during the period analysed. Garland's return to method and interrogation of 'culture' also betrays similar concerns that cultural investigations must be tied to a historical analysis and assessment of the mechanics of penal change. Essentially, they must be tied to an investigation of policy and the policy process.

In order to create the most multi-layered and accurate possible account of Irish, or indeed any, prison policy, it is necessary to address both of these elements: the social context and the particulars of policy formation. In particular, assessing the political processes by which policy comes about throws significant amounts of light on the content of that policy, its immediate genesis and the socio-political culture of the time in which such policy was created. In this way, a more precise picture of prison policy emerges, and a truly variegated account of that policy is achieved.

Not only is an approach that explores political reasons for change necessary to examine localised differences or variations in penal forms and culture across national boundaries, it is also vital to ensure that all planes on which penal change is played out are explored.

One good example of the debate in this regard comes from Beckett and Western's innovative analysis of the relationship between social policy goals and prison policy objectives and outcomes. The authors seek to test the general hypothesis that 'the social and penal spheres are components of a policy-regime concerned with the governance of social marginality' (Beckett and Western 2001: 35). To do so, they utilise a sophisticated statistical model to explore the specific correlations between the two in the USA, including a variety of variables.

An endeavour to make such concrete and empirical linkages between social policy change and prison policy is admirable. Their methods and conclusions have, however, been subject to criticism by Greenberg (2001), who argues that while modelling such as theirs can operate to predict a state's prison population, it will not work so well in explaining that change. Using welfare to predict imprisonment rates gives no indication as to why political actors decided to change their approach to both spheres. Moreover, among other excluded potential influences, the influence of policies pursued in other jurisdictions (or in the case of the USA, federal policies) is overlooked.

We could go much further and add a variety of 'political' matters that affect penal change, some of which are explored below. As Greenberg avers, to be confident about how these changes and features come about it is necessary to use 'qualitative analyses of how these policies were adopted' (Greenberg 2001: 73).

Ignoring the immediate political context of policy runs the risk of entering the realm of structural determinism and falling into the trap of positing that sociological changes and processes were conclusive in the formation of policy, without addressing the question of individual autonomy among policy-makers, politicians and administrators. This point is particularly well made in relation to Ireland where, as will be seen, there is a particularly close relationship between individual personalities in the policy-making field and the results of that labour.

Jones and Newburn sum up this purpose and approach well:

> In order better to understand the tensions between the global and the local, we argue there is a need to place the study of human agency and political processes closer to the centre of the account that is offered. This approach focuses more closely on the details of policy development and political influence, and moves from these to the broader issues of emergent social routines and cultural sensibilities.
>
> *(Jones and Newburn 2005a: 76)*

Linking structural change and political choice: policy analysis

Linking policy and investigation of the policy process with structural and cultural change is one way of resolving the concerns prominent in the minds of all those seeking to explain penal change. This work provides such a bridge in the Irish context, while also calling for others to follow these methods within analyses of punishment more broadly. As Jones and Newburn state succinctly, 'economic forces, social structures, cultural sensibilities do not lobby for penal innovations, frame legislation, pass sentences or vote in elections, people do' (Jones and Newburn 2002: 178), an approach that has some resonances with the 'radical pluralism' proffered by Cavadino and Dignan (2007), though with some important differences.

The approach conducted here also owes an additional intellectual debt to Tonry's penetrating critique of the convergence accounts of contemporary penality. His examination of the determinants of penal policies concludes, essentially, 'whether countries adopt more punitive policies turns on country-specific characteristics'

(Tonry 2007: 17) and that 'explanations may be found in distinctive features of national history and culture, in the influence of particular systems of religious belief, or ... in political culture' (Tonry 2007: 41, internal quotations omitted). As Tonry warns, we must understand much more about how these various elements interact and, essentially, how the mechanics of either punitive or liberal penal policies come to be formed. Though Tonry does not use these particular terms, it can be argued that he also advocates a form of multi-disciplinarity in penological scholarship, and, particularly, an approach that foregrounds investigations of how policy comes to be formed.

This work therefore involves the detailed examination of the particular and peculiar forces that impacted upon Irish prison policy from 1922 to the present and to 'reinsert' agency in order to provide a fuller picture of the way in which cultural formation works.

Given this, the policy-making process is another area germane to this analysis. Investigations of this process attempt to determine the immediate political, bureaucratic and administrative factors that lead to the creation of policy positions, concrete movements in, directions and guidelines for action in a particular field. Jones and Newburn state that 'few studies have provided detailed evidence about how penal policy comes to be the way it is. Although plausible claims have been made about the sources of influence over policy outcomes, these are rarely based upon systematic empirical analysis of the process of policy formulation' (Jones and Newburn 2004: 127), though the work of Ryan stands as a significant, and early, exception in this regard (Ryan 1978, 2003).

The usefulness of policy analysis is evident on several levels. First of all, it is imperative for historical accuracy, but it is also helpful in a more general way. Policy analysis facilitates researchers studying criminal justice to understand the way in which the political processes in this area operate, how they negotiate change, are constrained, are influenced by particular actors or players and how 'politics' shapes emergent criminal justice practice, exploring both the pragmatic elements of political compromise and the way in which political ideology might be brought to bear on criminal justice matters (Bottoms 1995; Solomon 1981).

Theoretical perspectives on prison policy and its formation

While this is so, analysis of policy is still relatively underdeveloped within criminology, which tends to overlook the 'nuts and bolts' of the making of political and administrative decisions affecting crime and responses to it. More recently, however, the work of Jones and Newburn in particular has provided a conceptual and methodological framework to carry out such investigations.

The nature of policy and its formation

The work of Kingdon (1995) has been used to great effect by Jones and Newburn in their work on comparative criminal justice and policy transfer (Jones and Newburn 2007). Policy-making analysis must take account of the policy process, or in other words the way in which policy comes to fruition, and the content of that policy. Two dimensions of policy are apparent, those of 'process' and 'substance'. These concern both the formation of policy and the operation of that policy respectively. The formation of policy can be conceptualised as a series of stages or streams that interact with each other to eventually result in a decision and direction for action.

Political theory and political science conceive of policy-making as a series of stages, with a finalised policy (itself subject to change and reformulation) being the result of a number of distinct but interrelated mechanisms. First, a problem comes to light, or is defined as such, then a series of alternative solutions are canvassed and explored, the implications of each are examined and finally the most suitable alternative is then experimented with. These are known as the problem, policy and political streams.

The creation of policy is generally far more haphazard and messy than this neat formulation might suggest. Negotiation pervades each element of the process. Toch states the dilemma succinctly, cautioning that 'those who look for philosophical consistency in prison policies are apt not to find it … politics as it affects policy is the art of compromise' (Toch 1994: 95).

Jones and Newburn also utilise Kingdon's concept of a 'policy window' to describe an opportunity to promote particularly favoured solutions, or ways of viewing a particular problem (Kingdon 1995: 166–9). These are opened up due to the congruence of a particular set of factual circumstances, which make policy-makers more receptive to tackling certain issues or creating certain responses. Into these windows step 'policy entrepreneurs', a concept familiar also from moral panic analysis and labelling theory. These invest a variety of resources in highlighting their causes and favoured responses, through promotion, publicity and lobbying. Overall, policy happens through a confluence of all of these elements, when the various 'Ps' collide: problems, policy proposals and politics.

Policy-making: the results

The results of the process – the substantive policy – can also be thought of in terms of 'levels', with the content of policy ranging from symbolism in policy, such as ideas and rhetoric expressed by policy-makers as grand statements of approach (Jones and Newburn 2006), to the more material and substantial elements of policy, such as policy instruments, administrative implementation procedures and policies in practice and in action. In addition, various 'strands' of policy may be present within the wider field of prison policy, with different purposes or directions being pursued in individual elements of the prison system. A 'punitive' approach may be taken in one area, for example in relation to imprisonment of sex offenders, while a reintegrative approach could be attempted in another.

A 'policy style' is also an important object of analysis as it betrays the way in which a policy-maker and political actors wish to be viewed, demonstrating a particular governmental 'style'. Policy goals are as important as policy content, as symbols and rhetoric are also explicatory of the direction of government and administration. Ideas, attitudes and the representation of 'sentiment' by policy-makers hold out explanatory potential.

Marion (2002) has also identified 'symbolic politics' as an important subject of assessment in policy analysis. This assumes that political acts are directed at the 'audience' of the general public, with the substance of the act being less important than the perception of its audience and their reaction thereto.

The question of symbolic policies and penal styles or the tone of penal policy begins to implicate many of the same questions and subjects of assessment as those studies that seek to place penal policy within its broader socio-political contexts. While this type of analysis is less developed in studies of policy *simpliciter*, much of the literature explores the more diffuse influences on the mechanics of the policy-making process, such as prevailing popular opinion or political cultures, or 'the national mood'. These elements can also be conceived of as constituting elements of the cultural space in which prison policy is created.

Influences on policy

Various agents and agencies have a role in the creation of policy, and the role of such bodies is obviously a prime area for investigation. A variety of sources and interactions are responsible for the identification of problem areas, suggestions for responses and the creation and implementation of final policy. 'Policy communities' or, more broadly, networks are made up of all those actors with a direct interest in the creation and implementation of policy, as well as those who are in a position to influence such policy. The interactions between each are variable and complex, with different sectors coalescing or in conflict at particular points and over particular issues (Cope 2001).

Ismaili (2006) divides the criminal justice 'policy community' into two main tranches. The first branch is that of 'sub-government', incorporating elected actors such as, in the US context, presidents, governors, mayors, legislative actors, major pressure groups, heads of government departments and agencies and key judicial actors. The second group is termed 'the attentive public' and is made up of the media, experts, academics and consultants, other pressure groups, interested members of the public, non-governmental organisations, and so on.

Another possible system of classification is given by Downes and Morgan (2007) who identify a series of bodies that have a prospective bearing on the creation of criminal justice strategies and plans. In addition to the party political dimension, penal interest and pressure groups, non-governmental organisations, think tanks, the mass media and the civil service all potentially play a role, while those who work within the prison system such as prison officers, governors, doctors and other staff have a part to play; this may be generally limited (Ryan 2003), however, though occasionally staff lobbies can have a consequential role. Even prisoners themselves, through their reaction to imprisonment, may on occasion force changes in prison policy (McEvoy 2001; Ryan 1978), though more often than not the voices of prisoners are largely absent from policy discussions (Ryan 2003).

The government and civil service

Clearly, the government, in terms of both elected representatives and the Cabinet, and the civil service are two of the main sources of policy developments, though this dynamic has shifted and altered over time; the 'policy networks' approach demonstrate that it is not just 'the government' that plays a role in governance. The power play between the executive and the legislature also has a bearing on the creation of policy (Oliver and Marion 2006), with some suggestions coming from Parliament – in Ireland the Oireachtas – while others are created by individual ministers (see further Jenkins 1975). In either case these may be subjected to a deliberative process, though in others they involve high-handed executive decisions, dismissive of the role of elected representatives.

The position of the civil service is particularly interesting and revealing, as a traditional source of policy ideas through briefings, memoranda and reports. Rock's (1995) analysis of the policy-making process highlights how the Criminal Justice Act 1991 was the culmination of ten years of study and exploration, driven and shaped by key civil servants (see further Goold 2004; Moriarty 1977; Rutherford 1996). Civil servants can play particularly creative roles, sometimes single-handedly energising entire arguments and assessments, or in the propagation of governmental messages (Morgan 2006).

As Rock notes, the viability of an idea is further affected by good timing, particularly when a new official is appointed or elected and brings his or her own reform agenda and inquiring perspective to the scene. This may be additionally contingent on the individual's personal characteristics, reputation and ability to influence colleagues. Persuasive ability exhibited by individuals may be as important as the empirical validity of their suggestions. Rock argues that such individuals may manage to break free of the traditional conservatism among policy-makers, who often find it safer to do nothing for fear of doing the wrong thing (Rock 1995: 7), though whether there is a similar reticence on the part of policy-makers within government to take action today is open to question.

Criminal justice practitioners and criminologists

Criminal justice practitioners, 'experts' and service providers may also operate to shape or suggest policy (Culp 2005; Fairchild *et al.* 1985; King and Jarvis 1977; Lewis 1997; Stolz 2002; Thomas 1977). Criminologists can have a role at governmental level, with James Q. Wilson and Lloyd Ohlin being two academics identified by Rutherford (1996) as key shapers of government policy. Criminologists may have a perhaps limited role in the formation of public opinion (Feilzer 2007; Groombridge 2007), though the decline in importance of such professionals has been well documented (Garland 2001), in some cases decried (Hood 1987; Hood *et al.* 2003; Radzinowicz 1965, 1999). Indeed there is a great deal of ongoing debate and controversy within the academy about what that role should entail (Young 2002a; Zedner 2003), the limitations on that role, the use made of criminological knowledge in political responses to crime (Loader and Sparks 2004) or even whether criminology continues to have a role in a 'post-crime' age (Zedner 2002).

Interest groups and influential individuals

As Stolz (2002) has shown, interest groups, from professional and business consortia to civic and victim and offender support groups, can have a major impact upon the criminal justice policy-making process. Within prison policy-making in the UK, interest groups such as the Howard League for Penal Reform have been around for several decades, with other groups such as the National Association for the Care and Resettlement of Offenders (NACRO) being established in 1966 and the Radical Alternatives to Prison (RAP) formed in 1969 (Ryan 1978). A variety of interest groups work in the field today. At their formation most such groups had the offender as their subject of concern, but victims' groups are a growing development in the UK also (Downes and Morgan 2007).

As Wilson warns, the 'lobby' for penal reform should not be conceived of as a monolithic entity, with all groups rowing in the same direction (Wilson 2001). Instead, it may be a fragmented and complex landscape, with varying degrees of closeness to government. In addition, the level of cooperation from government and the willingness to engage with such groups, perhaps to the exclusion of 'popular opinion', is another key variable impacting upon their potential to shape the penal agenda (Ryan 1996, 2003).

Ryan makes the very pertinent point, however, that the focus of much of the literature on 'interest' or pressure groups focuses on their ability to affect government attitudes and responses, something that overlooks some of the central elements of those groups' work. As Ryan (1996) shows in the case of INQUEST, its effort is not expended solely in the corridors of Whitehall. It also carries out key functions in the ignored sites of coroner's courts, prison cells and hospital wards, where state power is no less potent.

As well as through more formalised structures such as pressure groups, various interested individuals who have political or social influence can leave their mark upon prison policy. The most obvious are those closest to the process, such as particularly active civil servants, though as Rutherford (1996) demonstrates, individual criminologists or criminal justice practitioners can have a profound influence on the direction of policy. More broadly, penal reformers such as Howard, Fry, Crofton, Carpenter and de Tocqueville were particularly influential individuals. Throughout history literary figures have taken up the cause of penal reform and have prompted interest and advocacy regarding prison policies (Newburn 2003).

The media

The media, or more specifically individuals who express positions through use of the media, can play a key role in prompting governmental action, and in the formation of public opinion. 'Public opinion', for instance through polling, may also be expressed in this way, and have influence on policy, with a more deliberative public discourse being advocated (Barker 2006; Green 2006).

In the case of prisons, it is clear that current public understanding of such issues as shaped by the media 'remains suppressed to the point of ignorance' (Jewkes 2007: 448), and that much reportage of the prison system supports negative views of prisoners and unsympathetic responses thereto.

'Events'

Into this matrix come 'events', or what Downes and Morgan describe as 'matters of scandal and concern' (Downes and Morgan 2007: 731). These are the unpredictable variables that can overtake and subsume all forms of planning, and explode or charge onto the scene, often in the form of 'public opinion' or 'media attention'. Downes and Morgan identify four types of event that have 'trump card' effect over all other elements of policy formation, and can cause dramatic and unpredicted shifts in policy. These include prison escapes, high-profile crimes, miscarriages of justice and riotous assemblies, as well as altering political fortunes and eruptions. As Rock has commented, policy-making would 'be an otherwise smooth metamorphosis were it not for the sudden lurches and opportunities imposed by uncontrollable problems of timing and context' (Rock 1995: 16).

The matrix of policy formation

There is no doubting the 'messiness' or volatility of policy-making, which is as influenced by empirical evidence and knowledge as it is by moral sentiment, cultural changes, political opportunism and expediency, vested interests and 'habit' (Ruth and Reitz 2003). As such, the ways in which policy is debated, created and reshaped through implementation provide highly illuminating evidence for both the political dimension of prison policy, but also the wider social and cultural assumptions that impact upon that policy.

The Irish context

Academic literature on criminological matters in Ireland generally is somewhat thin on the ground, though there is now a developing corpus of work on many areas of Irish criminal justice policy and an increasing number of academics working in the field. Within this growing literature, contemporary prison policy has received much more attention than historical accounts, which is hardly surprising given the recent flowering of Irish criminological discourse and the need to provide analysis of current trends.

While the picture of Irish prison policy is less difficult to discern than was previously the case, it still remains true that a comprehensive and in-depth empirical assessment of the development of Irish prison policy such as this has not been previously attempted.

Moreover, there has not yet been a sustained assessment of the manner in which criminal justice policy-making occurs in the state. Some exploration has been carried out, with O'Donnell referring to the state's 'vulnerability to policy transfer from its larger neighbours (especially Britain and the US with whom a common language and legal tradition are shared)' (O'Donnell 2008: 129) and Hamilton to the specific instance of this in the creation of anti-social behaviour orders in Irish law (Hamilton 2007).

When it comes to policy formation in the Irish context, Chubb (1982) has provided an insightful analysis of the Irish policy-making process and the various stakeholders that take part in such a process. Chubb's work is a general thesis, rather than tailored to the criminal justice policy-making process. His typology is, however, generally useful in providing a framework to explore the key players in the Irish policy-making process. Chubb identifies Ireland's 'proximate policy-makers' as the members of the government (Cabinet) and ministers of state (this latter group were known as parliamentary secretaries for a large part of the period under analysis); the members of the Dáil and the Seanad (the lower and upper houses of Parliament) and some senior civil servants, including temporary advisers and some other public servants.

Each of these proximate policy-makers has a particular role within the process, though such roles are not fixed and are liable to change in particular circumstances. O'Halpin (1999b) considers the three main components in Irish policy-making to be the government, the civil service and interest groups, with voters, political parties, the media and the judiciary also having important roles at various times (see further the contributions in Coakley and Gallagher 2010).

Government and ministers

Having the greatest ability to effect change and access to resources and materials, the government is in the strongest position to create and alter policy. The government has, for example, a near monopoly on initiating legislation, one of the most obvious ways of forming and implementing policy. Ministers in government therefore have a very clear and potent function in this regard. Furthermore, ministers are responsible for the creation of secondary or delegated legislation to implement the 'nuts and bolts' of primary legislation. It has been noted, however, that the particular constituency demands on government ministers, which seem to be especially onerous in Ireland, have operated to constrain their ability to institute policy (Connolly 2004).

In the case of prisons, until 1924 the system was controlled by the Department of Home Affairs, which was renamed the Department of Justice thereafter. Until

1928 the prison system was administered by a General Prisons Board, a semi-autonomous body capable of ordering the everyday administration of the prison service, with the Department ultimately responsible for policy direction. At present, the Department is entitled the Department of Justice and Law Reform. The Irish Prison Service is responsible for operations.

The civil service

The professional civil service has a multitude of roles in the formation and implementation of policy. Finlay (1966) provided a classic text on the operation of the civil service, detailing its legislative base, work and staff, with Dooney adding to this work and providing insights into the manner in which the civil service operated in Ireland (Dooney 1976). Barrington's analysis of public administration in Ireland gives critical commentary on its performance until the 1980s (Barrington 1980).

The Irish civil service was the product largely of British practice and no fundamental alterations were made to its structure on Independence. After 1958 the civil service underwent a significant expansion. This was due to the increasing workload for the state in coordinating social and other policy, and also through the acceptance of the principles of a financial plan, *Economic Development*, which demanded planning for and appraisal of the development of the state by a professional group of individuals. Barrington asserted in 1965 that much policy-making in those years emanated from the civil service.

More generally, the civil service is actively involved in the collection and appraisal of relevant information, analysis of issues and suggesting potential approaches. Dealing with parliamentary questions, meeting deputations of interested groups and participating in committees are also central elements to this work (Dooney 1976). The collation and assessment of research is conducted by these individuals. The degree of 'success' that such research may have within government is variable, however. In the Irish context, the commission of research is inhibited by the perspective that the far greater output of research into criminal justice matters in the UK serves the needs of policy-makers here as well.

A constraint on action can be the traditions and attitudes of the particular department, or the 'culture' of the civil service and the section of operation involved. Historically, the civil service is considered to have inherited British traditions and attitudes, with these prevalent for several decades after Independence and being most obvious in the role of the Department of Finance (Dooney 1976; Fanning 1978).

The Oireachtas

The Oireachtas, or Parliament, is important to the policy-making process as it will debate, amend and ultimately pass or reject legislative proposals put before it (Gallagher 2004). However, its power in the independent creation of policy is somewhat limited, as through governmental majorities and party loyalty means it is difficult to have much impact on government bills when that government is ill disposed to accept suggestions, though this power becomes more potent at times of governmental instability. Depending on the nature of the government's majority, private members' bills are also hostages to governmental approval and are often utilised for the purposes of publicity as much as any serious attempt to shape policy. The role of the opposition is a factor in policy criticism or suggestion, given its ability to criticise, embarrass and give assistance to the government in the formulation of policy. The Oireachtas has had varying degrees of success in these regards in the realm of prison-policy making, as will be demonstrated.

Bills can be introduced in either the Dáil (the lower house) or the Seanad (the upper house) and if there is a conflict between the houses the Dáil prevails. There is a five-stage process for bills, involving debate and their passing. Bills then go to the other house and finally to the President who signs them into law. Rarely, a bill may be referred to the Supreme Court to test its compatibility with the Constitution. A member of the Dáil is known as a Teachta Dála, or TD, while a member of the Seanad is known as a Senator.

Other sources of influence

While the centres of power in the policy process are concentrated among a remarkably small number of individuals working within government, there are a number of constraints or sources of influence on these actors. A lack of professional expertise, finances or governmental support are obvious factors. Political support or opposition from the grassroots of an organisation is another very strong feature of political discourse and action. Party activists and annual conventions can be sources of ideas, or indeed pressure. These can also relay more diffuse or sectional interests from among the public.

'Pressure groups' or interest groups can act in this manner too, gaining weight 'on the inside' either through mediation with ministers or public servants or through criticism from the outside. Dealings with ministers and senior civil servants appears to be the most prevalent form of such activity, with formalised 'lobbying' of Oireachtas members less obvious, though interest groups have a significant influence over government (Murphy 2010).

Since 1994 the Irish Penal Reform Trust has advocated on behalf of prisoners' rights and for penal reform. Though it remains a small organisation, it has recently established a significant public profile and ability to engage with policy-makers.

Other influences include international treaties, particularly those to which Ireland is a party, and other international instruments that may have persuasive authority. EU law obligations are an obvious current force of influence. The Department of Justice is also cognisant of the variable over which it has no control – judicial application and interpretation of the fruits of their labour. Constitutional implications of legislative action are prominent in the minds of civil servants in the Department of Justice.

The policy process in Ireland is, of course, at an institutional level far from neatly reflective of any typology. As in any jurisdiction scandals, 'events', surges of public interest and crises can all overtake the best-laid plans, and action is often frustrated until funds, governmental support or public outcry demand it. Elections and changes of government are key variables both in terms of setting the 'mood' for public administration and changing policy goals.

Inertia is another characteristic of public service practice at various times, with a mentality of caution and restraint often prevailing over innovative sentiments. As will be explored throughout this work, the political landscape in Ireland is not noted for a strong ideological driving force, with pragmatic concerns and local or sectional issues resulting in greater political activity and change than the influence of political or economic schools of thought (Kilcommins *et al.* 2004).

Policy analysis and the sociology of punishment for Ireland

Prison policy has been affected by all of the groups, influences and features of Irish policy-making outlined above, with various groups or interests having differing levels of success at different times. The immediate inputs into the policy-making process regarding the prison system are vital to study in their own right in order to make the best sense of the developments and to be able to explain their unfolding. However, in order to attain the most explanatorily compelling account of Irish prison policy, the immediate context of the policy-making process must be examined along with the broader structural or cultural influences on this policy. This latter investigation is carried out here by reviewing a broad range of historical and sociological literature on the nature of the Irish state. By employing the insights of both perspectives, it is hoped that a multi-faceted or variegated account of prison policy in Ireland from Independence to the present day will be achieved. In this work, the policy determinants and results will be explored, before a socio-political and cultural context of the developments will be given for each period under investigation.

A word on methodology

This book advocates that penologists would do well to examine the process by which penal policy comes to be formed in greater detail. Such an approach has been followed in the course of this work. An archival approach was employed in order to provide the documentary evidence necessary to assess the factors at work in the creation of Irish prison policy. Key documentary sources sought out and analysed included government and opposition publications such as bills, Acts, discussion/consultation documents, manifestos, ministerial speeches, opposition speeches, parliamentary debates and reports, committee reports, pressure group and think-tank publications and the development of policy as reported in newspapers.

The methodological approach taken here had a theoretical underpinning, based in the work of Jones and Newburn, and Loader and Sparks. Both highlight the need for penologists to understand how policy actors themselves talk about and conceive of their actions and intentions. The process that Loader and Sparks term 'historical recovery' is described below:

> The procedure we envisage would subject ... events to more searching forms of historical research and reflection, aim to explore their interplay with extant political imperatives and programmes and seek to explore the ideas and meanings that actors mobilise to encode/decode events and 'name' the legitimate response.
>
> (*Loader and Sparks 2004: 15*)

Such a process of historical recovery was carried out here – one that sought to grasp the complexity and unevenness of the policy-making process.

In this regard, it should be noted that under the National Archives Act 1986 documents from departments of government that are more than 30 years old may be transferred to the National Archives for public access. Even documents that are 30 years old or more may be retained if a certificate is granted for their retention by the department on a variety of bases, for example if it is contrary to the public interest or if they would or might cause distress or danger to living persons.

Some documents have undoubtedly been retained by government. This would be particularly relevant to sensitive materials touching on the security of the state. It is impossible to know how many of these files were not accessible for the purposes of this research but it can be speculated that some of those bearing on the Civil War period, the Emergency and the 1970s were not available. Other archival collections have similar date restrictions. As such, the material in the later chapters of the book relies, by necessity, less on such documents and more on discussions within the Oireachtas, reports of pressure groups, academic accounts and media analyses to piece together the elements of prison policy. As the Bibliography makes clear, archival material from a wide variety of sources was obtained. Where available, prisoner testimony, memoir and media accounts were also used.

2

FROM INDEPENDENCE TO THE 'EMERGENCY'
Civil war and conservative administration

Introduction

This chapter begins with an introduction to the prison system as it stood when the Free State government took over its administration in 1922. It then explores the use of detention during the Civil War period (1922 to c.1924), examining the development of the burgeoning system of incarceration arising out of the bitter, violent and divisive war following the signing of the Treaty with Britain on 6 December 1921. The Treaty concluded the War of Independence, which had been fought since 1919. The chapter details the reaction of prisoners to their incarceration and examines the nature of their resistance. It then goes on to describe prison policy as created by an independent Irish government, noting that prison policy was a marginal area of public policy, exciting little interest and engendering few innovations for many years. The nature of the Irish state and its governance is examined along with the social, economic, political and cultural influences on the prison system and its slow pace of development.

Opposition to the Treaty leads to conflict

The Treaty split Irish opinion and its leaders, providing for the recognition of the King as head of state, establishing a Boundary Commission to draw a border with what was to become Northern Ireland and an oath of allegiance to the British monarch when members (TDs) would take their seats in the Dáil (the lower house of Parliament). The division between those who supported and those who rejected the Treaty between Ireland and Great Britain played out across all elements of Irish society. Its impact on the prison system was also significant, with the state's institutions being used to hold very large numbers of those who expressed their opposition to the terms of the Treaty by forceful means. These prisoners were known as members of the 'Irregular' forces among governmental circles and supporters, but conceived of themselves as 'Republicans'. The latter term and the more neutral 'anti-Treaty forces' are used in this chapter. Many of those imprisoned were prominent members of Irish society, and some of them would go on to become political leaders and penal administrators themselves.

During the Civil War period both the ordinary system of imprisonment and a network of military and quasi-military sites, which had previously been occupied by British forces and had been taken over by the Free State Army (the state being known as the 'Free State'), were utilised in order to respond to and quell the major disorder which was occurring during the conflict.

The prison system in the Irish Free State

The prison system inherited by the independent Irish Free State following the Anglo–Irish Treaty was, as Osborough has put it: 'the product very largely of English penological thought and practice. The nineteenth century origin of several of its principal features was equally obtrusive' (Osborough 1985: 181).

The new state, through its provisional government, took charge of several local prisons, at Dundalk, Galway, Sligo, Waterford, Kilkenny, Cork, Limerick and Tullamore. These held prisoners serving short sentences of imprisonment for minor offences. There were also four convict prisons, to which prisoners serving sentences of penal servitude were sent: Mountjoy; Maryborough (later becoming known as Portlaoise); and Cork male and female prisons. There was one Borstal at Clonmel as well as a host of other institutions of detention including three Bridewells at Ballina, Birr and Mallow. These institutions were administered by the semi-autonomous General Prisons Board, established in 1878. In the new administration Kevin O'Higgins TD became the Minister for Home Affairs, with responsibility for the prison system.

Architecturally and tangibly, the legacy of British rule was most apparent. The legal regulation and internal regimes of the prisons were the product of British administration and legislation.

One of the most striking features of the prison system when the Irish Free State came into existence was the parsimony with which it was used. In January 1922 a crude inventory of the prison population and the available spaces was taken, finding 462 prisoners in custody out of a total of 2,038 available places (JUS H78/17). The closure of Cork female prison and its merger with the male prison was mooted 'in the interests of better administration and economy' (JUS H78/21) and in June 1922 it was suggested that Dundalk and Waterford local prisons be closed.

The transfer of authority regarding the prison system from British to Irish Free State administration was relatively unremarkable. When the provisional government, made up of what became the Cumann na nGaedheal party, took over there was no rush to make alterations to the system or the manner of prison governance. The General Prisons Board remained in place and the change would have been largely unnoticed by those detained within the system. As the author

Brendan Behan acerbically put it, when the Free State took over, the only things that changed in the prison system were the 'badges on the warders' caps' (Behan 1956: 14).

The projected direction of Irish penal administration over the following decades was likely to continue in the vein established in the late nineteenth century. Low numbers and minor, though steady, welfarist-type reforms were to be expected. While, as will be seen, this state of affairs did eventually come to pass, the intervention of the Civil War had an acute influence on the nascent system in the immediate and longer term.

As a result of the events of the Civil War, however, the progression of Irish penal policy was quite literally violently interrupted and its subsequent trajectory is partly explicable by reference to this fact. As O'Halpin avers, 'the post-treaty conflict had a profound effect on the course of development of the state's public order and defence institutions, and on the system of justice' (O'Halpin 1999a: 1).

Detention during the Civil War

Security matters and the defence of the state

With the outbreak of Civil War the unremarkable passage in the state's assumption of responsibility for the prison system was forcefully ended. During previous conflicts, the British authorities had made a regular practice of sending politically motivated prisoners to English jails in prisons such as Wormwood Scrubs and Brixton. Once the Treaty was signed, this arrangement inevitably had to end. One of the first acts of sovereignty exercised by the state was to order the release of those detained for political offences in Ireland and receive Irish prisoners from Britain (McConville 2005: 764).

The Civil War period had an acute and immediate impact upon the prison system and prison policy. This was manifested in a number of ways. First, it set a precedent for the use by the state of its prison system as part of its security policy. Threats to the state, most visibly apparent during times of Republican activity, were countered through the use of, and within, the prison system and other sites of detention. During the Civil War period and in the years that followed, the penal and prison policies of the state were cleaved to its security policy. All were at the front line of defence as the Free State established itself.

The aim of suppressing disorder was the centrifugal force driving the various tactics employed within the system of detention. This objective and its spin-offs, involving emergency legislation, overcrowding, poor conditions, executions and criminalisation define the use of detention during and immediately after the Civil War.

Detention, both the fact thereof and the conditions therein, became an important front in a propaganda war between the pro- and anti-Treaty sides during the Civil War. The Civil War period was, moreover, the first example of a pattern in post-Independence Ireland whereby calls for prison reform would often be linked to situations in which there would be a 'political' dimension to such imprisonment.

When the Civil War commenced, the pace of change in the administration of the penal system in the Free State was exceptionally rapid. Mountjoy received its first Civil War detainee in June 1922 (Carey 2000: 198). By the end of the Civil War, over 12,000 individuals, including more than 400 women, were held in some form of detention because of their involvement or association with the conflict, though exact numbers are very difficult to verify (Lyons 1973: 462).

The precise numbers of sentenced prisoners are also difficult to discern as the Annual Reports on Prisons were not published by the Free State authorities until later in the decade and inventories were somewhat haphazard and inaccurate given the confusion and chaos prevalent within the sites of detention. It is clear, however, that the average daily population of the prisons increased significantly, though the vast bulk of those detained were interned without charge, trial or conviction.

Prison overcrowding

The number of prisoners – both those sentenced by the courts and those held extra-judicially – put enormous pressure on the state's sites of detention. The prison system was overwhelmed and it was soon apparent that the existing accommodation was hopelessly inadequate to house the large numbers detained. The government took steps to attempt to relieve the situation, with a definite eye to future increases in the numbers of detainees.

The authorities redesignated prisons and parts of prisons to be administered by the military authorities and began to recommission buildings that had formerly been used as places of detention to allow their use by the military. Kilmainham jail, disused since 1916, was reopened in July 1922, despite having been found in a state of wreck and wholly unsuitable for the reception of prisoners (JUS H78/25). A system of very basic facilities was also constructed to provide further accommodation, such as the Curragh internment camp, established in November 1922.

The most generally employed mechanism to deal with the large numbers in detention was, however, to overuse the already available capacity within the prisons and military institutions existent in the Free State.

Chronic overcrowding was a feature of Irish prison life throughout the duration of the Civil War and the strain on the system was immense, with Limerick holding eight men in one cell and Galway containing 30 'ordinary' and 248 military prisoners in 117 cells (JUS H78/25) in November 1922. By February 1923 Mountjoy held 674 military and 385 ordinary prisoners while having accommodation for less than half that number (TAO S1362/1).

The situation reached such a critical point that the provisional government was even considering reintroducing a form of banishment or transportation, with the Cabinet actively considering a suggestion to send prisoners to the island of St Helena to be detained there in late 1922 (*Irish Times*, 3 January 1925).

Conditions of detention

In such circumstances it is hardly surprising that the conditions prevalent in the prisons and other sites of detention were far from ideal. Reports abounded of inadequate ventilation, sanitation, food, clothing and bedding. Conditions in Kilmainham, to which female prisoners had been moved after protesting at their detention with 'common convicts' (McCoole 2003: 42), were particularly severe. One prisoner, Hannah Moynihan, noted at the time: 'this part of the jail to which we have been taken has long since been condemned as insanitary. It is a dark gloomy place with long dreary passages' (Kilmainham Jail Archives, uncatalogued). In Kilmainham there was one toilet for 130 women and almost every pane of glass in the building had been broken (McCoole 2003: 39). Kathleen Clarke described the conditions there as a 'chamber of horrors' (Clarke and Litton 1991: 199).

Decades later, a man who would serve many years as Minister for Justice in successive Fianna Fáil governments, Gerry Boland, recalled that after a riot in Mountjoy he and other prisoners were compelled to sleep outside in the yard in terrible cold and sleet (*Irish Times*, 9 October 1968). The author Frank O'Connor was imprisoned, despite his gender, in the Cork female prison in 1923 and described it as a 'dreadful place', overcrowded and infested with vermin (O'Connor 2005: 169). Newbridge camp, used to hold internees, consisted of a mixture of huts and old disused military buildings, with broken windows and primitive conditions, including the use of stables (MacBride 2005: 75). The North Dublin Union, another internment camp, was notorious, having neither bathing nor washing facilities (Buckley 1938: 61).

In Mountjoy, conditions were similarly dismal. Ernie O'Malley detailed that some prisoners were 'consigned to the basement cells, dirty, oozy, ill-ventilated, where they were ill-treated by officers' (O'Malley 1978: 201). Campbell argues that in certain circumstances the conditions of detention were used as a means of punishment, both individually and collectively, and were not just unfortunate spin-offs from the pressures of overcrowding (Campbell 1994: 227).

The conditions in all the state's sites of detention were undoubtedly more than grim. More disturbing, however, were some particularly troubling elements of penal administration pertaining during the period.

Deaths in custody and a policy of executions

The deep tensions and hostility heralded by the outbreak of Civil War were replicated in the policies conducted within the prison system and sites of detention, a proportion of which can only be described as atrocities.

O'Halpin estimates that as many as 150 prisoners, internees or persons otherwise in custody, were killed either while detained or while allegedly evading capture (O'Halpin 1999a: 34). Seventy-seven anti-Treaty prisoners or detainees were executed between November 1922 and May 1923 (Lee 1989: 18). Many more were sentenced to death, but remained in prison. It is clear that the use of executions was a further military tactic employed in an attempt to end the hostilities by cowing those engaged in such operations against the government.

Reaction of detainees: resistance and organisation

A vital element of the climate surrounding the implementation of the government's policies within the prisons and internment camps is the vociferous reaction of a great many of those detained. These prisoners and detainees were highly organised within the prisons and effective in activating crucial channels of publicity and support outside. The prisoner support machine was also well oiled from years of practice from the War of Independence and before. Their reaction involved the rejection of prison policy, which had to accommodate and usually attempt to overcome or defeat it.

Prisoner resistance

McEvoy (2001), in a work of considerable depth and insight, assesses the nature of politically motivated prisoners' responses to various tactics or epochs in imprisonment in Northern Ireland in the period from the 1960s to the 1990s. McEvoy conceptualises the response of paramilitary prisoners in four principal ways, all of which centre around the concept of 'resistance': resistance as political struggle; resistance as a struggle to neutralise or limit the power of prison authorities; the collective nature of prisoner resistance; and resistance as part of political conflict. This was similarly reflected during the Civil War period. Other protests involving political prisoners have comparable resonances (McConville 2005; Radzinowicz and Hood 1979).

Among Republican prisoners in Northern Ireland in particular, McEvoy notes a number of facets to the manifestation of this resistance, some of which were overt, vivid and often had tragic consequences. They included hunger-striking, the control of space, escapes and escape attempts, and the use of violence. Others were more subtle, and involved the education and training of prisoners by prisoners. Similar techniques were used by anti-Treaty prisoners in the Free State.

Solidarity, protest and escape

The chaotic conditions extant in the country's makeshift places of detention posed a number of problems for the prison authorities. High levels of inter-prisoner solidarity flourished in spite of, or perhaps because of, the disarray and disorder. Furthermore, these conditions allowed for incessant attempts by prisoners at escape through tunnelling, break-outs or any other means at their disposal.

In such conditions, the military structure into which many detainees fell was most valuable in providing a coherent and efficient mechanism of voicing complaint and registering dissatisfaction. Often this took the form of simple destruction of their cells and other areas. In August 1922, for example, Portlaoise prison was set on fire by Republican prisoners (TAO S1369/1) after the prisoners issued an 'ultimatum' to the authorities to recognise political status (MacEoin 1987: 99).

McEvoy's hypothesis that politically motivated prisoners utilise escape and escape attempts as means of 'resistance as ridicule' was certainly borne out during these years. Peadar O'Donnell recalls that prisoners in Mountjoy spent inordinate amounts of time burrowing through the walls of their cells in 'D' wing, making both discipline for the Free State authorities and privacy for the imprisoned. One imaginative and elaborate attempt at escape was carried out in Mountjoy prison in 1923. Over thirty prisoners were involved and a conveyor belt system was established to remove the dirt collected. Prisoners worked on rotation day and night, with meticulous cleaning operations for clothes used in the operation (MacBride 2005: 79–81). It was unsuccessful.

Resistance through ridicule was also evident in the amusements and diversions participated in by the prisoners. A carnival was organised in 'C' wing of Mountjoy in August 1923. The cells and landing were decorated and the prisoners wore festive costume. Fortune-tellers, gamblers and tricksters plied their trade, plays were staged and a procession was held. In the evening they even held a dance with some of the prisoners donning handkerchiefs on their heads to take the role of women. Never missing an opportunity to make a political statement, this procession included 'representatives from the British Empire and other uncivilised countries' (O'Malley 1978: 253).

O'Malley reports of prisoners making poteen, or hooch, in their cells, while he and Peadar O'Donnell produced the wonderfully entitled 'Book of Cells', which lampooned Free State ministers and carried caricatures both written and illustrated, and in which O'Donnell made his writing debut.

Education, prison policy and politics

In Mountjoy, classes were held daily in subjects such as wood-carving, macramé and the making of replica Tara brooches (Ní Chuilleanáin 2001). Greek was taught in Ernie O'Malley's cell in 'A' wing of Mountjoy (UCD Archives P/06/1/754) and a 'Revolutionist History' class was given by Dorothy MacArdle in Kilmainham (McCoole 1997: 46). Prisoners established games such as rounders and handball and staged plays (TCD MS 10056). Talks were given on topics as diverse as the military situation, the ordination of women into the Catholic Church and the position of women in industry (Ó Drisceoil 2001: 68). Some of the prisoners in the Newbridge military camp were receiving instruction in constitutional law, local government and Irish history (Garvin 1996: 136). O'Connor went so far as to describe life in the Curragh as 'the nearest thing I could have found to life on a college campus' (O'Connor 2005: 179). Most significantly, in light of the impact on the future direction of Irish politics, prisoners in Mountjoy began to establish Sinn Féin cumainn (branches) with an eye to maintaining these groups upon release.

It is clear that within the prisons, prisoners themselves were important mediators of policy, making it very difficult for its imposition at prison level, and were also catalysts for political change (Hopkinson 2003), with many of the prisoners involved going on to shape Irish politics in the years ahead, though not in the area of prison policy.

One of the most arresting examples of prisoner organisation and mobility during this period was the putting forward of prisoners as candidates in the general election of 1923. Eighteen prisoners were elected as Sinn Féin TDs. Part of the platform on which they ran was to secure their release, though their central focus was on the ongoing dispute over the Treaty.

Peadar O'Donnell and Liam Mellows wrote a number of publications on social and political matters while imprisoned in Mountjoy. One such was 'Notes from Mountjoy', which was a political programme for a Republican government. It was smuggled out in 'comms' by instalments. The prisoners had ingenious methods of keeping the channels of communication open both within and without the walls, with letters, newspapers and orders being smuggled in and out, for example in laundry, soap or tobacco or, occasionally, the crust of a pie (O'Malley 1978: 206).

Accounts of ill treatment of detainees were stock fare for sympathetic publications, and posters and pamphlets would be regularly posted on the walls of Trinity College Dublin and other high-profile locations by members of Cumann na mBan and others. The voices of prisoners in the debates about prisoner issues were loudly heard and, as will be seen, comparatively significant, though ultimately largely unsuccessful.

Prisoner grievances

The question of political status

Given the prisoners' self-conception as military insurgents fighting an illegitimate governmental authority, it was inevitable that, as Campbell remarks, 'the status issue was certain to become a bone of contention' (Campbell 1994: 227). A passage in Ernie O'Malley's *The Singing Flame* encapsulates these feelings: 'Men who had been sentenced for civilian offences were also sent to Mountjoy; they added to the known touts and pigeons amongst us. A few non-political prisoners had been placed in our wing. Probably it was a prelude to treating us as criminals' (O'Malley 1978: 232).

This account by O'Malley is typical of the 'othering' engaged in by the Civil War detainees towards the civilian prisoners. It is apparent that many could not empathise with such prisoners and seemed either to pity or to scorn them (Buckley 1938: 254). Within Mountjoy, the Civil War detainees refused to wash the corridors as requested to do so by Deputy Governor Paudeen O'Keefe, who arranged for the women convicts to do so instead (NLI MS 43245).

It appears that for much of the Civil War period *de facto* prisoner-of-war status was granted. Later changes to this policy, as will be seen, had serious ramifications.

General conditions of detention

As well as their demands for political status *per se*, the prisoners put forward their grievances about the manner of their detention more generally. A letter sent 'on behalf of the Irish Republican prisoners' to the provisional government by Oscar Traynor, then detained in Kilmainham and who later became a Minister for Justice, is typical of the numerous such communications made during the Civil War period (Kilmainham Jail Archives, uncatalogued files). In this letter Traynor complained about the standard of food, the fact that prison officials were opening prisoners' post, and the restrictions on the number and duration of visits the detainees could receive.

Public sympathy: prisoner support Networks

In keeping with the division of popular opinion about the Treaty itself, there was a significant degree of sympathy among a large proportion of Irish society for the prisoners' position. A number of groups and individuals were exceptionally active in presenting their views on prison policy, internment and the conditions pertaining within the sites of detention. Most of these had strong political affiliations, often over and above their commitment to the prisoner issue. These included the Political Prisoners' Committee, which had been affiliated with the Sinn Féin party and later the anti-Treaty section of that organisation, the Republican Prisoners' Dependents Fund, the Prisoners' Defence Organisation, and other organisations such as Cumann na mBan and the Irish White Cross.

The Women's Prisoners' Defence League

The most notable and enduring of them was the Women's Prisoners' Defence League, known colloquially as 'the Mothers'. This interest group and source of agitation was established by Maud Gonne MacBride, a long-time campaigner in various Republican struggles and a former prisoner, after she was refused permission to bring food and clothes to her son, Seán MacBride and his future wife Kid Bulfin, who were both in prison at the time. Its members included Charlotte Despard, later active in the Workers' Party, who occupied the position of president, and other high-profile Republican figures such as Helena Molony, Dr Kathleen Lynn and Dorothy MacArdle.

The League's members would take to the streets of Dublin regularly in order to protest against and highlight the plight of the detainees. These protests would often involve stirring speeches and symbolic remembrances of the prisoners, with women holding crosses to represent those in prison. They were active in visiting prisoners and assisting their families (Ward 1983) and writing letters to the press and political notables (NLI MS 33675/A/1).

These women created some of the greatest contention and consternation, with Ward describing them as 'a decided embarrassment to the Free State Government'

(Ward 1983: 190). Many of their demonstrations were broken up, with protestors shot at and hosed in efforts to disperse them. Their actions demonstrably upset at least one member of the Dáil, when Alec McCabe TD declared: 'why not let out these prisoners and put an end to the campaign of these wild women who spend their Sundays and the time they should spend in their homes, orating from the ruins in O'Connell Street?' (Dáil Debates, vol 7, col 1135, 21 May 1924). The Minister for Home Affairs, Kevin O'Higgins TD, took a similarly dim view of this activity, describing them as 'hysterical young women who ought to be playing five-fingered exercises or helping their mother with the brasses' (*Éire*, 19 February 1923).

Impact on prison policy

While Ward avers that without the interventions of the Women's Prisoners' Defence League the conditions of prisoners would have been far worse (Ward 1997), it is difficult to find evidence of this. Although there was a high level of interest in the conditions of imprisonment and detention, and a number of interest groups used all means possible to put the case of the prisoners, as well as significant agitation by prisoners themselves, the effect on prison policy was largely nugatory. The Republican and radical credentials of those involved were a most unattractive combination in the eyes of the government. As such, these grievances were always ill placed to elicit a favourable response.

One way in which this agitation did have a bearing on governmental action was at the level of reassurance, and public statements regarding prison conditions described complaints as propaganda (TAO S1369/1).

In many ways, however, seeking to discern an impact on policy-making would be to miss the point of the organisation, the members of which would have been somewhat aghast at the thought of becoming part of a cooperative, working relationship with the government. Rather, it had some successes in maintaining popular interest in prison conditions, linking this to political aims and putting forward a rival conception of the situation to that propagated by the government.

The huge level of interest in detention is further evidenced in the fact that the government decided to sanction the intervention of the International Red Cross Committee and agreed for it to make a report on the Irish conditions of detention, which became the Haccius Report (NLI MS 43124, translation from French by the author). This was carried out in April and May 1923. While the Committee accepted that there were grounds for complaint in relation to overcrowding, and that the ventilation in Mountjoy was inadequate, it went on to say that 'the treatment of these prisoners is devoid of all hostile spirit and the general principles adopted by the Red Cross are observed'.

The situation at the end of the Civil War

What is to be done with 12,000 detainees?

Though figures vary, by the end of the Civil War over 12,000 people were held in custody. The declaration of an end to martial law resulted in a crisis for the government regarding what to do with the vast numbers detained. The result was the introduction of legislation that regularised continued internment. In August 1923 the Public Safety (Emergency Powers) (No. 2) Act came into force.

The government approved of continued detention, but it was also aware of the need to begin a speedy and widespread process of release, both from a practical point of view and as a means of beginning some sort of reconciliation with the opponents of the Treaty. As O'Halpin points out, the government reconciled these positions by letting 'the republican rank and file go free in dribs and drabs' (O'Halpin 1999a: 42).

The declining numbers of internees and sentenced political prisoners removed some of the pressure on the state's system of detention and its prisons in particular. However, the presence of the large numbers who remained continued to have an impact on prison policy in the immediate aftermath of the Civil War. These prisoners and detainees became increasingly disgruntled with their ongoing detention.

Change of policy: prisoner frustration and agitation

The fact that there had not been a general amnesty was a continuing source of anger among many prisoners and their supporters. It appears that during the Civil War proper, *de facto* prisoner-of-war status was granted to anti-Treaty detainees, who were allowed to form their own military structures and in the main deal with the prison authorities as a unit. From mid-1923, however, these unspoken assumptions no longer had currency. A change of leadership in Mountjoy prison sparked the genesis of a new approach. From then on, the authorities pursued a policy that refused to acknowledge the existence of an internal military structure or prisoner organisation, which Minister for Home Affairs Kevin O'Higgins described as a 'deliberate policy' (Dáil Debates, vol 6, col 1574, 28 February 1924). For their part, the prisoners equated this with a strategy of criminalisation and they displayed significant resistance to this tag.

Hunger strike

Such was the level of bitterness among some detainees and their supporters about their ongoing detention and the conditions in Mountjoy in particular, that one of the most tragic incidents of the period began in October 1923. This was a hunger strike, which originated in Mountjoy. The strike was begun as an attempt to secure unconditional release for all the remaining prisoners and was framed as the only passive weapon left to them (UCD Archives P17A/43).

The hunger strike has a particular appeal and resonance with Republican protest and imprisonment, carrying a long history and near reverence within those circles. Its power lies in the transformation of 'the body' into a site of resistance, protest and political struggle (McEvoy 2001; Sweeney 1993) and the quasi-religious allegory of self-sacrifice. In addition, the hunger strikes of Ashe and MacSwiney were also comparatively fresh in the memory of the prisoners of 1923.

The strike spread rapidly from Mountjoy to other prisons and places of detention, including the very large sites at Tintown A and B, Hare Park, Gormanstown camp and Newbridge barracks. At one stage 8,000 internees and sentenced prisoners were on strike. The involvement of such enormous numbers was in fact a flaw in the prisoners' strategy rather than a strength (O'Donnell 1965: 96).

The events surrounding the hunger strike caused huge outrage within anti-Treaty circles and beyond, and created another front in the ongoing propaganda war. In fact, Bowyer Bell describes the prisoners' release campaign at this time the 'only virile, practical Republican activity' being conducted in Ireland during that period (Bell 1998: 43).

The hunger strike was poorly organised and considered, and collapsed under its own weight within six weeks, after the deaths of two men, Dennis Barry and Andy O'Sullivan. The prisoners became painfully aware that the Free State authorities were unwilling to make concessions and the strike was called off on 23 November, after 41 days with no definite promise of release (*Irish Times*, 24 November 1923).

The end of the hunger strike signalled a decline in much of the prison agitation. Over the next year or two the majority of prisoners were released, with the numbers remaining falling steadily during the spring of 1924, and the prisons being returned to civilian use. Eamon de Valera was one of the last to be released, on 16 July of that year (Coogan 1995; Longford and O'Neill 1974).

The plight of 'ordinary' detainees

Prisoners who were incarcerated in Irish jails during the Civil War for reasons other than those related to the unrest were almost entirely overlooked by the prison authorities, policy-makers and the public during this time. They were generally only referred to or intruded on the consciousness of such groups and individuals when some connection with the effects of the Civil War was established. In effect they were forgotten.

Due to the enormous overcrowding, huge influxes into the state's prisons and the creation of a temporary penal complex in the form of barracks and camps, those convicted under the ordinary criminal law were essentially squeezed out in the ensuing crisis. At a very basic level, there simply was not the space for them and it appears that many were released to allow for more 'dangerous' individuals to be held. Ordinary prisoners were often kept in Garda barracks and in makeshift accommodation within the prisons.

The General Prisons Board petitioned the Ministers for Justice and Home Affairs in periodic attempts to have some accommodation set aside for civil prisoners, most of which requests were in vain (JUS H78/3). The situation had already reached acute proportions by October 1922 when Thomas Direen, a police inspector, wrote to the Department of Justice, informing it: 'there is no accommodation for civilian prisoners in Limerick prison presently … We are holding them in William Street [a police barracks] until we get further instructions' (JUS H78/33). A secretary in the Department of Home Affairs added the following memorandum to the report from the inspector when petitioning the Department of Defence for more spaces for ordinary prisoners: 'the state of affairs described would become a serious public scandal as well as an obstruction to the due administration of justice' (JUS H78/33). It is clear that ordinary prisoners were either being turned away, released early or held in deeply unsatisfactory conditions during these months.

Eventually, with the release of increasing numbers of anti-Treaty internees and prisoners, the Department of Defence began to decommission the buildings from military authority following increasingly urgent requests from the General Prisons Board. In December 1923 several prisons were transferred back to civilian control, with Mountjoy and Kilmainham finally following in 1924.

The re-establishment of normality

In the circumstances of the Civil War, the creation of prison policy proper was next to impossible. There was neither time, resources nor interest in altering the regimes or assessing the prevalent prison system, its use or future direction. The only discernible trend in prison policy during this period was that of security, the suppression of disorder and the assertion of the government's legitimacy to govern.

In calmer times that followed the new state had the opportunity to put its own stamp on Irish prison policy. Once the chaos had dissipated, however, the breathing space afforded to the authorities did not result in any great examination of the system or its direction. The immediate problems facing penal administrators were the results of the shambolic state of much of the accommodation after the disruption involved in the Civil War.

There are relatively few developments to relate regarding prison policy or innovations therein during this time. This lack of penal discourse is telling in its own way as it indicates both the attitude of penal administrators to their task and the lack of political will to create change. What is most surprising about this assessment is the fact that many of those who had first-hand experience of the prison system during the Civil War period, and indeed previously, were not prompted by those experiences to create change in the prison system, with Margaret Buckley an exception (Buckley 1938). No penal reform interest groups were established and those sitting in government who had been in prison exhibited similar apathy. The 'othering' of ordinary prisoners engaged in by those who considered themselves engaged in military action and prisoners of war is partially responsible for this, but wider factors that inhibited change in the Irish prison system were also influential. Part of the reason may have been fatigue at the end of a number of campaigns that resulted in imprisonment, including the Civil War, the War of Independence and the Easter Rebellion. Another possible explanation may be that the driving force behind prisoner campaigns in previous periods – that of Republican sentiments – was channelled into other areas of political and cultural life, and without this, sustained interest in the prison system was unforthcoming. Though perhaps overstating the situation, one senator related:

> There is no doubt at all, no doubt whatever, that if there had not been a Civil War in 1922 there certainly would have been an inquiry into the prison system. There was a certain kind of enthusiasm, a certain kind of high-spirit at that moment, which would have brought about an inquiry into the prison system among other things, and one of the effects of the Civil War, apart altogether from the human lives that were lost and the material damage done, was the postponement of certain matters of that kind.
>
> *(Seanad Debates, vol 31, col 2181, 12 June 1946)*

Tomlinson states that 'once the civil war was over, the now divided Irish prison system largely faded from view' (Tomlinson 1995: 185), while McCullagh argues: 'the issue of prison and of prison reform was not a major one on the agenda of the new state' (McCullagh 1988: 155). Both these assessments are largely accurate. In 1922 the Minister for Home Affairs, Kevin O'Higgins, described penal reform as:

> A big question and an interesting question, but scarcely a question for a transitional Government. I think that everyone here would agree that we should aim at improvement and reform in the existing prison system … But one does not attempt sweeping reforms in a country situated as this country is at the moment. One does not build or try to build in the path of a forest fire. This question and many other interesting questions will have to be postponed until the situation alters.
>
> *(Dáil Debates, vol 1, cols 2311–12, 28 November 1922)*

In reality, these matters were postponed indefinitely. After the high levels of committals and daily averages in the prison system, the numbers of those detained began to tail off in 1925. The first Annual Report on the prison system of the Free State was published in 1927 and related to the year 1925–26. This year is the first that can be considered 'normal' in Irish penal administration, recording an average daily population (including the Borstal) of 922 prisoners (*Annual Report on Prisons*, 1927).

On the conclusion of the Civil War there was a great deal of continuity in the administration of the ordinary detention system from the days prior to

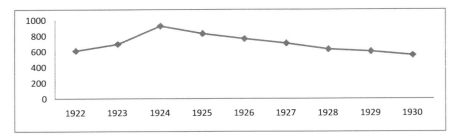

FIGURE 2.1 Average daily prison population 1922–30

Independence. The system was administered by the General Prisons Board until 1928, under the overall direction of the Department of Justice and its Minister. Within the prisons the regime for ordinary prisoners was little different from that which went before under British rule, being governed by prison regulations promulgated by the General Prisons Board in 1895, 1902 and 1915. The industries in which prisoners were engaged included agricultural work (mainly at Portlaoise), mailbag-making for the Department of Posts and Telegraphs, wood-chopping, tailoring, baking, basket-making, mat-making, shoe-making, tailoring and weaving. Females were engaged in sewing, knitting and laundry work. Both sets of prisoners also worked on general prison maintenance.

The General Prisons Board and the 'ethos' of prison policy

Despite this general continuity, the General Prisons Board, the body in charge of the administration of the prison system, made a number of changes to the internal regimes and treatment of prisoners in the period following the Civil War. These reflect a desire to 'humanise' or ameliorate conditions within the state's prisons and included the abolition of the sentence of hard labour and the introduction of sprung mattresses and iron bedsteads for prisoners, replacing the plank beds that had been used for years before (JUS H248/32A).

The Prisons (Visiting Committees) Act 1925

Probably the most important change made by the new authorities in the area of prisons was an Act passed in 1925 providing for the statutory establishment of visiting committees for each prison. Under the Act, visiting committees were appointed to carry out a number of functions: inspecting prisons to ensure that conditions were satisfactory, reporting abuses, conducting disciplinary hearings, hearing complaints from prisoners, and awarding 'privileges' in particular circumstances.

The duties and powers of the visiting committees reflected the twin elements of their roles, which were often in contradiction to each other. The roles of both 'watch-dog' and imposer of punishments and privileges was an obvious tension inherent in the task of such committees. The independence of the committees from the Minister for Justice, given the manner of their appointment, was another area open to criticism, a point made at the time by the Labour leader Tom Johnson (Rogan 2009b).

The introduction of the 1925 Act can be read as involving a genuine desire, in the aftermath of Civil War and amid allegations of ill treatment and worse within the state's prisons, to introduce an outside method of accountability and inspections. This concern for oversight and independent investigation of prison conditions, the lack of which was sharply felt during the Civil War period, was the explicit purpose for the legislation as introduced by the Cumann na nGaedheal government (Dáil Debates, vol 10, col 264, 18 February 1925).

On closer inspection, however, while these may have been sincerely held reasons for change, it is apparent that more prosaic considerations prompted the introduction of the legislation. The files on the matter reveal that the Department of Justice requested the drawing up of a bill to establish visiting committees to update the existing system, which was based on British legislation, in order to reflect the transition to the Free State. The archaic nature of these regulations required updating and this was the official reason given for the request to the Office of the Attorney General to draft legislation, though the heightened awareness of the need for oversight in prison administration may have been responsible for the timing (OAG 2000/22/127).

The rules that were drawn up to govern the function of the committees were framed in a style that would not have been out of place in the nineteenth century, involving the upholding of discipline and the encouragement of 'labour' and prevention of 'relapse'. However, the rules sought to ensure that prison conditions fulfilled basic, uniform standards. Matters such as diet and the material conditions of the prison were key foci and the committees were also to ensure that labour conducted while imprisoned prepared prisoners to earn their livelihood on release. As such, they reflect what may be seen as a Victorian ethic, which pervaded 'ordinary' prison policy throughout these years, emphasising order, cleanliness, uniformity, legal justice and work.

Declining prisoner numbers and closure of prisons

The lack of vision for the prison system evident during the post-Civil War period was also a product of a lack of necessity for the employment of imagination or planning for a system. Similarly, the 1930s display a great deal of continuity with the previous decade both in terms of penal developments and as indicators of prison policy. Many of the same themes, issues and difficulties that typified prison policy in Ireland in the aftermath of the Civil War remained prevalent. As one member of the Dáil put it in 1930, 'the question of penal reform is a burning question in every country except Ireland' (Dáil Debates, vol 34, col 2506, 23 May 1930).

This state of affairs provided further comfort to administrators who could happily 'forget' about a system that was no longer causing problems or headaches. It also allowed for one clear policy direction – that of prison closure.

A number of prisons were closed after the Civil War, reflecting the greater normality and the lessening of pressure on space within the system. Tullamore prison and the Bridewells at Ballina, Mallow and Birr were long disused but were not finally closed until 1924. Many of the state's smaller prisons were shut and others were reduced to minor status under which they could receive only prisoners sentenced to imprisonment rather than penal servitude. In 1926 Dundalk prison was reduced to minor status, from then on receiving only prisoners on remand and those serving sentences of less than one week. Sunday's Well women's prison in Cork was empty by 1926, while Kilmainham and Kilkenny prisons were finally officially closed in 1929, though both had been disused for years.

Further closures were contemplated by the Department of Justice, with the prospect of reducing the penal estate to three prisons countenanced, one for Leinster, one for Munster and one for Connaught and the remaining counties of Ulster (Dáil Debates, vol 11, col 674, 30 April 1925).

The Prisons Act 1933 was introduced to validate the closure of certain prisons and the transfer of their use retrospectively. Closure of prisons remained a feature of the penal scheme during the 1930s, with Galway and Waterford prisons closing then (TAO S13879).

Prison closure was not conceived of as part of a determined policy to eradicate the institution of imprisonment and provide alternatives. The purpose was to take advantage of the coincidence of reducing prisoner numbers and effect significant financial savings in terms of the upkeep of prisons and the replication of services. However, the proposal to reduce the penal estate to three prisons was scuppered on further investigation by the Department of Justice when it discovered that the economies that would result from the arrangement would be offset by the extra expense involved in transporting prisoners over long distances.

The passage of the Prisons Act 1933 through the houses of the Oireachtas could have afforded its members an opportunity to engage in a comprehensive review of penal matters and establish a vision for the state's prisons for the future. This was not taken. In the Dáil debates on the issue of prison closure, there is only one call for the establishment of an inquiry into the penal system. This suggestion came from TD James Dillon of Fine Gael (which party had been formed through the merger of Cumann na nGaedheal and the Centre Party in 1933), a figure who was a regular contributor to debates on prison matters and particularly vocal on the appalling conditions in the state's industrial and reformatory schools (Manning 1999). No such commission was established.

The dissolution of the General Prisons Board

The General Prisons Board fell victim to the uncompromising hand of cut-backs and centralisation in 1928, when the resignation of its chairman presented the opportunity for the Board to be wound up (TAO S5578). It was estimated that a saving of 1,700 pounds per year could be made in the event of such abolition with other savings possible.

In addition, unnecessary duplication in public service was frowned upon within administrative circles, and as an extra layer of management in the functioning of the penal estate the General Prisons Board was an obvious candidate for those tasked with effecting economies and reducing surplus in public administration. The government was seeking to 'slim down' public administration and reduce the number of boards dealing with a variety of matters and to incorporate them departments. As a memorandum on the future of the General Prisons Board demonstrated, it would be 'more in consonance with general policy that [the Minister] should assume direct control and responsibility' (TAO S5578).

After the abolition of the General Prisons Board, the prison system was run solely by the Department of Justice until the next century. The Department of Justice thus gained a monopoly on prison policy-making.

The Department of Justice and prison policy

The new masters proved to be wary of either extensive change or even minor amendments to the existing regimes within prisons. While the Prisons' Section of the Department (known as D6) had a comparable level of staff to the General Prisons Board at transfer, within the Department the administration of prisons was just one element in a remit that extended over the Gardaí, the courts, the land registry, registry of deeds, the public records office, law reform, petitions for mitigation of penalties, immigration and charitable donations and bequests (TAO S15059A).

It can be posited that the absence of a body with embedded expertise, developed over decades on prison matters with energy and resources directed entirely to such affairs, was one reason why innovation was so scarce. However, while it is true that the General Prisons Board had administrative control over the system, Ryan argues that the comparable authority in Great Britain was not independent of the Home Office, which retained ultimate control over the system (Ryan 2003). In light of the later attitude of the Department of Justice, it can be argued here that the Department of Justice would, regardless of the views of the Board, have implemented its conservative agenda.

The record of the Department of Justice during the 1920s and 1930s is one of limited efforts in the penal realm. Conservatism permeated its approach and it was particularly averse to instigating changes or reforms of any nature. A strategic examination of the system or of its operation, effects or reflections on its aims is strikingly absent from official discourse during this period. The Department did not take any opportunity to engage in such an assessment or consideration. It did not seek outside assistance to investigate the prisons, nor did it compare in any meaningful way the efforts being made within the Irish system with those that pertained abroad. It is not the case that innovations were attempted and were then neutralised within the Department or were abandoned after implementation. They were simply not even conceived of.

One of the rare insights into the workings of the Department of Justice in these years comes from reminiscences by a civil servant who worked in Justice from 1927 until 1971. Peter Berry, who eventually rose to become Secretary, the most senior civil servant of the Department, and had a profound impact upon prison policy in later years, recalls a very small unit, housed on the top floor of government buildings on Merrion Street, Dublin. The Department had few staff, with Berry moving around to fill in gaps whenever he was needed. Resources were difficult to come by, and the overall impression is one of wariness and reluctance when it came to change (Berry 1980).

The transfer of functions from the General Prisons Board was carried out with the intention of cutting costs, minimising staff and generally reducing the resources available to the administration of the prison system. The Department continued these tasks with a kind of zealousness in restraint.

This attitude was already apparent in the period directly prior to transfer. The Department, particularly through the offices of its Secretary, S. A. Roche, sought to negate outside suggestions for modifications to the prevailing practices and was itself loathe to effect transformation from the inside. Even if the government had desired penal reform, of which there is minimal evidence, long-serving Secretary Roche nipped suggestions for reform firmly in the bud. In 1932 the Department assessed the potential for increasing the facilities available to prisoners. Roche informed the Minister of the day:

> One of the great difficulties in giving prisoners more facilities is expense … the more liberty a prisoner gets the more warders, paradoxically enough, must be employed and paid … whether our present system is harsher or less reformative than it should be cannot be considered by any reasonable person as a matter of immediate urgency.
>
> *(TAO S6296)*

In 1932, shortly after the first electoral victory for Fianna Fáil, a party established in 1927 and opposing the Treaty, the new Minister for Justice directed Roche to conduct a preliminary examination of allegations of ill treatment against prisoners during the tenure of the Cumann na nGaedheal government (TAO S6296). Roche made it clear that the Department was keen to negate any overactive tendencies that the Minister might present. Caution was strongly advocated and Roche advised his Minister to get involved in delaying tactics:

> I suggest that on this point your reply should be that you propose to treat the general question of prison reform as a subject obviously requiring long and patient consideration and a thorough examination of details. It would be wrong to assume that the Department of Justice has never before considered the merits of other prison systems.
>
> *(TAO S6296)*

It appears that the Department was not only reluctant to implement changes suggested by interested bodies, it was anxious to deflect any other sources of suggestion before they could be made. The reports of the Visiting Committee for Cork prison, for example, had begun to be published in local newspapers and this was frowned upon by officials, being considered 'open to grave objection' (JUS H248/32A). The same committee around this time was deprived of the services of one individual, a member of Cork City Council, because, as the prison governor reported, he was reputedly of 'a disagreeable, fiery and erratic manner' and had 'consistently opposed and obstructed the City Manager in the Municipal government of the city' (JUS H248/19). Such attributes were highly undesirable in the mind of departmental officials of the day.

The prevailing attitude within the Department of Justice was, unsurprisingly, replicated in ministerial pronouncements about the prison system, which displayed a similar anathema towards change or innovation. Kevin O'Higgins' successor (after O'Higgins was assassinated), James Fitzgerald-Kenney TD, was particularly *laissez-faire* when it came to prison policy matters.

Fitzgerald-Kenney was one of the few members of Dáil Éireann during these years who had never spent time in jail. Nor did he appear to desire an increase in his knowledge of the system. He admitted to never having visited the prisons during his first year in office, and further contended that it was not his duty to do so (Dáil Debates, vol 34, col 1819, 14 May 1930). Moreover, it was alleged contemporaneously that the Department had the true control over the running of the prisons and that the Minister for Justice was merely a conduit for their decisions and a messenger to the Dáil. This charge was made at various points throughout the history of penal policy, but first achieves prominence in 1930 when Seán Lemass TD put it to Fitzgerald-Kenney that he had 'absolutely no voice in the decisions of his Department or any control over its activities; and, secondly, that there were many things done by his Department which could not possibly be brought into the light of day' (Dáil Debates, vol 34, col 837, 21 February 1930). Lemass' key point related to the position of the Department on 'political' prisoners, and his claim is difficult to test. However, it is apparent that the Department had significant influence over the appointment of visiting committees and the opinions of the Department regarding costs and minimising innovation or change certainly held sway during the period, whether ministers acquiesced in them or actively promoted them.

When Fianna Fáil took over after the 1932 general election, its record shows a similar attitude in terms of lack of interest and innovation within penal affairs. This is surprising, given the level of concern about the detention of Republican prisoners among Fianna Fáil members and supporters.

Intriguingly, de Valera's official biographers reveal that he had sent some of his ideas on prison reform to Sir Samuel Hoare, the British Home Secretary who was drafting the Criminal Justice Bill of 1938. Hoare described himself as being 'delighted' with his views, as he knew 'quite a lot about the prisons of England'

and incorporated these ideas into the bill (Longford and O'Neill 1974: 358). De Valera did not put any of these ideas into practice in Ireland, however, nor is there any indication that he sought to influence the operation of his Ministers for Justice.

Under the Fianna Fáil administration, the policy on prisons remained remarkably consistent with that which had prevailed under the previous government. The emphasis continued to be on economy and aversion to change. No new programmes were instigated. No new categorisations of prisoner or new classes of prison staff were introduced. No new 'experts' began to work in the prisons and no experiments were attempted regarding rehabilitation or reform.

The traditional occupations remained the only forms of activity for most prisoners. Farm work occupied the 'ideal' type of activity in the Irish prison system. Many prisoners continued to be occupied by breaking sticks in the prison yard, as brought to light by the first, unsuccessful, Irish case to litigate prison conditions: *O'Conghaile v Wallace* [1938] IR 256.

These pervasive attitudes of inhibition when it came to change are exemplified by a Department of Justice file from the 1930s entitled 'Prison Reform in the Free State'. This file contained two pages – itself symbolic – which were two letters from the Department to interested persons explaining why prison reform was not necessary (JUS 248/58).

Prison policy in the post-Civil War period: caution and conservatism

The absence of voices calling for innovation the prison system, an absence also reflected in the dearth of academic or media comment about such matters, and the overriding attitudes of caution and conservatism displayed by both ministers and departmental officials resulted in a time of great quiet and essential stasis within prison policy. Making sustained or effective efforts at reform through work and education were considered to be 'hardly worth' the attempt, being frustrated by lack of imagination, finances and a preponderance of short sentences.

The rhetoric of policy-makers: reform and moral regeneration

While there were few actual changes in prison policy and administration during the years following the Civil War, the small changes implemented were aimed at the betterment of prison conditions and a dedication, at the rhetorical level at least, to assisting the prisoner to return to society on release. All those with an input to the policy-making process exhibited 'humanitarian' feelings regarding imprisonment and a wish to alleviate the pains of confinement. The particular form in which this desire was expressed was dressed in moralistic language of reform and salvation. As such it is reminiscent of Victorian ideals of penality, involving moral regeneration, 'saving' and the power of work.

Fitzgerald-Kenney, despite his general disinclination to instigate reforms, proffered his own opinions regarding the point of imprisonment. He averred in 1928:

> In dealing with prisoners the main object is to endeavour to reform them, to endeavour to bring home to them that though a man may have fallen he can rise again; that though he may be down he need not be down for all time … Our idea is to try to save these prisoners, to do everything we can, so that when they go out again into the world they will be able to have something like a fresh start.
>
> *(Dáil Debates, vol 27, col 268, 16 November 1928)*

This approach was shared by those in opposition and there was a fairly consistent conception of the objectives of imprisonment across party lines. Mr Little TD, for Fianna Fáil, stated his belief that reform should be a cardinal principle of the system, arguing that 'the basis of the attempt at prison reform is the moral regeneration of the prisoner, and the belief that hope should be used as a more powerful agent than fear' (Dáil Debates, vol 34, col 2498, 23 May 1930). These ideas again exhibited a large element of Christian sentiments rather than a broader, or indeed secular, notion of 'social rehabilitation'. Nevertheless, it is the lack of a punitive or harsh tone in Little's analysis of the issue that is most interesting. While the suggestions made are almost 'twee', their importance lies as much in demonstrating an absence of draconian feelings regarding prisoners as illustrating the limited advancements hoped for in the Irish system.

Voluntary organisations

The conceptualisation of prison policy as one in tune with Victorian ideals of charity, redemption and moral salvation through work is further strengthened by another feature of the system during these years. A significant degree of reliance was placed on voluntary organisations regarding the after-care of prisoners by the Department of Justice (Dáil Debates, vol 27, col 390, 16 November 1928). These organisations, many of which had an explicitly religious ethos, filled the gap in after-care for some prisoners, something that the state was quite happy for them to do, having no formalised provisions or structures of support for released prisoners.

Limited interest and few changes

The years following Independence were therefore rather quiet in prison policy terms. Financial considerations, a reliance on the voluntary sector, an aversion to innovation, the lack of voices pressing for change and the low numbers within the system all combined to create a system in which little changed and little was said about the prison system.

If we conceive of policy regarding public administration as involving decisions regarding direction of particular institutions with a vision of what those institutions are designed to achieve, policy regarding the imprisonment of ordinary detainees during the late 1920s was quite weak under this test. The central concerns of administrators at this point were those relating to internal administration and matters of daily, small-scale importance, such as diet and the physical infrastructure. Each year, the developments reported in the annual statements relating to the prisons consist of matters relating primarily to the maintenance of prisoners in terms of their physical comfort and the maintenance of the prisons themselves.

Another factor was present during these years, however, which lent a further layer to the nature of Irish prison policy and also accounts in many respects for the limited nature of the developments related. This involved continued unrest and disorder, ripples from the Civil War years that continued to be felt.

Republican disruption and disorder

Prison policy was buffeted at various times during the remainder of the 1920s by the hangover from the Civil War. After what appeared to be the dying down of disturbances in the country in 1923–24, the *bête noir* of Irish public administration at this time – security – reared its head once again in 1926. The continuing ability of the IRA to create disruption and disorder was evident throughout this period and prompted yet more emergency legislation and draconian responses by the government. The Public Safety Act of 1927 was an enactment of comparable severity to those that had preceded it. This Act allowed *inter alia* for the establishment of Special Criminal Courts, to operate in addition to the by this stage traditional military courts.

Those who were sentenced or interned continued to pose the usual problems for prison administrators, eliciting a security-conscious and defensive approach, while at the same time deflecting attention from the 'ordinary' prison system. A statement from the Minister for Justice in 1930 acts as a useful summary of the approach to prison policy generally in this period. After a fairly wide-ranging debate on many prison issues, in which 'political' imprisonment was a comparatively small matter for discussion, Fitzgerald-Kenney stated: 'this debate has divided itself into two parts, the question of prison administration and the question of the so-called political prisoners in Mountjoy and Portlaoighse. I will deal with the latter part first' (Dáil Debates, vol 34, col 2512, 30 May 1930). This division of interest and priority in approach were replicated throughout the decade. As one TD declared in frustration:

> Apparently the only people who take any interest in the matter are those agitating on behalf of political prisoners. No one ever looks at it from the humanitarian standpoint at all. Apart from our views on the ill-treatment of political prisoners, I think the treatment of prisoners generally should be taken in hand.
>
> *(Dáil Debates, vol 34, col 2507, 23 May 1930)*

The deputy's hopes would remain unfulfilled for some time to come. The atmosphere in the Free State's prisons remained tense throughout the 1920s with escape attempts and protests regular occurrences. The IRA successfully organised the escape of 19 prisoners from Mountjoy prison in November 1925. In 1927 32 prisoners in Portlaoise began a non-cooperation strike. Hunger strikes took place intermittently, aimed at securing release or the amelioration of prison conditions.

Concern about other political groups

In the 1930s the Department of Justice began to be concerned about groups other than the 'mainstream' Republican entities. For the first time communist groups, some of which also had Republican leanings, became official subjects of concern. The establishment of Saor Éire in particular was watched keenly by security officials (English 1994).

The degree of anxiety that the Cumann na nGaedheal government felt about these movements is betrayed in a memorandum sent by President W. T. Cosgrave to the Catholic Archbishop of Dublin, Archbishop Byrne, in September 1931. He wrote that 'a situation without parallel as a threat to the foundation of all authority has arisen' and listed four sources of potential disorder within the state. These were the IRA, Cumann na mBan and their associates, specifically including the Women's Prisoners' Defence League and the Prisoners' Dependents' Organisation, Fianna Éireann and 'a number of Communistic groups' (DDA, Archbishop Byrne Papers, Government Box 1).

The climate of near paranoia about such groups within the Executive Council is clear. Ten organisations were banned, including Cumann na mBan and the Women's Prisoners' Defence League, in October 1931 (JUS S9472). Clearly, organisations seeking change of the penal system were highly undesirable in the eyes of the government.

Policy on Republican prisoners

Like the Cumann na nGaedheal government, and despite its protestations on behalf of Republican prisoners in the 1920s, upon assuming power in 1932 Fianna Fáil proved itself to be unafraid of using the prison system and detention generally to secure the state. To deal with IRA and Blueshirt activity, the Public Safety Act 1931 was reintroduced, the IRA was banned and 451 people were convicted under this legislation. The Women's Prisoners' Defence League reappeared, meeting weekly in Cathal Brugha Street, Dublin. Republican prisoners and their credentials with government were now poor. The marginalia of a Department of Justice official on one newspaper report is typical: 'these are IRA auxiliaries: So far as I know they assist *only* IRA prisoners' (JUS 8/425, emphasis in original).

This was somewhat surprising given the history of the Fianna Fáil party and its interest in prisoners. The imprisonment of Republicans had in fact become a factor in the general election of 1932. Cumann na nGaedheal and Fianna Fáil sought to make political capital out of such events and, indeed, fears. It is interesting to note the linkage between criminal justice matters and electoral affairs appearing so early in Irish history. Cumann na nGaedheal utilised security as a key plank in its attempts to garner popular support, emphasising its credentials as a party of law and order that would crush the communist and Republican threats to the country (Lee 1989). For its part, Fianna Fáil attempted to walk a tightrope of currying favour with those who supported the IRA, Saor Éire and the other organisations, while still attempting to distance itself from them, particularly from the more radical elements.

Cumann na nGaedheal took out newspaper advertisements warning that voting for Fianna Fáil meant the release from prison of communists and terrorists. One such advertisement ran: 'How will you vote tomorrow? The gunmen are voting for FF. The communists are voting for FF' (Dunphy 1995).

Fianna Fáil ran, *inter alia*, on the promise that it would clear the jails of those prisoners remaining after the Civil War and under the various Public Safety Acts and other emergency legislation. Manning makes the remarkable statement that '"open the gaol gates" was the great cry of this election' (Manning 2006: 44).

Fianna Fáil achieved an impressive result in the 1932 general election, being able to form a government with the support of Labour. One of the first acts carried out by the new administration was to send members of the new government to the Dublin prisons and effectively to 'open the gaol gates', fulfilling its electoral promises and continuing de Valera's plans to 'woo' Republicans towards the Fianna Fáil party through such conciliatory gestures (O'Halpin 1999a: 107). Immediately upon taking office, the government ordered the release of 17 Republican prisoners under free pardon. Shortly afterwards, 97 remaining IRA prisoners were released. One of the prisoners to benefit from this envoy was Frank Ryan, who was carried shoulder high from Arbour Hill prison into Dublin city centre where a reception was held for him. Peadar O'Donnell and Maud Gonne addressed the throng of up to 30,000 people who had gathered to greet the released prisoners.

After the release of these prisoners, the prison numbers were further depleted by an amnesty for ordinary prisoners given on account of the Eucharistic Congress which was held in Dublin in 1932, amid scenes of huge religious fervour. It was decided that clemency ought to be extended to a number of prisoners who were then released on licence (JUS H248/57B).

Retrenchment and rectitude

Besides the question of subversion, retrenchment and rectitude were key themes in the administration of the Irish prison system during this period. The combined effect of the sensibilities of the Civil War and the continuing conflict as well as the conservatism in administration of the ordinary prison system gave prison policy during this period its particular characterisation.

While the prison system was utilised regularly in defence of the state, besides this very little occurred and the period can accurately be considered, as O'Donnell relates, one of 'stagnation' (O'Donnell 2008).

Interestingly, some comparatively radical efforts in other areas of the administration of justice were made, fundamentally restructuring some of the state's institutions of law and order. A new police force, the Garda Síochána, had been established to replace the contentious Dublin Metropolitan Police and military-style Royal Irish Constabulary. A new army was also established, known initially as the Free State Army (Allen 1999; Garvin 1996).

While the most obvious and disliked symbols and emblems of British rule, including the police and military forces, were eradicated and replaced, the less conspicuous or prominent remnants of that legacy were not altered. The prison system is in a peculiar position within this framework. Irish prisons had palpable associations with British rule, housing many of Ireland's most famous Republicans, and being the final resting place for significant numbers of those individuals. Yet the prison system was not overhauled after Independence, nor were there any efforts made to create new regimes, principles of punishment or institutions.

One significant reason for this was the 'solidity' of the system. The physicality of the prison system in terms of bricks and mortar lent that system a degree of inertia that should not be underestimated. Pragmatic requirements to use any available and even remotely suitable building during the chaos of the Civil War made those institutions indispensable and their removal unthinkable; the diminishing numbers of prisoners made it unnecessary.

As well as these immediate influences, there were other operating factors that account for the character of Irish prison policy during these years. What Kilcommins *et al.* describe as the 'calcification' of penal policy (2004: 41) owes its origins, in large part, to an obsession with the politics of fiscal rectitude and conservatism in social policy regarding the role of the state in improving the lot of its citizens during the 1920s in particular. These motivations were grounded in the cultural sensibilities and preoccupations of the time.

The nature of Free State public administration

The manner in which prison policy developed during this period can be assessed in tandem with wider developments in social policy and political culture during the Cumann na nGaedheal era. The later period during the 1930s under Fianna Fáil is characterised by a more expansionist approach to social welfare provision. However, while there were no attempts to make conditions in Irish prisons harsher during that period, nor were there sustained or serious attempts at penal reform either. In this regard, the attitudes and activities of the Department of Justice had a major impact on mediating broader social change within the prison system.

Financial concerns and the neglect of the prison system

After the Civil War, the Cumann na nGaedheal government became inordinately preoccupied with recovering from this situation, and balancing the state's books, arguably more so than even the state's financial status required (McCashin 2004: 29). It viewed this task as the core element of state-building and was particularly concerned to illustrate its ability to maintain the finances of the state as a form of proof to the wider world of its capability to govern. It was particularly hoped that the maturity and responsibility of the new government in rigorously pursuing economic caution and financial restraint would demonstrate that Ireland was capable of governing itself in a prudent and successful fashion. Vigorous economic retrenchment was considered to be the ultimate benchmark of fitness to govern.

The civil service, which administered the formation and implementation of policy, continued to operate along British style lines after 1922 (Coakley 2004b). One of the most important consequences of this was that the Department of Finance operated in a manner similar to the British 'Treasury' (Lee 1989). This attitude affected the Department of Justice in the same way as it affected every other Department in the new administration.

Ernest Blythe was appointed Minister for Finance in 1923. He along with other high-profile civil servants and ministers ensured 'that the new state would concentrate on rigorous retrenchment'. The goal of cutting costs and slimming down public administration was pursued with a dogged and ruthless efficiency, becoming an overarching focus that would permeate and shape all aspects of governmental administration (Bew 2007: 444; Meenan 1970).

The economic orthodoxy of this period can be characterised as stridently *laissez-faire* and Victorian in style and content, cutting income tax and government expenditure in very stringent fashion (Ferriter 2004: 304). Fanning sums up the Finance 'attitude': 'Finance officials made their mark upon the Irish Free State less by what they did than by what they prevented others doing. Defenders of the established socio-economic order, theirs was no brave new world envisioning Independence as an opportunity for change' (Fanning 1983: 64).

In a climate of such coldness to innovation and change, the fact that there is so little to report from prison policy in the post-Civil War years is, with hindsight, somewhat predictable. The finances were simply not available, even if prison reform had been desired. Moreover, incurring the wrath of the Department of Finance for suggesting such action would have required a Department of Justice that was far bolder and more imaginative than that which ran the prison system. Allied to this, and in many ways largely responsible for it, was the particular character of Irish social policy during this period.

Social policy and attitudes to the poor and marginalised

Ó Gráda assesses the approach of the Cumann na nGaedheal policy-makers to social policy thus: 'True, they were fiscally constrained by the needs to repair civil war damage and to establish an economic reputation. But there was a hard edge too to the pronouncements of government spokesmen such as Ernest Blythe, Kevin O'Higgins and Patrick McGilligan' (Ó Gráda 1995: 91).

This 'hard edge' was a distinctive attitude to social policy, welfare expenditure and also to the Irish working classes and the poor (Breen 1990). Such an attitude is reflected in some very shocking statements uttered in the Dáil during this period regarding the proper role of government in making improvements in living conditions for the state's poor. Some of the more outrageous statements can only be characterised as based on a callous conservatism. McGilligan's statements that the government had no role whatsoever in the provision of employment, the expression of the sentiment that 'people may have to die in this country and die of starvation' (Dáil Debates, vol 9, col 562, 30 October 1924) in response to one such death, and the infamous reduction of the old age pension are some of the more colourful examples of the often harsh position of that government on social policy and social supports (Bew 2007: 444; Foster 1990: 512; Lee 1989).

It is clear that the early years of the Free State registered few developments that could be characterised as progressive elements of social policy. Social welfare provision was very slow to develop. Cousins argues, for example, that its course was also affected by the outbreak of political violence (Cousins 2002: 24). The provision of health care was framed in the language of economy and the expansion of unemployment assistance and injured workers' compensation were also strongly resisted. The development of public housing was neglected, despite the high levels of slum dwelling registered in the state (Ferriter 2004: 239).

Keogh argues that in fact, 'with certain exceptions … the government of Saorstát Éireann was far from being innovative' (Keogh 2005: 37), while O'Halpin says of these new rulers: 'they had no desire to transform Irish society, no intention of restructuring the economy' (O'Halpin 2003: 96).

A parallel can be drawn between the chasm separating the idealism of the pre-Civil War period and reality of the implementation of social policy in the post-Civil War period; and the same chasm is evident between idealism and reality in penal administration. Many of those who were part of the movement that gave rise to the Democratic Programme, which was filled with socially progressive ideals, and many of the new state's prison governors, had experienced the prison system from the inside themselves. On assuming office, however, reforms that might have been expected given such personal histories failed to materialise. As Kilcommins *et al.* state: 'despite the potential for reform introduced by the existence of an independent Irish government, the prison system and particularly its internal regimes, remained relatively unchanged' (2004: 47).

This social conservatism was compounded by the absence of a strong labour movement in Ireland during these formative years (Farrell 1970; Keogh 2005; Puirséil 2007). This factor can also be linked to the peculiar nature of Irish politics in the post-Civil War age which coalesced largely around the 'national question' rather than exhibiting a more usual split along class lines. The trade union movement was also internally divided and provided little in the way of either opposition or alternative ideas (Keogh 2005: 39). Although the welfarist settlement in Britain was a product of various administrations – Liberal, Conservative and Labour – the impetus behind the establishment of welfare state policies came largely from the desire to achieve a consensus between all elements of the social spectrum and to ensure a form of social safety-net for workers in particular. There was no comparable movement in Ireland.

Fanning argues, moreover, that socialism in Ireland was unable to surmount three hurdles: the continuing adherence to 'Civil War' politics in the new state, a Catholic bias against state planning, and the agricultural nature of the economy (Fanning 1983: 41). Radicalism in Irish politics during the post-Civil War years was confined largely to republicanism rather than social policy, and even within that group there was serious disagreement about the social aims it should pursue (English 1994).

Although the Fianna Fáil administration took the same conservative approach to prisons as the Cumann na nGaedheal government, there were some interesting differences in its overall attitude towards social policy. Compared with the austerity of Cumann na nGaedheal's approach to social provision, the verdict that the Fianna Fáil administration took a 'progressive' line on such matters is not unwarranted (Foster 1990: 546; Puirséil 2007: 40). The new government took action to implement a number of commitments it had made regarding social policy during the 1932 election, for instance the Workmen's Compensation Act and in 1936 a Widows and Orphans' Pension Scheme came into operation. A range of measures were introduced regarding public housing, the health service and the distribution of land, particularly to farmers from poorer agricultural regions in the west of Ireland, and public works were provided for employment purposes. Cottages for agricultural labourers were constructed, the provision of which had been a prominent electoral issue.

Social expenditure generally increased in the early years of the Fianna Fáil administration (Ferriter 2004: 397). Cousins describes these innovations as involving a 'dramatic change in the approach to social services' (Cousins 2002: 83). Barrington agrees that during the 1930s, 'considerable administrative activity was devoted to the laying of the foundations of an industrial community, and in developing such welfare services as housing' (Barrington 1967: 84). Girvin also asserts that the Fianna Fáil administration of this period was more socially interventionist than its predecessor (Girvin 2003). This was partially inspired by the party's relationship with Labour, which had supported Fianna Fáil's minority government in 1932 on the basis of the implementation of socio-economic reforms. Fianna Fáil was also not unaware that its activity in this area would be attractive to Labour supporters. In fact, its actions had the effect of attracting a large amount of that party's support base.

The greatest activity in the social policy realm was witnessed in the immediate aftermath of Fianna Fáil's assumption of power. The party's first budget contained a number of increases in social welfare allowances and the summer of 1932 'saw a raft of progressive legislation passing through the Dáil' (Puirséil 2007: 40). Dunphy argues, however, that the social radicalism of Fianna Fáil in its early years of power dissipated by the end of the 1930s and that the promulgation of the Constitution signalled the end of the party's ambitions for social change (Dunphy 1995: 208). After 1936 much less of the type of activity that had marked the early part of the new administration occurred. The Constitution promulgated in 1937 did include a commitment to principles of social improvement, for example, but these were contained in the firmly non-justiciable 'Directive Principles' by which the state *ought* to live, rather than being legally obliged to implement.

Towards the end of the 1930s Irish politics became more concerned with the 'economic war' with Britain whereby retaliatory tariffs and protectionist measures were imposed by each state over the refusal of the Irish government to pay over land annuities as agreed by the Anglo-Irish Treaty of 1922, dismantling the remnants of that Treaty through the Constitution and the threats to the state posed by subversive organisations.

Ireland was still, moreover, in an economically perilous position, which was compounded by these financial disagreements with Britain. A supplementary budget was introduced in 1939 and an Economy Committee was established to recommend cuts in public spending. During the later part of the 1930s there were fewer developments in social policy. By this time the old reliable economic and ideological arguments against state intervention and public spending had made a comeback (Fanning 1978: 631). Emigration was also a feature of the 'hungry thirties' and unemployment remained high, compounded by a worldwide economic depression (Ferriter 2004: 272).

Though Irish social policy was altered significantly during the 1930s in comparison with the austerity of the previous decade, it would be an overstatement to suggest that these innovations heralded a hegemonic commitment to the principles of 'the welfare state', for example, or to strong action in the realm of social provision.

Many of the factors outlined in relation to the characteristics of governance during the Cumann na nGaedheal era apply to this period as well. As one commentator puts it, 'the issues which dominated the politics of the 1920s – most notably stability and security – continued to be equally relevant' (Ferriter 2004: 359). Fanning argues, regarding the Department of Finance, that 'although much has been made of the significance of the 1932 change of government as a watershed in the Department's history, the strength of continuity binding the two decades cannot be lightly dismissed' (Fanning 1978: 353). The social reforms, when taken together with other economic developments and policies during the period, represent a curious mix of philosophies rather than exhibiting a coherent motif.

The period has been summarised by Ferriter as one of contradictions (Ferriter 2004: 359). On the one hand, socially progressive legislation was enacted, but self-sufficient, frugal living was mooted as the ideal way of life and censorship laws continued to prop up a conservative cultural scene (Brown 1981: 45) where sexual morality and its institutional regulation remained key concerns, and the place of women within the home was protected by the Constitution. The right to private property was given constitutional recognition, but de Valera could also praise James Connolly, the executed Republican socialist without feeling any apparent contradiction.

This is another important factor in the socio-economic landscape of Ireland in the 1930s. 'Pragmatism' is a word that has become indelibly associated with Fianna Fáil, and it was clearly in evidence during the 1930s. The actions taken by Fianna Fáil were responsive to the most pressing needs and most popular causes. Its economic policies of self-sufficiency and protectionism were based on Republican sentiments rather than rigorously empirical economic modelling (English 2006: 319). It adopted the language of social radicalism and implemented mild, gradualist social reform but did not fundamentally disturb the prevailing *status quo*.

Overall, the social change of the period seemed to satisfy both the political elite and the majority of the electorate. The melange of positions has been summed up by Dunphy thus: that Fianna Fáil 'took advantage of the weakness of class politics in Ireland by developing a language which seemed occasionally socialist, but practices which were comfortably capitalist' (Dunphy 1995: 164).

Social change and prisons during the 1930s

The lack of translation of the social progress that occurred during the 1930s into the prison system can be explained by the comparative perceived importance of both realms. The social reforms that were introduced in the 1930s were far more pressing than any movements in relation to 'ordinary' imprisonment at any rate.

This increase in social compassion during the 1930s did not, however, completely bypass the prison system. The changes in expectation about living standards and what was an 'acceptable' level of social provision altered the benchmark by which prison conditions were judged. Though none of this was made explicit, it was clear by the actions taken that a belief in limited liberalisation of prison regimes was present.

Attitudes within the Department of Justice must again account for some of this inactivity. During the period under consideration that Department was continuing its mode of cut-backs and caution, but its efforts were also taken up with analysing the emerging threats to the state from the IRA and other groups, receiving information from the Gardaí on such matters, drawing up legislation to deal with these threats and working on the drafting of the Constitution. With so many other drains on its resources, prison policy was ill placed for sustained action. Radicalism was not something associated with the Department more generally. In the mid-1930s it put forward the view that an absolute ban on the importation and sale of contraceptives was desirable (Ferriter 2004: 402) and it also pursued a very restrictive line on immigration into the state.

More than this, however, the pragmatism that characterised Fianna Fáil's policies during the 1930s left prison policy without a set of background assumptions by which it should be governed and civil servants could therefore have a very decisive role. The caution of the Department was, furthermore, unchallenged by political necessity, there being little in the way of advantage to transform the prison system as compared with, for example, pension provision. Without any of these pressures for change, the lack of innovation or guiding principle for prison policy becomes more explicable.

Forms of control outside prisons and concerns about 'deviance'

It is an incontrovertible fact that while the prison system was contracting in Ireland during this era, a system of detention outside the prison system was in place that had an enormously extensive reach over the population of the state, particularly, of course, those whom that state deemed 'deviant'. While prisons were under-populated, the industrial and reformatory school system, mental hospitals, county homes, mother and baby homes, Magdalene laundries and others held increasing numbers.

Most of these institutions did not require any kind of judicial sanction in order to be received into them, and all were hidden from public view. Revelations about the extent of abuses perpetrated on children and other inmates in these institutions have emerged only in recent years.

O'Sullivan and O'Donnell (2007) and Kilcommins et al. (2004) argue cogently that Irish society was highly regulated and used incarceration in various forms to a strikingly high degree during this period and for several following decades. Given this over-confinement of Irish society and the methods employed to restrain deviance, the prison system was largely unnecessary for the maintenance of Irish social order.

With the exception of subversive crime, the prison system was not required to control deviant populations to any great extent. They could be taken care of far more effectively through these other institutions. This is particularly true in the case of women. These institutions aimed to manage, control, 'reclaim' and neutralise the threat posed by individuals and groups who were considered a threat to the state's social order. Many of these individuals were children from backgrounds deemed to be irregular, girls and women who had 'fallen' from societal grace, victims of family feuds over money and land, and others considered to be social 'misfits'. The methods resorted to were often brutal but had the objective of religious and moral reclamation rooted in the Victorian and religious origins of the institutions and the particular relationship many of them had with explicitly religious motives. The sharp edge of social control that the prison system could otherwise provide was rendered essentially useless in a system that had so many other mechanisms of securing compliance or containing deviant populations.

Many of these sites were focused upon matters of sexual immorality. This preoccupation had a further impact on social life, allowing, additionally and consequentially, social problems to be kept in the background for decades.

This situation was partly a reflection of the reliance on the non-state sector that characterised Irish social provision. The state was content to delegate control of these institutions to religious and other organisations which operated an almost 'shadow' welfare state in the absence of governmental provision.

Insularity and the British inheritance

A further characteristic of Irish public administration was insularity in approach and outlook. There is no evidence that Irish policy-makers looked abroad for ideas regarding emerging movements in social policy. This is certainly true of the penal system. The Department of Justice officials, like their counterparts in the other elements of public administration, were trained within a framework peculiar to British ways of conducting public policy. When they took over the running of the prison system, they largely continued to operate the procedures that had pertained prior to the establishment of the Free State.

The Brennan Commission of Enquiry into the Civil Service (1935), conducted between 1932 and 1935, recognised that while the passing of control to a native administration may have been revolutionary in principle, it entailed, broadly speaking, no immediate disturbance of any fundamental kind in the daily work of the average civil servant.

As for prison policy, administrators continued to operate these systems without adding an 'Irish' dimension to them, or, in addition, even keeping abreast of developments within British policy, which is even more remarkable given these prior connections. It is perhaps the case that in the quest to establish a separate 'Irish' identity for the Free State and to demonstrate its independence from Britain, British ideas were not considered worthy of inquiry and policies propagated there would have been frowned upon.

This was also due, in part, to the generally insular and conservative nature of public administration during the period at issue. Barrington's verdict on the work of the public administration during this period is damning. He argues that the civil service was bereft of internal imagination when it came to planning for economic and social affairs, though this problem, he suggests, was structural rather than a lack of individual talent or initiative (Barrington 1967: 85). Its effect was, however, to frustrate the instigation or development of radical or visionary policies, which was most apparent in the realm of prison policy.

The absence of a wider 'community of ideas'

If personal experience had no effect on the thinking of Ministers for Justice regarding penal innovation and reform, it was improbable that other sources of information regarding the prison system and prospects for reform could have convinced them or their Department of the need to instigate change. However, even if there had been openness to new ideas at official level, there were very few sources from which they could come.

There was a professorship of Penal Legislation, Constitutional and Criminal Law at Trinity College Dublin (the Reid Professorship), later renamed the Professorship of Criminal Law, Criminology and Penology, but the various incumbents of this position during the 1920s and 1930s do not appear to have had much impact on either the Department of Justice or wider public discourse surrounding the prison system. There were no other academics working specifically in the area at the time.

Moreover, the education system generally reflected the conservative and traditional nature of Irish society. Third-level education remained reserved for those with significant financial means. The universities produced graduates mainly for the professions, medicine, law and clerical positions. There were few other graduates and most arts graduates went on to become teachers (Coolahan 2003: 763; Lee 1989: 131). The sciences, and particularly the social sciences, were sorely under-represented. The academic landscape was therefore an infertile one for ideas about prison policy and its direction.

Given its central role in the administration of many regulatory institutions, the Catholic Church might have been expected to have become involved in agitation about prison conditions, but apart from its important chaplaincy function this was not really apparent. The other religious denominations were generally in a similar position. Their input remained largely through other non-prison sites of regulation.

Newspaper coverage of the prison system was taken up mainly with the more exciting topic of 'political' imprisonment than any review of the state of Irish prisons generally. Censorship was also a prominent feature of Irish cultural and intellectual life. This operated to deny the state of many works of artistic endeavour, and also stultified social comment more generally. Added to this was the general distrust of groups associated with prisoners' rights or prison reform. At a time when a Minister for Justice had been assassinated, sympathy with such pleas was hardly to be expected. These conditions also fostered a large degree of suspicion regarding groups with 'left-wing' leanings. It can be posited that the combination of these factors had something of a 'chilling effect' on those who might otherwise have voiced concerns about the prison system and suggested change.

Stability, security and caution therefore constituted the symbiosis that defined the period. They combined to make retrenchment and rectitude key themes in the administration and direction of the prison system. Concerns over the secure custody of Republican prisoners were another underlying factor. Ultimately, the Fianna Fáil government of the 1930s decided to consolidate and make permanent emergency legislation in the form of the Offences Against the State Act 1939, the most significant piece of anti-terrorism legislation in the history of the state and the blueprint for subsequent enactments. The 1939 Act solidified the sense that prison policy in Ireland would continue to be influenced by concerns about security. This sense was borne out in the following years.

3

THE 'EMERGENCY'
The recurring effects of subversion and stagnation

Introduction

The 1920s and 1930s were times of caution in prison policy. However, the decades were also peppered with outbreaks of violence, disorder and fears of threats to the very foundations of the state. In 1939, this response would once again be employed in the context of the outbreak of World War Two or the 'Emergency' as it was known in Ireland. Prison policy was affected by such attempts to neutralise the threats from growing IRA activity and to counter the fears of a British invasion on the grounds of IRA collaboration with Nazi Germany and otherwise maintain neutrality (Bew 2007; Bowman 1982; Girvin 2006; Wills 2007).

This chapter commences by assessing the early impact of the Emergency on prison policy and the interconnections between the security of the state, the integrity of the prison system and the suppression of prisoner protest. The next section looks at the developments that occurred within the ordinary system of detention during these years. Finally, the chapter assesses a profoundly influential event on Irish prison policy that came at the end of the Emergency and at a time when there were stirrings of penal reform more generally. This arose from the death of an IRA prisoner in Portlaoise prison and the subsequent inquest into the circumstances thereof. The combined effect of these changes resulted in some official action in the prison arena, including the introduction of the Prison Rules 1947.

Imprisonment and internment: securing the state

Prison policy during the period of the Emergency was affected significantly by the conflict between the government and the IRA and the ongoing tensions this engendered. Security policy included the use of executions, imprisonment and internment. All three methods were used to remove IRA members from circulation, to crush opposition and to reaffirm the power and authority of the elected government.

As had been the case in the previous decade, during the Emergency the Fianna Fáil administration was unafraid of using the prison system and detention generally to secure the state. This took on a renewed impetus when the IRA began to amass support and materials again in the late 1930s, commencing a bombing campaign in Britain in 1938. The introduction of the new Constitution, called Bunreacht na hÉireann, in 1937 was a further factor. Through it, the Fianna Fáil government could assert that a break had been made with the past, particularly the British elements of governance within the state. As such, the defence of the state was now cast as a defence of a system of government established through popular consent.

In the early stages of the Emergency the numerical impact of its events on the ordinary prison system was relatively minor. As well as sentenced prisoners, however, large numbers were interned under Emergency legislation, mainly in a large army camp established at the Curragh, County Kildare. Some internees were also held throughout the state's prisons.

The number of detainees held under the powers of internment is difficult to calculate and it is similarly difficult to account for the proportion of the sentenced population made up by IRA prisoners. It is clear, however, that large numbers were interned under the extensive powers of the Offences Against the State (Amendment) Act 1940. By 1941 the number of internees was over 400 and the number sentenced by the Special Criminal Courts had exceeded 200 (Maguire 2008: 245). Overall, the average daily population in the institutions run by the Department of Justice went up from 544.68 in 1941 to 739.36 in 1942 (*Annual Reports on Prisons*, 1944). Thereafter, following a reduction in activity by the IRA, internees began to be released, initially in small numbers, with the camps empty in mid-1943. The average daily population in the prisons also began to drop.

The political status of prisoners and the authority of the state

Within the various sites of detention, prison policy came into collision with the resistance of the detainees involved. This resistance was a feature of prison events right from the outset.

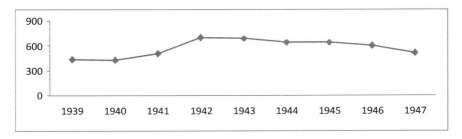

FIGURE 3.1   Average daily prison population 1939–47

Hunger strikes

Con Lehane, a solicitor and later co-founder of Clann na Poblachta, went on the first reported hunger strike of the Emergency directly upon his internment in Arbour Hill military prison in September 1939 (*Irish Independent*, 20 September 1939). Initially the government took a position of no compromise and announced that no releases would be ordered of those who went on hunger strike (*Irish Press*, 1 November 1939). The refusal of the government to grant political status to prisoners involved prompted a huge outcry among the parts of the population sympathetic to the demands (TAO S11533), but also from less obvious quarters including the leader of Fine Gael (TAO S11533). The government relented in this instance and released the men who remained on hunger strike by mid-November.

The government would later come to regret this display of clemency and it would not be repeated. This stance was emboldened by further activity by the IRA, particularly an audacious raid on the army's ammunition fort at Phoenix Park, Dublin. In the aftermath of this deeply embarrassing incident, the Taoiseach warned the IRA that the policy of 'patience' was at an end (Fanning 1983: 170) and a toughening of attitude was thereafter apparent (O'Halpin 1999a).

A further hunger strike took place in the spring of 1940. The government gave no concessions this time, despite renewed outcry and calls for release. Two men died, Anthony D'Arcy and Jack (Seán) MacNeela. In the aftermath of their deaths, the IRA called off its protest without achieving any of its goals within the state's sites of detention.

Prisoner resistance

Along with the drastic measure of the hunger strike, other forms of prison protest were regularly employed by the prisoners and their supporters, posing a variety of problems for prison policy-makers and administrators and engendering a number of responses. In Portlaoise, for example, several prisoners refused to wear prison clothing, instead donning blankets, and this went on for several years.

Within the prisons and the Curragh camp, the prisoners engaged in a wide variety of techniques to frustrate the intentions of penal administrators in the imposition of prison order and authority. The inmates in the Curragh were described by Máire MacSwiney-Brugha as a 'motley crowd' (MacSwiney-Brugha 2006: 191). Undoubtedly they were an unusual bunch. Members of families with long-term Republican connections such as George Plunkett, Ruairí Brugha and Dom Adams (the uncle of Gerry Adams, President of Sinn Féin since 1983) were detained alongside literary notables such as Mairtín Ó Cadhain and Brendan Behan.

Conditions were also rather peculiar. Ó Cadhain taught Irish to university level while Brugha taught it to primary level. The inmates were affiliated to a myriad ideologies. There were many splits in the camp between communists, socialists, Trotskyists, IRA supporters of Germany, IRA supporters of the Allies, devout Catholics and others, all of whom established their own networks.

The material conditions in the Curragh have been described by Ó Cadhain as 'the Siberia of Ireland' (cited in Wills 2007: 346). The environment of the Curragh was oppressive. Cold, lack of food and outbreaks of dysentery combined to make life difficult.

Boredom was one of the greatest problems faced by many of the internees and this led to some 'mischief' with very serious consequences, such as the burning down of a hut (Maguire 2008). Less consequential mischief involved the making of poteen and bestowing the lavatory with the name 'Bolands', after the Minister for Justice (Behan 1990: 66). Escape attempts were also frequent and tunnelling was widely practised (Maguire 2008).

Prison regime

There is little contemporary evidence of the regimes applicable to IRA prisoners, which is partly due to the government's policy of censorship of material regarding prison affairs. As became apparent after the Emergency, political status was not granted to these prisoners, and instead 'criminalisation' was evident in the government's approach. Portlaoise had a particularly rigorous regime (Ó Longaigh 2006), which came to light in dramatic circumstances, recounted below.

Brendan Behan has provided an account of life in Mountjoy around this time. Many of the conditions he describes applied equally to ordinary prisoners, though Behan was there by sentence of the Special Criminal Court. He too recounts the monotony, slopping out and the cramped living conditions (Behan 1990). There, those who like Behan had been sentenced for activities relating to IRA membership occupied themselves as a group by taking handicraft classes such as embroidery and basket-work.

Prison protests and censorship

Protests about the treatment of Republican prisoners and conditions were maintained throughout this period. However, much of the activity remained out of public discourse due to the zealous operation of wartime censorship restrictions. Censorship during the Emergency was widespread, covering matters deemed to relate to Ireland's neutrality and items considered to be capable of disturbing public order more broadly (Ó Drisceoil 1996). The imprisonment of IRA members was considered to fall directly within both categories.

One of the largest protests concerned the fate of one prisoner – Charlie Kerins from County Kerry who had been sentenced to death. Numerous interventions were made on Kerins' behalf in the Dáil and a petition was signed by thousands calling for a reprieve (TAO S13567 C–G). Riots occurred in Dublin and three Deputies were suspended from the Dáil when pleading for clemency on his behalf in the hours before he was due to die (Dáil Debates, vol 95, cols 1137–40, 29 November 1944).

The government was clearly more than fearful that the death of Kerins would rehabilitate the IRA in the eyes of the public. This fear was reflected in the government's censorship policy on the reporting of Kerins' actions and the punishment he had received (JUS/OWC R47). Reports on speeches made on behalf of Kerins were censored, with even advertisements for Masses for the prisoner not being immune from interference (JUS/OWC R48). The efforts on his behalf were to fail as Kerins was hanged in Mountjoy by Pierrepoint, the state's official executioner, on 1 December 1944.

The censorship surrounding death sentences extended to protests about prison conditions and almost any reference to the prison system. As will be seen below, the circumstances of imprisonment in Portlaoise prison were not reported on until after the end of the war. Prison matters were therefore self-consciously intertwined with the defence of the state and the nullification of protest was a key weapon in this campaign.

While the 'Republican' factor was a key element of the later discussions, the Emergency also witnessed increasing interest in prison conditions more generally and the content and purpose of prison policy. These changes occurred largely separately and independently of the policies pursued in respect of Republican prisoners but eventually converged with the issue of the detention of Republicans to create the conditions for change in the Irish prison system later in the 1940s.

'Ordinary' imprisonment: liberalisation of prison regimes

In the early 1940s a trend of slow but apparent liberalisation of prison regimes began to appear. It is important to note that for ordinary prisoners, there was no attempt to make the conditions in which they lived deliberately harsh. While those conditions may not have been particularly luxuriant, there was at least no punitive intent motivating penal administrators visible. Oireachtas debates and Department of Justice documents reveal a desire to alleviate prison conditions and a hope that reform could be achieved. There is certainly a dearth of calls for a solely retributive system or a movement towards denial of basic conditions to inmates.

In 1941 the first buds of this movement were reported by the Minister. In that year, prisoners were given the facility to associate for two hours in the evenings out of their cells, having been previously locked up from 4.30 p.m. (Dáil Debates, vol 83, col 1272, 28 May 1941). In 1942 prisoners began to receive a light meal at 7.30 p.m. in keeping with the relaxation of the evening routine in the state's prisons (Dáil Debates, vol 86, col 1552, 5 May 1942). Wireless sets and gramophones were installed.

It appears that these changes were prompted not from any empirical investigation, debate or deliberation about their potential effect on reoffending, but from a notion that it was 'right' to alleviate some of the rigours of punishment. These developments were exclusively instigated by the Department of Justice and there is little evidence of extensive deliberation within policy-making circles before implementation.

The particular changes that accrued at this time cannot in any way be described as sweeping innovations designed to remodel and recast the face of Irish imprisonment. Most were minor and rooted in administrative concerns, internal regimes and regulation. While the government was moving to effect change in the criminal justice system, this was done in an immensely cautious manner. These small beginnings were constantly overshadowed by the threats of 'economy', which were biting with ever greater vigour during the financial difficulties of the Emergency years. The Minister for Justice felt a recurring need to justify his actions on financial grounds, particularly around the time of the 1943 general election. He was undoubtedly conscious of the opposition's potential to decry his efforts on the basis of extravagance during a time when even basic commodities were difficult to come by (Dáil Debates, vol 86, col 1564, 5 May 1942).

The Department of Justice was also suffering from a reluctance to provide investment. In 1942 there was only one principal officer within the Department, who was in fact on loan to another Department, compared with three of that rank in 1928. In a Department with a wide brief, few staff and concerned about economy, prison policy would inevitably struggle to come to the fore. Moreover, departmental officials were actively engaged in receiving and collating intelligence reports on IRA activity and on anyone suspected of having communist sympathies.

Increased interest from outside the prison system

The small changes to prison regimes were accompanied by modest investigations of the prison system from sources outside the Department of Justice. These publications attracted attention from both academic and philanthropic circles, and among the wider public. While there was little official examination or research conducted on the prison system, there were a number of somewhat basic but comparatively mould-breaking assessments of the Irish prison system.

'The Prisons' and The Bell

In 1940 a series of articles by Edward Fahy, the Reid Professor of Penal Legislation, Constitutional and Criminal Law and the Law of Evidence at Trinity College Dublin (from 1940 to 1945), was carried in *The Bell*. *The Bell* was an important periodical in which some of the vital first steps in documenting and investigating Irish affairs, particularly regarding social and political issues, as well as broader cultural items, were taken. The writer Seán Ó Faoláin, then editor of *The Bell*, commissioned the pieces involved.

Fahy was aware of the originality of his examination and the resulting piece, declaring: 'so far as the writer of this article is aware, nothing exists in print which can be called an examination of our Prison System' (Fahy 1940: 18).

Fahy was complimentary of many elements of the system, such as the provision of meals, but he criticised other penal practices and the Department's record on penal reform more generally. He was particularly severe on the lack of stimulation and the monotony of prison life. In providing evidence that 'it should be realised by even the most hard-hearted that life today in Ordinary and Convict Prisons in Éire is not exactly a picnic' (Fahy 1940: 24), he reported that there was nothing in the way of 'amusements' or recreation provided, apart from a few entertainments at Christmas. Exercise was difficult in most prisons because of a lack of space and prisoners spent large parts of their day locked up. Food was served in the cells, resulting in further isolation. One of the greatest defects in the system, according to Fahy, was the idleness and lack of activity among prisoners.

However, the Reid Professor was patently aware of the objections that would be made to his recommendations for reform, demonstrating the preoccupations of the time – those of economy regarding extra prison staff and salaries.

Fahy was a voice in the academic wilderness given the absence of intra- or inter-academic discussion on Irish prisons or the purposes of penal policy. This was not, in truth, unique to Ireland. Britain lacked a criminological academy of any size until the 1950s or beyond. However, the point remains that academic input on the formation of prison policy cannot be identified as being either existent or important during these years.

It is difficult to assess the impact that Fahy's piece had and if it can be characterised as having stimulated an atmosphere of inquiry and curiosity about penal policy. Certainly, it is apparently unmentioned in official Department of Justice files or in the Dáil reports on the penal system. He was not invited, for example, to examine the prison system by the Department of Justice nor to discuss his work with officials and he had, therefore, no official or direct impact on the formation of prison policy.

The impact of the prison memoir: I Did Penal Servitude

While Professor Fahy's work remained confined to relatively small and homogeneous circles, another publication had a far greater and more widespread impact on the popular imagination and, indirectly, parliamentary discussions of Irish penal policy.

This piece was carried in a series of articles in the 1944 volume of *The Bell* and later published as a pamphlet following the great interest aroused by its original appearance: *D83223: I Did Penal Servitude: Journey to Fear* (Mahon-Smith 1945). The author, Walter Mahon-Smith, had spent time in a number of prisons in the state, including Sligo local prison, Limerick, Portlaoise and Mountjoy, for fraud offences. Mahon-Smith's writing was an account of his time spent in these institutions and the impressions formed thereby. His account of the prison regimes tallies with that provided by Fahy to a great degree. He worked, for example, chopping wood, was provided with the Bible as his sole reading material and wore a rough grey frieze with a thick dark stripe.

He detailed a life where four hours of education per week was obligatory for the 'illiterate' convicts and those with a low standard of education were also expected to 'improve themselves', while the prison industries remained basic and old-fashioned. The publication of Mahon-Smith's account and views caused something of a stir, which in terms in the Irish prison policy of the 1940s was quite significant.

I Did Penal Servitude was explicitly picked up on in a Dáil debate, but not until 1947 (Dáil Debates, vol 105, cols 207–314, 26 March 1947). However, the publication did elicit some immediate public debate regarding the prison system generally. *The Irish Times* related: 'it raises … a much larger issue, which must be considered by the Government sooner or later – the whole question of prison policy,' and called for a thorough overhaul of the system through the establishment of a government commission (31 May 1945). Seán Ó Faoláin's preface to the book was reprinted in this review, in which he explained the interest generated in the writing as being the result of the Irish people's first exposure to the suggestion that the state was imprisoning potentially excellent citizens and that nothing was being done to rehabilitate them (*Irish Times*, 5 January 1946).

The publication of Mahon-Smith's account and the interest it engendered among the public and commentators, combined with a number of other incidents, instigated a kindling of interest in penal matters immediately after the Emergency. In the short period from 1945 to 1947 the prison system was held up to increasing scrutiny through critical publications, commentary and the impact of the visit of a Catholic priest with internationally recognised reformist credentials.

The visit of Fr Flanagan

The famous Irish-American Catholic priest, Fr Flanagan, founder of Boystown, Nebraska, came to visit Ireland in 1946. Fr Flanagan's visit is most remembered for his denunciation of the country's industrial and reformatory school system, but it is clear he also had something to say about the prison system, and his visit was a further factor in kindling interest in penal affairs.

Keogh reports that Fr Flanagan described the prisons in the state as a 'disgrace to the Christian nation' (*Irish Times*, 6 September 2004). There is some dispute of the exact chronology, but it does appear that Fr Flanagan was influenced by *I Did Penal Servitude*, which he described as a 'horrible statement' of prison conditions which 'tore the heart out of him' (Raftery, *Irish Times*, 9 September 2004). So moved was the priest that he deplored the prisons of Ireland at public meetings as 'a disgrace, unChristlike and wrong'.

Fr Flanagan's visit and comments caused a great degree of consternation within governmental circles and the Minister for Justice strongly refuted Fr Flanagan's claims and criticisms, which apparently had been warmly welcomed by members of the public on his speaking tour (Keogh 2004). This reaction must, however, be placed within the context of the time. As Keogh asserts, 'prison reform was a sensitive issue for the government in the summer of 1946' (*Irish Times*,

6 September 2004). The reasons behind this sensitivity add a further layer of interest in penal affairs which, as will be shown below, explains the developments of this period to a large extent.

Inquest and inquiry following the end of the Emergency

On the cessation of World War Two, the numbers in Irish jails began to fall, as the crime rate also steadied. In 1944 the *Annual Reports on Prisons* were published once again after a five-year break.

Internees began to be released in 1944 (Maguire 2008). Prison conditions generally became tolerable, but it was a very different picture in Portlaoise. The events there and the effect they had on public opinion are a vital part in understanding the developments in penal policy during this period.

In 1945 it was admitted by the Government Information Bureau that nine prisoners in Portlaoise had been confined to their cells for several years without outdoor exercise. Many letters were written to the newspapers complaining about these conditions, but also, and significantly in light of later government action, the fact that prisons were still being administered under British prison rules (*Irish Times*, 1 November 1945; TAO S12579A). This 'British' factor still had potency in Ireland, where the War of Independence remained in people's memory and there was a deal of support or at least sympathy for IRA actions and aims. When the full extent of the treatment of IRA prisoners in Portlaoise came to light, the issue became a lit taper.

The death of Seán McCaughey

These matters did not come to a head, however, until another tragic drama unfolded within the Irish prison system. In 1946, Republican prisoners in Portlaoise staged another hunger strike in protest at their continued detention and at prison conditions. A number of prisoners there had refused to wear prison clothing for many years in protest at their treatment as 'criminals', instead donning prison blankets.

One such prisoner was Seán McCaughey from Belfast and a member of the IRA. He died on 11 May 1946 after 22 days on hunger strike; for some of this period he was also on thirst strike, in an effort to secure his unconditional release. McCaughey had spent almost four years without clothing in solitary confinement, inducing a significant toll on his mental health. Noël Browne related later that he visited the cell in which McCaughey had been detained and described it as a 'deep cell underground, a truly awful place in which to die, hungry or not' (Browne 1986: 89).

The conditions in which these prisoners were held were entirely different from and far more unpleasant and severe than those experienced by Mahon–Smith. In fact, it is remarkable that Mahon–Smith said nothing about these prisoners. It is possible that even *The Bell*, which was very keen to push the boundaries of restrictions on freedom of speech, was either fearful or victim of the wartime censor.

Protests were made during the latter part of McCaughey's strike. A petition signed by members of the Oireachtas was presented to de Valera and a march on Leinster House, the seat of Parliament, was attempted (Maguire 2008: 57). However, the government was resolute in its stance and McCaughey did not succeed in his endeavours.

The inquest into McCaughey's death is famous for the work of Seán MacBride SC who appeared for the relatives of the dead hunger striker. Liam Hartnett was junior counsel at the inquest. Adding to the drama, the inquest was held in Portlaoise prison itself, involving a large number of police and military officers. The inquest is most noted, however, for the startling statement made by the prison's doctor. Under sustained questioning from MacBride, he admitted that he would not have kept a dog in the conditions in which McCaughey was held (*Irish Times*, 13 May 1946) and this made front-page news. The jury stated that in their opinion, 'the conditions existing in the prison were not all that could be desired according to the evidence furnished'.

Seán McCaughey's death and the subsequent inquest aroused huge interest among the public. MacBride was accused of using the inquest in order to stir up a wider debate about prison conditions (MacBride 2005: 135), and if this was the aim then he was certainly successful.

MacBride recalled later that the interest stirred was heightened because, due to the censorship involved, the public was unaware of the extent of political imprisonment and the conditions in which such prisoners were held. The ban on reporting of such matters had been lifted just before the inquest. The prisoner issue, in effect, 'crystallised' (Jordan 1993: 83) around the death of the Belfast man. This had significant ramifications for the debate on prison conditions and the government's attitude towards prison policy.

Undoubtedly, the vanguard of the interest in prison conditions in 1946 was sparked by Republicans and their supporters. Immediately following the inquest the Republican Prisoners' Release Committee, a group acting to promote the rights of Republican prisoners, organised a meeting in Dublin that was attended by around 3,000 people. Calls were made at it for a public inquiry into the conditions at Portlaoise (*Irish Times*, 20 May 1946).

Into this context of concern and agitation, the comments of Fr Flanagan resurfaced. Fr Flanagan's criticisms were reported in the Irish media during his visit earlier in 1946, but the greatest consternation seems to have been caused when he repeated his comments in the *New York Press* on 17 July 1946, after the death and inquest of Seán McCaughey. In the Dáil later that month, the Minister for Justice's attention was drawn to the statements. His reply was combative and defensive. He stated that Fr Flanagan had not visited any of the prisons or the Borstal while on his visit, and expressed his opinion that he was 'surprised that in these circumstances an ecclesiastic of his standing should have thought it proper to describe in such offensive and intemperate language conditions about which he has no first-hand knowledge' (Dáil Debates, vol 102, col 1135, 23 July 1946).

On 29 May 1946, shortly after the conclusion of the inquest, the Farmers Party and the Labour Party called for an inquiry into conditions at Portlaoise prison. This was defeated, however, with Fine Gael voting with the government. Seanad Éireann, on the other hand, passed a motion calling for such an inquiry (Seanad Debates, vol 31, cols 2120–204). Significantly, in light of later developments, the debate in the upper house focused on the provisions of the Prison Rules under which the prisoners were held and the unavailability of copies of the relevant rules. Consequentially, this was the first time the term 'rehabilitation' rather than 'reform' was recorded in parliamentary discourse. It is probable that the senators involved had read about changes in Britain, or Mahon-Smith's claims, and were taken by this 'new' approach to imprisonment. The term was, generally, still very much a novelty.

A matrix of sensitivity and negative comment

It appears that around this time the government and Department of Justice began to feel beleaguered by the mounting criticism of the prison system. Criticism of prisons was ill tolerated and viewed almost as an attack on the state and its good name internationally. Letters sent to the newspapers and other material deemed 'sensitive' on the topic were kept on file in the Department (TAO S1144).

The calls for investigation and the specific establishment of an independent committee to assess the conditions within the prison system were initially resisted by the government. Fianna Fáil was, however, vulnerable to the censure being expressed, given that much of it came from its natural support base, particularly when viewed in light of an upcoming general election and general dissatisfaction among its voters about its achievements.

The ongoing condemnation of the conditions at Portlaoise, which exploded when the veils of censorship were removed, and the concomitant desire to assuage the worries of its supporters, acted to compel the government to allow an investigation into the conditions in that prison.

The Labour Party Report

On 28 May 1946 Minister Boland announced in the Dáil that he had been asked by members of the Labour Party to investigate the conditions in Portlaoise (Dáil Debates, vol 101, col 882, 28 May 1946). His response illustrates the cautious approach of the government about prison matters at this time. The Minister was anxious to ensure that only members of the Oireachtas and no other interest groups would gain access to the prison. However, it must still be noted that allowing such an inquiry was unique and is further evidence that the government wished to assuage public opinion.

The names of four TDs were submitted to and approved by the Minister, and they conducted a hasty inquiry into conditions in June, the results of which were published in August 1946. The title of the report itself betrays its origins: *Prisons and Prisoners in Ireland: Report on Certain Aspects of Prison Conditions in Portlaoighse Convict Prison* (Labour Party 1946).

The report was originally intended for circulation exclusively among the Labour Party and the Minister, but such was the demand for copies of the document that the Labour Party was compelled to publish it as a pamphlet.

The extent of the investigation was limited on many levels, being confined to a seven-and-a-half-hour visit to a single prison. While the report owed its origins to the debate on the detention of IRA prisoners, the authors did not confine themselves to this issue only and the report covered three main topics.

First, it evaluated the conditions of non-political prisoners. Their account confirms much of what was stated by both Mahon-Smith and Fahy in their descriptions of prison life. The report also made some criticisms and recommendations. It was felt that prison dress had a depressing effect and there was a lack of recreational facilities. Prisoners were found to be parading in single file around the building in an aimless manner, and the food was also unrelentingly monotonous. The impression given is one of extreme boredom among prisoners, compounded by the absence of tobacco. The report recommended that the food be increased and the lights not be extinguished until 10 p.m.

Political prisoners comprised the second key topic dealt with. By this time, seven persons remained in Portlaoise who continued to claim political status. These seven were still wearing a smock fashioned from a blanket and the report was the first to reveal the extent of the difficult conditions extant in that prison. The prisoners involved were subject to special observation, which involved strip-searching at frequent intervals and the switching on of the light in their cells every 15 minutes during the night, whereas the norm was every two hours. Up until 1943 at least they were locked in their cells for 24 hours per day, could not send or receive letters, nor take visits or read newspapers. Their only contact was with officials of the prison. They were furthermore not allowed to exercise in the open air, or even outside their cells. After May 1943 these prisoners were allowed to associate within the prison for three hours per day except on Sundays or holy days, but were still denied access to the prison grounds and exercise outside. The authors concluded that they should be transferred to military custody in the Curragh.

Finally, the report contained some broad recommendations about the penal system. The authors were convinced that the system as it then stood was not the optimum one for combating crime and was, in fact, 'demoralising and outmoded'. Corporal punishment and dietary punishments that were still being used in the prison system should be abandoned, along with solitary confinement, they concluded.

The Labour Party members then set out their vision for the penal system, which was officially adopted as party policy on the prisons, the first time that a general position on penal reform was included in the policy of any Irish political party:

> The chief aim and object of all penal process, it has been said, should be the recognition of the general principle of dividing all offenders into two categories, first, those who ought never enter a jail; and second, those who ought never be allowed to leave it. But if the chief aim of penal legislation is to keep jails empty, as we believe it should be, the present system of imprisonment, so far as Penal Servitude prisoners are concerned, must be abandoned.

Specifically, the report called for the establishment of 'colonies' rather than jails, which would allow for segregation and the provision of work and training of a 'beneficial character'. Long-term prisoners should be kept under the care and guidance of a doctor and psychiatrist and should be equipped by moral and physical training to make a fresh start and establish a 'normal' life on release (Labour Party 1946).

The government defends its record on prisons

The Dáil was in summer recess when the Labour Party Report was published and so the Oireachtas did not debate its contents immediately. However, interest in prison conditions endured into 1947. In the aftermath of the report and in the face of critique within it, from sections of the media and Fr Flanagan, the government was keen to put the best spin on its record regarding penal reform. In the *Annual Report on Prisons* for the year 1946, published in 1947, for example, the usual litany of short and repeated statements about the prison food, industries, prisoners' health and so on was interrupted by a précis of the improvements to prison conditions over the previous 20 years. It can be speculated that the decision to include this statement was made with the knowledge that the events of that year would make the *Annual Report* a more enticing read than normal.

The Oireachtas debates the prison system

When the Oireachtas came to debate penal affairs in 1947, two Dáil deputies who had spent time in Sligo prison over disputes regarding land annuities, along with some of the Labour TDs who had visited Portlaoise prison the year before, and the leader of Fine Gael, W. T. Cosgrave, sought a prison commission to investigate and reform the conditions in the state's jails.

The majority of comment by the members of the Dáil was critical of prevailing penal conditions and supportive of investigation and reform. In spite of all these criticisms, the government refused to contemplate the establishment of a prison commission.

One of the main objections to the establishment of such an investigation was outlined by the Minister: 'The position is that we find it impossible to keep certain types of people who should not be on commissions off them – soft-hearted and soft-headed people. That is my opinion. It would be impossible to keep those people off and the last position would be worse than the first' (Dáil Debates, vol 105, col 595, 16 April 1947).

While the Minister declared that 'further improvements may be found to be practicable and desirable', it was felt that these could be implemented and enough information obtained 'without resorting to the appointment of a formal commission … I think it would be much better to leave things as they are and if things are to be done they can be done by administrative action' (Dáil Debates, vol 105, col 595, 16 April 1947).

The Minister's preferred course of action was the one utilised to effect some small changes. Administrative action was the chosen method to update parts of the prison system and the regulations that guided its functioning.

Administrative changes within the prison system

In 1946 and 1947 a number of administrative decisions were taken within the system that were aimed at improving the material conditions of the state's penal institutions and modernising its industries and regimes. Writing 25 years later, O'Flynn described this period as being one of 'liberalisation of the regimes' in prison (O'Flynn 1971: 5), which, as has been seen, was already in evidence in the early 1940s.

While there is no indication on record that the recommendations of the Labour Party were directly taken into account in making the relevant decisions, many of the amendments effected were along the lines of those proposed by the report. These alterations to prison regimes were those most easily, cheaply and least obtrusively implemented. They acted to alleviate some of the most visible and criticised facets of prison life and to deflect criticism in this way without overhauling the entire official approach to prison policy.

Shortly after the report's publication, the regulations regarding visits and letters were revised and liberalised. In July 1946, not long after the inquest of McCaughey, the early lock-up that had existed on Sundays and holy days was abolished. In August, 'lights out' was put back from 8.30 p.m. to 10 p.m. At Christmas all prisoners were now allowed to receive parcels of fruitcake and other 'small luxuries'. Later, this concession was extended to Easter and Halloween. The parcels were provided by prisoners' families while the Society of Friends and St Vincent de Paul provided for those who had no outside support.

Over the next few months, other moderate efforts were also made. In Mountjoy new industries were established. Carpentry and smithing were introduced along with the feeding of pigs. Arrangements were made to introduce electric washing machines to the women's prison to improve the laundry facilities, and for finishing machines in the shoe-making workshops and more power-driven sewing machines in the men's prison.

A recreation yard was erected at Sligo prison. Radio sets were provided and the libraries in all the prisons were substantially restocked after the neglect forced by wartime rationing.

In June 1947 long-term prisoners in Portlaoise were given permission to smoke. Clothing was also subject to change. Suits of a similar cloth and pattern to those worn by 'civilians' were issued to Portlaoise prison, which were to be worn during the evening recreation period and on Sundays and holy days.

Responding specifically to the Labour Party Report, the Department of Justice investigated the possibility of establishing farm colonies for prisoners it described as being of the 'incidental' type, defined as those with a previously good record and who were unlikely to offend again. The extent of these inquiries was explicitly preliminary and consisted of an inventory of the numbers of prisoners who might be suitable for such a scheme. The fruit of this labour was that only 20 suitable prisoners were detained in Ireland at the time and the project was not viable (TAO S13879). As such, while the report prompted investigation and change, the factors of economy and low prisoner numbers continued to act as constraints to action.

The Prison Rules 1947

One area in which legislative effort was engaged and that did affect the overall prison system was the introduction of the Prison Rules in 1947. It is an irony of the history of prison policy that while 'political' imprisonment had deflected attention from ordinary prisoners, the interest sparked by such detention had the greatest impact on the ordinary prison system.

On 5 June 1946, in the month after McCaughey's death, James Larkin Junior TD put down a question in the Dáil inquiring as to the various sets of prison rules, where these could be found and when they would be placed in the Oireachtas library (Dáil Debates, vol 101, col 1309, 5 June 1946). A list of the rules was circulated to all members of the house who were present, and it was revealed that all of the rules bar one had been made by the General Prisons Board when Ireland had been under British rule.

Given the history of Ireland, British treatment of Irish prisoners was certainly not the desired comparison for a Fianna Fáil administration that was beginning to feel the heat regarding its Republican credentials.

Amazingly, there were no spare copies of the rules available in the Department of Justice to place in the Oireachtas library. The discovery of this fact in itself may provide a partial explanation for the development of new rules. Eventually, the Department decided that a mere reprint was not suitable, and modernisation and improvement were called for, requiring a full redraft. The official change of heart regarding the revision of the rules resulted in an overhaul of the existing regulations. They were finally signed by Minister Boland on 16 September 1947.

The new Prison Rules covered all aspects of prison life and the internal administration of penal regimes and activities. It is, however, difficult to discern a particular philosophy of imprisonment or vision of its objectives from the rules. Their overarching purpose and function were essentially purely administrative, laying out in detail the particular regulations to govern every element of the running of prisons from day to day and were largely a consolidating and updating measure of the rules already in existence, taking the rules promulgated for internees under the Offences Against the State Act 1939 as their inspiration.

There was a patent concern in the rules with hygiene, cleanliness and good order. The rules begin with a section on 'accommodation' and require, for example, that each cell only be used for a prisoner when certified by the Minister to be of such a size, and to be lighted, warmed, ventilated, and fitted up in such a manner as may be requisite for health, and furnished with the means of enabling the prisoner to communicate at any time with an officer of the prison. Furthermore, under the rules as originally enacted, each prisoner was to occupy a cell by himself, unless in association.

There is little attention devoted to the question of 'treatment' of prisoners of any nature. Instead, the rules are aimed at the regulation of the needs of prisoners and to provide a statement of their entitlements while in custody, regarding food, clothing (which allowed certain prisoners to wear their own clothes) and cleanliness.

Cosmetics and consolidation rather than innovation

The Prison Rules did not herald or embody any great reformative zeal or drive in the prison system. The rules were primarily a consolidation of a scattering of rules and sources of administration and obligations dating back to the Prisons Act of 1826. The rules in the main reproduced these provisions, rather than effecting any great innovation in the system. Their content reflects largely Victorian notions of penal regulation, and the main changes brought in by the rules involved a culling of provisions from the old regulations that had been rendered obsolete by improvements carried out by administrative action over the years since Independence, such as the removal of the plank bed, and abolition of bread-and-water punishments, hard labour and corporal punishment.

The rules further reflect the tenor of Irish penal policy at this time. They highlight a greater focus and interest in material prison conditions and an undoubted desire for the amelioration of life for prisoners. However, they are unimaginative and conservative in their aims. Improvements in material conditions were the motif of this period, rather than a transformation, or even a consideration, of radical changes in philosophy or practice. Official thinking about punishment was still far too underdeveloped to create the conditions for such change. To a certain degree, the introduction of the rules was a largely cosmetic exercise, instigated by a degree of embarrassment felt by the state about the existing ones.

Fianna Fáil loses Republican support

Towards the end of Fianna Fáil's tenure during this period, the prison system began to receive greater attention and, more significantly, greater action was taken. This was very much a product of the particular circumstances which involved IRA detainees, increased public interest in prison conditions and deaths in dreadful circumstances of prisoners on hunger strike. This combination of events appears to have forced the Department of Justice into action it would otherwise have resisted. However, such a confluence of events was not novel in the history of Irish prison affairs. The fact that action was taken in the late 1940s and not before reflects a change in Irish political, social and intellectual culture during this period.

Fianna Fáil had started its time in power with a nod to its Republican support base. It was still concerned with its electoral appeal on 'national' matters and the dangers of losing this source of support. The establishment of a new political party proclaiming Republican ideals and courting Fianna Fáil voters, Clann na Poblachta, in 1946, not long after the death of McCaughey, was another factor for disquiet in this regard (Bowman 1982: 262; Lee 1989: 270).

Clann na Poblachta had some quite direct links to the politics of imprisonment in Ireland. One of its main founders was Seán MacBride. Two other founders of the Clann were Con Lehane and Noel Hartnett, who had also worked alongside MacBride at the McCaughey inquest. Peadar Cowan was another involved from the outset. He would later write an influential pamphlet on prison conditions. Noël Browne, a Clann Minister in the Inter-Party Government formed in 1948, would also show a keen interest in penal reform and prisoners' rights and welfare throughout his career in public service.

The Clann was formed, as Lee states, on the 'the basis of committees formed to help Republican prisoners during the war' (Lee 1989: 286). A significant source of support for the Clann came from those disenchanted specifically with Fianna Fáil's treatment of Republican prisoners, as well as dissatisfaction with the lack of progress on many of the Republic's radical social ideals (Rafter 1996).

Dissatisfaction with the government also accounted for a minor resurgence in Labour Party support (Puirséil 2007: 89), with that party accused of utilising popular disquiet over the hunger strikes to improve its standing (Lee 1989: 223).

This disquiet over slippage in support for the country's largest party was not groundless. In the general election of 1943, which Fianna Fáil had contested on the basis of its record on security, arguing that a strong government was required in turbulent times, that party witnessed a 10 per cent drop in its support, losing ten seats. Labour and Clann na Talmhan, a party set up to defend rural interests, were the main winners. Puirséil links the success of Labour in part to the tumult over the 'Republican' issue of the day, arguing that 'Labour's assiduous adoption of the prisoners issue garnered it at least one new seat ... where Dan Spring won a seat for Labour in the Republican heartland of Kerry North' (Puirséil 2007: 89).

De Valera, concerned to head off the Clann's rising popularity before it reached troublesome levels, called an election for 1948. Before this, however, the government felt itself compelled to take action on the prison question in order to deflect suggestions that it was as coercive and draconian as the Cumann na nGaedheal administration, a charge that would have been anathema to most Fianna Fáil supporters. The 'green' or Republican card and concern over Fianna Fáil's electoral fortunes trumped resistance to reform in a way that had not been seen either under Cumann na nGaedheal or Fianna Fáil in the mid–1930s, nor indeed was it seen again in later years.

'Liberalisation' and changes in Irish social policy

The political massaging of Fianna Fáil supporters cannot account solely for the definite moves towards the embryonic efforts at altering the administration of the prison system that began at this time. Contributions on the prison system in the houses of the Oireachtas and within the media were generally sympathetic to the needs of ordinary prisoners and there was a consensus that conditions should be improved. The fact that the sentiments being expressed in that debate were largely 'progressive' should not be taken for granted. Policy-makers were capable of espousing 'policy styles' that were distinctly tough when it came to Republican prisoners.

During the mid–1940s debate about provision for the state's poor, ill and unemployed continued to build, partially fuelled by contemporaneous developments in Britain. As one commentator notes, 'in a sense, Fianna Fáil was entering the second period of expansion in social welfare legislation from the early 1940s on' (Ferriter 2004: 402).

Debates on social security became more frequent. Political pressure was mounting to take action in this regard and in 1947 a separate Department, Social Welfare, was established to cope with the extra demands for social services and to administer the developing system, and have a *locus* for planning and thinking. Public health was under increasing focus after decades of neglect. As Lee notes, no Irish government 'took much interest in health until the Second World War' (Lee 1989: 313). Very high levels of illness, particularly tuberculosis and rickets, were prevalent among the poorer sections of Irish society, due to ongoing high levels of squalor and malnutrition (Barrington 1987: 154). A Public Health Bill was introduced in 1945 in an attempt to foster a preventative approach to public health, envisaging a free scheme without a means test for mothers and children up to the age of 16. A Department of Health was also, finally, established in 1947.

A very significant development was the introduction of a Children's Allowance in 1944, which occurred before a similar measure was brought into British social policy. The factors behind this successful major social reform are indicative of the character of Irish social provision during this period and are illuminating when contrasted with the realm of prison policy and the nature of the Fianna Fáil government's approach to policy change more generally. Lee (1989) and Bew and Patterson (1982) conceive of the reasons why the Children's Allowance came about as a struggle between the forces of modernisation and resistance being fought out within the Fianna Fáil party itself.

The Minister in charge of the venture was Seán Lemass. Predictably, the Department of Finance vociferously opposed the measure (Cousins 2002: 81) and this was one of the rare battles that it lost. The political attractiveness of the allowance safeguarded its passage, something that prison reforms could not hope to achieve.

Resistance to change

As well as being grounded in party politics and electoral appeal, the introduction of the Children's Allowance stands as something of an exception rather than part of a full-blooded commitment to an Irish 'welfare state'. When compared with the events occurring across the Irish Sea, the picture of Irish social policy was far less innovative or transformative. Ireland avoided the disaster and upheaval attendant on the war experienced elsewhere. This had the effect of removing another potential source of change. The 'revolutionary moment' largely passed Ireland by. As Puirséil puts it, 'in Ireland, the inclination of many Irish politicians was to reach for their darning needles' (Puirséil 2007: 116).

The general hesitation to social expansionism or policy transformation was reflected in the official reaction to the Beveridge Report published in the United Kingdom. Its recommendations received extensive coverage in the Irish press. Within Fianna Fáil, however, the two factions representing modernisation and continuity were again at odds. Seán MacEntee, the Minister for Finance, was opposed to its introduction in Ireland, citing its emphasis on dependence on the state for benefits and his opposition to compulsory insurance benefits. McElligot, the Secretary in that Department, was advocating a 'good fright' for the people so that the 'apostles of expansionism would see where the country stood when they realised that existing and practically essential services were being cut to the bone' (quoted in Fanning 1978: 320). Other opponents of Beveridge based their hostility on interpretations of Catholic social doctrine, being particularly resistant to what was perceived to be impermissible state interference in family life and a suspicion of state 'planning' – something then associated with communist regimes (Dunphy 1995: 246). In a budget speech in May 1945, the Minister for Finance Seán T. Ó Ceallaigh dismissed the possibility of introducing a scheme of social security akin to Beveridgeism on the grounds that it was impracticable and unsuitable in the Irish context, particularly given the financial position of the state (Bew and Patterson 1982: 12).

The Public Health Bill 1945 mentioned above received enormous opposition from Fine Gael on the basis of its perceived incompatibility with Catholic social teaching. Its reintroduction, after the establishment of the Departments of Health and Social Welfare, was resisted by the Irish Medical Association, a powerful lobby representing doctors, and the Catholic hierarchy (Whyte 1980). The bill to establish the Department of Social Welfare was criticised by the opposition along similar lines.

There remained no radical transformation of Irish social policy akin to the introduction of the British welfare state, there was no recasting of the social scene or realignment of social interests or classes, and 'full scale modernisation remained a long way off' (Ferriter 2004: 497). The political elites remained resistant to change and class-based politics did not become a feature of the Irish political landscape. The Labour Party suffered a debilitating split in 1944 and maintained its fear of being considered either too radical or too close to its sister party in Britain.

Unlike in Britain, there was no major expansion of state functions, nor finances assigned to such a task. Patterson argues that such a move was further inhibited by an aversion to increasing the tax burden on the Irish higher classes, which Fianna Fáil was trying to court during these years (Patterson 1997: 150).

Instead of social or economic transformation, there was a series of individual measures exhibiting elements of a commitment to greater intervention in social life and endeavour aimed at improving the living conditions of Irish citizens, though poverty, infant mortality, slum accommodation, unemployment, poor health and a reliance on charity continued. The industrial and reformatory school system endured and the country's mental hospitals and other sites of detention remained largely immune to change.

The policies to tackle Irish social ills were implemented as much for political reasons as they were a demonstrable vision of social transformation. Fanning argues that the state's response to the Beveridge Report was 'not so much an overall economic plan for the post-war years as piecemeal proposals in particular areas based on the response of individual departments' (Fanning 1983: 150).

Within prison policy, the changes made were similarly *ad hoc* and piecemeal. Like developments in the social policy area, they had the aim of 'improvement' in common, without representing any innovative or radical departure. Pragmatism and electoral politics, rather than philosophical commitments of any description, were characteristic of the changes made in both areas. In 1948, political change was, however, on the horizon. Its impact on prison policy is assessed in the next chapter.

4

THE 1950s
Low numbers and limited interest

Introduction

This chapter assesses prison policy in Ireland from 1948 until 1958, a decade in which there were unprecedented changes on the party political front. However, these political shifts were not replicated in the realm of prison policy, which exhibited a remarkable degree of continuity over the decade, being notable chiefly for its stagnation and official neglect. The numbers in prisons fell to remarkably low levels and the gradualist approach to improving prison conditions was also maintained.

The first Inter-Party Government

The political system in Ireland underwent a shock when the country went to the polls in February 1948. In that election Fianna Fáil was unable to secure an overall majority and the previously unthinkable came to pass. A coalition government of Fine Gael, Clann na Talmhan, Labour, National Labour, Clann na Poblachta and

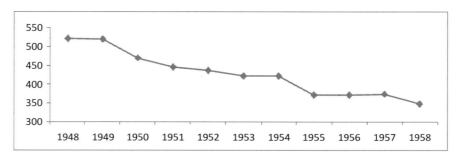

FIGURE 4.1 Average daily prison population 1948–58

a number of independents was formed. It was the first Inter-Party Government in the state's history.

Though possibly an obvious choice with his legal background and experience, the new Minister for Justice was not to be the leader of Clann na Poblachta, Seán MacBride, but came from the Fine Gael party in the shape of General Seán MacEoin. MacBride assumed the position of Minister for External Affairs and John A. Costello of Fine Gael became Taoiseach.

An early act of the new administration was to give an amnesty to the remaining IRA prisoners in the state's jails. This decision was prompted in particular by the desire of the Clann na Poblachta segment of the new government to affirm its qualifications as a Republican party and to effect what many of its supporters would have wished (Girvin and Roberts 2000).

A new Minister for Justice: a new vision for prison policy?

Besides this significant move, General MacEoin's stewardship of the system continued the previous administration's efforts to effect small reforms within the prison system.

No large-scale reforms were attempted under his leadership, but the government did make a couple of changes to the system. In the early part of his tenure, MacEoin sought to remedy what were considered faults in prevailing prison administration. One of these was directly related to the McCaughey furore discussed in the previous chapter. It was felt that the lack of official oversight of the prisons had allowed for the manner of his confinement to be hidden from public view. In his first Estimate (Budget speech) as Minister in 1948, MacEoin announced that his government proposed to appoint an Inspector of Prisons for the first time in the history of the Free State (Dáil Debates, vol 111, col 1550, 23 June 1948). This was an innovation, in fact, first mooted by the Fianna Fáil administration before its departure from office. The Inter-Party Government viewed it as long overdue. It was to be a full-time appointment, though its actual fate is unclear. The position was not actually filled until 2002.

MacEoin's second announcement involved a proposal to change the name of the Borstal to St Patrick's Institution, Clonmel. This was designed to erase the British associations with the name of the institution and was another plank in the assertion of Republican credentials by the new government, which was, in fact, the first to declare Ireland a Republic.

Besides these changes, the new Minister for Justice did not rush to lay out the new government's philosophy of punishment or any radical new plans for reform of the penal system. The Inter-Party Government's position in this regard was therefore very much in the mould of that which had prevailed previously. There was a desire to improve conditions, but no evidence of a great deal of thought or deliberation beyond altering the material elements of the penal system. These themes are well brought out by the Oireachtas debates on the first Justice vote overseen by the new government.

In this debate, the Labour Party called for a system of 'rehabilitation' to be introduced into Irish prisons to prevent recidivism (Dáil Debates, vol 111, col 1678, 23 June 1948). 'Rehabilitation' was still a new and unfamiliar term, and it is unclear, and apparently unlikely, whether the deputies involved had considered the differences between it and reformation, or what the term involved more generally. The 'modern' nature of the word may have, in truth, been its greatest appeal, but the alteration in language is nonetheless significant.

An insight into both governmental and departmental thinking at this time comes from a speech delivered by General MacEoin to the Dublin Chamber of Commerce in October 1950 on 'The Work of the Department of Justice' (TAO S15059A). In this speech MacEoin evinced an attitude to innovation in penal policy most compatible with the tenor of debate regarding the prisons thereto. The Minister was evidently anxious to demonstrate to his audience that the Department was doing its utmost to improve prison conditions, providing examples from improvements in work and the alleviation of material deprivations while in custody.

The statements of policy suggest a desire to be perceived as humane and modern, to appear understanding of prisoners and to assist in reforming them; sentiments that had persisted from previous years. At the point of implementation, however, once again the changes were incremental and modest, being carried out mainly at the administrative level.

In Mountjoy, Limerick, Portlaoise and St Patrick's, film projectors were introduced to show films in the evenings (JUS 2002/2/60). In addition, permission to smoke was introduced to all prisons, while in Portlaoise those sentenced to penal servitude received a ration of tobacco or cigarettes. Additional games and recreational items were provided in Mountjoy and Portlaoise and in 1948 improved clothing for prisoners was introduced. Finishing machines for tailoring arrived in Mountjoy and Portlaoise workshops and the mailbag-making machines there were replaced. In addition, in an important symbolic effort the use of the terms 'warder' and 'wardress' was ended and members of the prison staff would therefrom be known as 'officer' (TAO S15059A). The Prison Officers' Association was formed during this year. In 1949 two handball alleys were erected in Mountjoy and in the same year a new recreation hall was added to Limerick prison.

One most significant change introduced in 1949 was the abolition of the 'ticket of leave' system which had prevailed for convicts who were granted release before the expiration of their sentence. Under the previous provisions, any such convict had to report to the police on a regular basis. MacEoin announced that from 1949 on, convicts were to be released unconditionally (JUS 93/182/1).

Departmental inquiry into prison conditions

While much of the effort expended during the years of the first Inter-Party Government regarding the prison system were localised, maintenance-focused and mild, the new Minister for Justice did watch over the first departmental investigation of the prison system for many years.

The Department of Justice conducted a comprehensive survey of the prison system as it then stood in 1949. Though it is not made explicit on file, it can be speculated that this was at the behest of the new administration, engaged in audit of past events and 'climate setting' for the future (unreleased files, JUS 93/182/1).

This inventory reported that the system had changed little in the decades since Independence. The Department was, however, satisfied that conditions had improved, emphasising the greater freedom experienced by prisoners and the introduction of association at work, recreation and exercise. Most revealing, however, are the statements made reflecting on the purpose of imprisonment and the penal system more generally. The memorandum averred, eschewing the language of 'rehabilitation', that 'the aim of the penitentiary and penal system is to protect society against the depredations of the criminal population in the country'. The official thinking was that imprisonment involved two main objects: 'the protection of society and the reclamation of the offender'. Reformatory efforts were stated to be centred on the work of the prison chaplains, voluntary workers and religious organisations.

The position of the Department in 1949 could as easily have been stated 50 years earlier. As is a common thread through much of this period, there was no desire to make conditions purposefully harsh or degrading, but equally there were no expansionary tendencies in the other direction either. One statement is emblematic: 'with regard to future reforms nothing specific is contemplated at the moment. Reforms are seldom planned, they evolve gradually as public opinion becomes more divorced from the old idea that prison should be made a place of rigorous punishment to deter the evil doer' (unreleased files, JUS 93/182/1). With these sentiments operating on official action, it is hardly surprising that there is minimal change to report during these years.

One innovation that was introduced and which affected the running of the Department of Justice over future years was the requirement to submit a regular 'progress report' every couple of months. These reports do not reveal much in the way of penal innovation during the period between 1948 and 1951. One exception comes from the report for the two months ending in March 1950, which stated that the question of amending and consolidating all the various enactments dealing with prisons and prisoners was being actively considered and preliminary assessments of the work had been made (TAO S15059A). There is no evidence that this amendment and consolidation ever went beyond such a preliminary stage. A change in government in 1951 was perhaps responsible for the abandonment of these plans and, as will be seen in later chapters, it was not mooted again until 1969.

Public comment on the prison system

Public comment on the prison system as administered by the first Inter-Party Government is scarce. In 1949 an article was carried in *The Irish Times* that reported on a meeting of the Statistical and Social Inquiry of Ireland which had been addressed by Thomas Malony, Bart, a former Attorney General and Chief Justice of Ireland. This was a rather contented and somewhat complacent affair, with Malony reciting the improvements that had taken place within the prisons since the foundation of the state and statistics from the annual reports. Besides this, there is apparently no academic comment on the prison system to report during the period of the first or second Inter-Party Governments, nor indeed under the Fianna Fáil administration. The lack of development of or modification in the system is also reflected in the absence of media coverage of penal affairs. The reportage that does exist is invariably uncritical and reflected the almost 'twee' view taken of prison matters during those years. What is most striking about such coverage, however, is the complete absence of a punitive or even questioning tone regarding what were considered to be 'luxuries' for prisoners in a time of general austerity.

Without the political will to translate these almost 'kindly' sentiments into practice to any large degree, the prison system was again allowed to drift along without any particular guiding hand or exercise of political agency. As Carey posits, quietness descended over the prison system (Carey 2000: 146).

Declining prisoner numbers, financial restraints and enduring conservatism

One factor that allowed for the complacent and untroubled attitude by departmental officials was the fact of low prisoner numbers during these years. After the turbulence of the Emergency, prison numbers began to fall and a generalised sense of greater normality within the prison system began to reappear.

One major factor in this decline was the introduction of increased remission under the Prison Rules. Remission had previously been fixed at one-sixth of a sentence in the case of prisoners serving sentences of ordinary imprisonment. This was increased significantly to one-fourth for such prisoners in 1947. The changes in remission had not been debated in the times of heightened interest surrounding prison conditions; it was an administrative innovation introduced by the Department of Justice. Furthermore, it was a development upon which the official thinking was apparently silent, though it was in keeping with the trend towards incremental liberalisation of prison regimes. Its introduction had, however, probably the most widespread and enduring results on the prison system as a whole over the next decade or more, and inadvertently acted as a factor that drained that system of interest and the necessity for change during those years.

This decline in numbers was continued by a ministerial action at the end of 1949 which had its roots in an ecclesiastical event. On Christmas Eve 1949 the

Minister for Justice granted remission to prisoners serving sentences to mark the beginning of the Roman Catholic Church's 'Holy Year' in 1950. This was carried out as 'an indication of the Government's complete harmony with the spirit of the Holy Season', hastening the decline in the prison population further (*Annual Report on Prisons*, 1950).

In fact, Minister MacEoin felt: 'the stage has been reached here, when we will have to consider seriously turning our provincial prisons into remand prisons, and keeping all sentenced prisoners in one or two central prisons' (TAO S15059A); this change was never implemented.

This manner of development was, of course, also firmly rooted in the criminal justice landscape of the period. As O'Donnell (2004a, 2008), O'Sullivan and O'Donnell (2007), and Brewer, Lockhart and Rodgers (1997) note from official crime rates, crime was almost astonishingly absent in the Ireland of the 1950s and that which did occur was generally of a minor nature. The effects of such low crime figures plus the apparent phenomenon that many of those who might otherwise have been sent to prison decided to emigrate beforehand meant that the numbers in prison hit record low after record low over these years. As well as a lack of political desire, there was no pressure from within the system to effect changes in approach.

Moreover, a continued key priority for the government remained the reduction in expenditure on the prison system and the apparatus of criminal justice as a whole, including a freeze on Garda recruitment. The Minister for Justice made several speeches in which he lambasted the previous administration for its wastage, highlighting a putative proposal for a Borstal at Chapelizod, County Dublin which, he argued, would cost 1.5 million pounds (Dáil Debates, vol 122, col 1119, 7 July 1950). Departmental reticence and governmental financial caution combined to neutralise change during these years.

Hesitation and conservatism also endured. MacEoin, alluding to criticism aimed at his Department for not using the services of psychiatrists and probation officers sufficiently, stated that the Department had 'deliberately gone slow' (TAO S15059A). The reason for such tardiness was that it was felt that better results could be achieved by employing voluntary probation workers and that the strong religious influence in Ireland meant that the services of professionals were not required to the extent they would be in more secular societies. The Minister was reluctant to employ more psychiatrists as even the Department of Health had not yet established psychiatric clinics (TAO S15059A). The penal system was certainly one of the most ill-placed *loci* to lead the way or break new in such techniques.

Impact of the first Inter-Party Government on prison policy

Penal administration appears to have been somewhat low on the list of priorities for the Inter-Party Government. This is surprising given the attendance at Cabinet of Seán MacBride and James Dillon, two men who were well versed in penal affairs and the need for reform. Moreover, its Minister for Justice, General MacEoin, had himself been imprisoned in Mountjoy during the War of Independence, reflecting a similar experience with members of earlier governments.

Overall, the first change of government in 16 years made a relatively negligible impact on prison policy, leaving a minimal mark on the direction, rhetoric or practice of penal affairs. As will be seen in the remainder of this chapter, however, compared to the rest of the 1950s the first Inter-Party Government was rather energetic and forward-thinking.

Fianna Fáil return to power

Penal affairs slip further down the official agenda

In mid-1951 Fianna Fáil was returned to power in the aftermath of the fall of the Inter-Party Government. Gerry Boland TD also returned to the Department of Justice, where he had a further chance to implement his ideas on penal reform. However, his tenure is characterised by contraction of the prison system and stasis in its administration.

In the Minister's first few speeches on the vote for his Department, a notable feature of his statements is the absence of prison affairs. A good example of this comes from one exchange with a fellow party member in the Dáil, Colm Gallagher TD, who was a social worker and newly elected representative for Dublin North Central. He appealed to the Minister to introduce occupational therapy and better and more varied trades, as well as an improved after-care system (Dáil Debates, vol 126, col 1421, 11 July 1951), statements that were probably received with some incomprehension and puzzlement. No reply of any description was made to Gallagher's suggestions and the debate was taken up with speed limits and a proposal to establish a High Court in Cork. On resumption of the debate, other TDs sought to appeal to the Minister to improve and reorganise the prisons. Again the Minister chose not to enlighten the Dáil in any way with his opinions on the topic.

The whole of 1952 passed without a comment on the prison system beyond the perfunctory recitation of the monies required for the Estimate in the Oireachtas. The 1953 Estimate also recorded a decrease in expenditure but the only comment of the Minister in relation to prisons was to ridicule a suggestion made by Seán MacBride that some offenders serving short sentences should be allowed to serve their sentence over a period of a year (Dáil Debates, vol 138, col 526, 22 April 1953). The worrying of sheep by dogs received greater attention in the debate on the Estimate than the penal system.

In 1951 Cork and Sligo prisons were reduced to minor status on the basis that their small prison populations did not justify their continuance. Sligo female prison was shut down completely, a 'good sign of the times' according to the Sligo Visiting Committee (*Annual Report on Prisons*, 1952). It was also welcomed by the government for the economies it facilitated in the reduction of staff. The year

1953, further, started a trend of year-on-year record-breaking for the lowest daily averages in the history of the state.

The Criminal Justice Act 1951

In 1951 a Criminal Justice Act was passed which, *inter alia*, provided that the power to remit a sentence imposed by a court could be exercised by the President in all cases, and on 'other authorities' in non-capital cases. This power was delegated to the Minister for Justice. This Act gave the Minister the power to remit sentences on conditions as the Minister saw fit, adding to the pre-existing provisions on remission contained in the 1947 Rules. Section 23 of the 1951 Act was another example of a small, unobtrusive, administrative effort to facilitate the running of prisons. It also furthered attempts to 'humanise' prison life by allowing for full or partial remission of sentences when the occasion arose.

The second Inter-Party Government

The second Inter-Party Government took office in June 1954. The pattern of the 1950s continued steadily. The government oversaw ongoing decline in prisoner numbers and there is very little evidence of any developments in prison policy under its tenure.

The year 1954 saw the daily average in the prison system drop to 398; 1955 recorded 356 and 1957 338; this trend was interrupted in 1956 when the figure went up to 373. In 1954 only one prisoner in the entire system was serving a sentence for over ten years, with the majority of sentences being for three months or less.

Closure of prisons

Prison closure – also a feature of earlier actions taken by legislators in the penal realm – was one policy direction that resulted from the conditions of the 1950s. When James Everett of the National Labour Party took office as Minister for Justice in the second Inter-Party Government in 1954, he declared that one of his priorities was to investigate the closure of some of the state's prisons in view of the continually falling numbers.

As had been common since Independence, a new Minister for Justice did not take the opportunity of his first extended statement on the Department of Justice's activity to elucidate a new strategy for the penal system, preferring to maintain the existing system and to reduce its operational capacity (Dáil Debates, vol 152, col 684, 13 July 1955). The decision to investigate the possibility of closure was prompted by concerns regarding administrative efficiency and economy. The United Nations Minimum Rules for the Treatment of Prisoners, signed in 1955, do not appear to have elicited any interest whatsoever.

Everett signed closure orders for Cork and Sligo prisons on 21 February 1956. In 1955 their daily averages had been 15 and 8 prisoners respectively. In that year, what had been the Borstal institution at Clonmel was closed and the boys transferred to the women's prison at Mountjoy. The women were then moved to a basement of St Patrick's Institution, the replacement for the Borstal on the site of the Mountjoy prison complex. As Quinlan states, this was 'probably the worst accommodation available within the prison system' (Quinlan 2003: 3), instigating decades of even more pronounced political neglect than that relating to the prison system generally. By this time there still remained a capacity for 1,200 prisoners within the system, three times more than was contemporaneously required.

The Prisons Act 1956

The closure of these prisons left an administrative and logistical predicament for the government. The inmates at Cork and Sligo prisons were to be transferred to Limerick and Mountjoy. The question arose as to what was to become of those sentenced to imprisonment in areas that had previously sent their convicted prisoners to Cork and Sligo prisons and who needed, at that time, to be transported directly to a prison that was now some distance away. To deal with this situation, a Prisons Bill was introduced in 1956 and passed in the same year. It introduced a provision to allow for a person to be detained in lock-ups in Garda stations or other locations for a period of up to 48 hours, pending their removal to prison.

The government felt rather pleased with itself regarding the state of affairs that this bill reflected. Minister Everett stated: 'I think we must all feel very pleased at the fact that we have now reached a stage in our history where we are in a position to close up some jails. It speaks well for the country' (Dáil Debates, vol 154, col 995, 29 February 1956). However, how much credit the government could legitimately take for such a state of affairs was less than clear. There was certainly no claim that prison policy was responsible for the low crime rate.

The 1956 Act got through all the stages of enactment in a single sitting with no assessment of the potential for penal reform in Ireland or any in-depth analysis of the prison system. The prison system was undoubtedly continuing to operate in an atmosphere of 'stagnation' (O'Donnell 2008).

The Border Campaign and its effect on prison policy

This contentment was disturbed somewhat by the resurgence of IRA activity during the latter half of the 1950s, and these Republican activities affected prison policy yet again. This was the time of the 'Border Campaign', when the IRA began to make border raids to attack RUC and British army targets as well as strategic sites such as bridges, transmitters and roads. During the five-year campaign six RUC men were killed, and eight IRA members died, mainly in accidents during the preparation of or involvement in such attacks (Moloney 2007).

The campaign continued into 1957. In that year there was also an election, after Seán MacBride withdrew the support of Clann na Poblachta for the second Inter-Party Government. Fianna Fáil won a large overall majority. Oscar Traynor TD was appointed Minister for Justice and no qualms were evident in his decision to reintroduce internment in July of that year, under the Offences Against the State (Amendment) Act 1940.

As with previous Republican campaigns, it is difficult to assess the impact that such events had on the wider prison system and ordinary detention. Certainly the broader context of heightened security, a tough attitude to IRA activity and a general strengthening of the criminal justice system to respond to such activity all affected the discourse surrounding the prison system in terms of both tone and content. Furthermore, the average daily prison population in 1956 did rise slightly.

It is clear, however, that the Border Campaign and those detained on foot of it had a far less significant impact on the prison system than previous actions taken by the IRA. The Fianna Fáil government had well-oiled machinery to deal with such individuals and a significant amount of practice, and no quibbles, about taking stringent action against them.

The Border Campaign, despite its long duration, did not impact upon the ordinary system of detention to any large degree. Its main effect was internal to the individual prisons in which IRA members were held. Some of those detained as a result of the campaign created disruption within Mountjoy and Portlaoise through hunger strikes, an escape from detention while a prisoner attended the Mater Hospital, and Ruairí Ó Brádaigh's escape from the Curragh during a football match (White 2006: 85). Punishments and loss of privileges were regularly ordered for prisoners who attempted to escape or caused disruption. However, it appears that *de facto* special status was granted, in contrast to previous experiences with prisoners of that type (TAO S11564G). Overall, the prison system continued on, attempting to accommodate the small numbers of prisoners who refused to accept the regime, but without being significantly bothered by them.

Eventually, all internees were released in late 1958 (O'Halpin 1999a: 300) and the order to 'dump arms' was given in 1962.

Reflecting its negligible impact, the lowest average daily population in the prison system in the history of the state was recorded during the Border Campaign, this being 369 prisoners in 1958. Minister Traynor reported his own happiness at the low numbers in the prison system in 1957, as his predecessor James Everett, had done before him. Traynor stated: 'the fact that we have been able to close at least three prisons is a step forward for this country. We should pat ourselves on the back for that fact. I do not suppose there is another nation in the world that is in the happy position of being able to close prisons' (Dáil Debates, vol 161, col 423, 26 March 1957).

Again, the presence of low prisoner numbers in the state's prisons was cited as a constraint against acting boldly in the area of prison policy. The Fianna Fáil administration of the late 1950s believed that it was committed to 'penal reform', or, broadly, to the improvement of conditions within prisons and attempts at rehabilitation, but the combination of limited resources and low numbers militated against the implementation of any such action. Traynor related: 'Our resources do not permit of experimentation to any large degree and the numbers of prisoners under sentence are too limited to permit of diverse classifications. Moreover, most prisoners are not long enough in custody for any training or rehabilitation measures to take effect' (Dáil Debates, vol 161, col 233, 26 March 1957).

Stasis in prison policy 1948–58

During these years, as has been indicated, the prison system in numerical terms contracted significantly, but the policy behind it remained in suspension, moving in no particular direction.

The declining prison rate was certainly a key factor in keeping the prison system out of the public eye and in allowing penal administrators and politicians to largely forget about it. However, other factors contributed to the general inertia within prison policy-making circles. At an immediate level the Department of Justice was, again, very content to maintain this picture and its officials never took it upon themselves to advocate a new policy vision for the prison system.

The Department of Justice's workload seems to have attracted less and less attention throughout this period. Without the interest of their political masters to prod the civil service officials into action, they reverted to a state of inaction. The Department was keen not to draw attention to itself and its staff appear to have been focused on maintaining the existing system, ensuring its smooth administration but studiously avoiding the avocation of reforms. This was not a Department that sought to make waves. For example, in 1952 the Secretary of the Department wrote to the Private Secretary of An Taoiseach stating:

> The Department of Justice is a regulative department and unlike some other departments … does not normally undertake projects of a social and economic betterment of a kind that appeal to the man in the street … Our activities important though they may be, have no popular appeal … All things considered, I think the less that is said about our plans the better. Our primary job is to protect the public from force and fraud and this, I think, we are doing.
>
> *(TAO 15059A)*

It is hard to decipher whether this attitude was a product of systematic departmental protocol or a combination of a particularly unadventurous, cautious or tentative collection of individuals, or a lack of direction from a series of ineffectual ministers. However, the results of their efforts are incontrovertible – no departmental activities were deemed worthy of a progress report during the entire decade.

Political culture and social policy: drift and decay

While there were very pragmatic reasons for the absence of innovative penal developments, this particular trajectory for prison policy reflects, in many ways, the same stagnation within the state's social policy, political character and cultural make-up during this period.

Initial signs under the first Inter-Party Government were that social welfare reform was to be a key priority for the new office holders. Its programme for government was based on a 'ten-point plan' which included commitments to introduce a comprehensive social security system and modification of the means test for various pensions (McCashin 2004: 38). The Labour leader, William Norton TD, was installed as Tánaiste and Minister for Social Welfare to implement these proposals.

There are some signs that Ireland appeared to be moving in something of a welfarist direction on social policy. For example, the first Inter-Party Government's Minister for Finance, Paddy McGilligan TD, gave an uncharacteristic speech, drafted by T. K. Whitaker, on 3 May 1950. In it he stated: 'the modern democratic state is ... rightly expected, not only to maintain the essential liberties of its citizens, but to take an active part in securing conditions favourable to their material well-being. This entails a continuous survey of the economic and social scene' (quoted in Fanning 1978: 457). The Taoiseach, John A. Costello, stated in a speech in 1949 that: 'the government must budget primarily to allocate a certain part of the nation's finances to public purposes' (quoted in Fanning 1978: 457). Statements such as these, coming from members of the Fine Gael party who were far less enthusiastic about such matters than their colleagues in government (McCullagh 1998: 187), hint at the fledgling commitment of the Irish state and its governors to a more socially reformist and interventionist policy.

These tendencies were, however, truncated by other events. External circumstances militated against the first Inter-Party Government's introduction of social welfare measures, as this government itself fell in 1951. The end to which this government came, in the wake of the Mother and Child Scheme debacle (the failure of the plan to introduce free health care for mothers and children up to the age of 16) demonstrates the lack of readiness of the majority of those with power in the state for social reforms (Browne 1986; Lee 1989: 317).

The first Inter-Party Government had produced a White Paper in 1949 which aimed to reform social welfare provision and also envisaged the introduction of legislation to increase its scope. This paper, strongly opposed in characteristic fashion by the Department of Finance, envisaged the extension of social insurance to all employees, to increase benefits and to introduce new benefits on marriage, maternity provision and in old age (Cousins 2002: 154–5). Stalling tactics meant that it fell with the government in 1951. This government also restarted a drive to provide more houses and reclaim large tracts of land in the west of Ireland (Lee 1989: 313). Some progress in social reform was made. The number of houses built with state aid increased in the 1950s (Ferriter 2004) and orphans' and widows' pensions were augmented under the first Inter-Party Government (Cousins 2002: 153).

When Fianna Fáil returned to government in 1952, it introduced legislation that became the Social Welfare Act 1952. This Act was a milestone in social welfare provision in Ireland and was the result of a build-up of expectation and reform, consolidating and introducing benefits such as disability and maternity benefit and laying the foundations for social welfare provision in future years. The Act was, however, a lot less expansionary than that proposed in 1948 and thereafter very little in the way of reformist legislation or policy was introduced. The period from 1948 to 1951 was significantly more interventionist in social policy terms than the rest of the 1950s, which was a far more 'regressive' (Kennedy 1975: ii) period. After 1952, for example, hospital building slowed down, partly due to lack of funding, education policy remained cautious and expenditure on housing decreased. The Social Welfare Act 1952 marked the conclusion of the post-war welfare state development in Ireland (Carey 2007: 211). As Cousins notes: 'the Irish system remained essentially fragmented and shared little commitment to inter-class solidarity' (Cousins 2005: 20).

More extensive reorganisation of social policy, even public agitation against unemployment, risked the label of 'socialism' which, particularly as the Cold War got under way, was considered effectively equivalent to communism in certain sectors of Irish society, a most undesirable classification, particularly for the Catholic Church. Puirséil puts the matter starkly: 'for the purposes of Irish Catholicism, Clem Attlee was placed on an ideological par with Joe Stalin' (Puirséil 2007: 145).

Financial difficulties

As well as the ideological resistance to and lack of political will for greater social interventionism, the financial stringencies that were thereby required meant that whatever welfare reforms were introduced in Ireland were postponed and severely restricted. As Whyte avers, all the events of these years were coloured by a 'serious and intractable economic crisis' which involved a series of industrial disputes, a rising cost of living, serious balance of payments deficits, calls for cuts in public expenditure and a series of stiff budgets (Whyte 2003a: 281). Ferriter notes that in the 1950s, 'what many ... other countries had that Ireland lacked were healthy, if not booming, economies in the post war period' (Ferriter 2004: 467).

The 1951 Budget was one of the harshest in the history of the state. Economic growth was almost non-existent and there were grave balance of payments deficits. There was a sterling crisis in 1952 and the state's balance of payments deteriorated significantly. The Budget of that year has been described as one of 'unusual severity' (Fanning 1978: 482). It halted a trend in welfare provision that had become apparent of increased public capital spending and heralded almost a decade of stagnancy in Irish economic development. Irish economic growth became slower than in any other Western European country during this period

(Ó Gráda 1997: 48). Government spending overall fell by 15 per cent between 1956 and 1958 (Walsh 1979: 27).

Seán MacEntee, reinstalled as Minister for Finance under Fianna Fáil in 1952, began to seek the balancing of the budget in an aggressive manner. Social and economic disaster was predicted unless greater savings were made across government departments. A memorandum from the Department of Finance to all departments is illustrative, directing: 'the more uneconomic and wasteful elements in the capital programme should be curtailed or abandoned … new commitments, whether of a capital or a recurrent nature, should be avoided' (quoted in Fanning 1978: 482). The Finance Department was also frightened rather than inspired by the prospect of the inflow of Marshall Aid to the country, fearing that it would incite politicians to come up with schemes to spend it (Lee 1989: 569). Its impact on all departments, including an already cautious Department of Justice, would have been keen.

The need for restraint was reiterated by the second Inter-Party Government's Minister for Finance, Gerard Sweetman, who in another memorandum to the government pleaded: 'every aspect of expenditure must be critically examined, all procedures carefully scrutinised and any charge on public funds that is not absolutely essential must be eliminated or retrenched' (quoted in Fanning 1978: 500).

Emigration

The Ireland of these years was in a dire financial position. Social and economic progress were twin chimeras. The state was haemorrhaging people, with thousands of young people unable or unwilling to put up with the high levels of unemployment and poor prospects choosing to leave. In 1957 there were 78,000 unemployed in a year when emigration was responsible for a net loss in population of 54,000 (Brown 1981: 18; Sexton 2003). Around one in eight of the population emigrated during the 1950s. Interestingly, this did not translate into votes for the parties on the left of the Irish political spectrum, with Labour continuing to suffer from its perennial 'weak' classification. More generally, the political authorities seemed at a loss to stop it.

Emigration operated as something of a safety valve for the state, allowing it to avoid bankruptcy and the very serious questions that would otherwise have been posed to its system of social provision (Daly 2007). It did, however, operate to drain Ireland of much talent and energy that might otherwise have been expended on innovation or social agitation (Coogan 1966; Whyte 2003a), having a depressing effect on national morale (Healy 1968, 1978; Lee 1989: 384). Its existence also highlights a lack of social solidarity in Irish society at the time, itself an impediment to greater social welfare expansion. Content to allow thousands of its young people to emigrate to keep a minimum standard of living for those who remained, there was no comparable attempt to eradicate the Beveridgean 'giants' here. As O'Connell and Rottman state: 'most Western European societies emerged from the Great Depression and the Second World War with commitments to both extend social rights and abolish unemployment. Ireland was an exception' (O'Connell and Rottman 1992: 231). There was certainly no attempt to lift all boats or to extend assistance to all of the state's citizens, and the class structure of the period was largely stable as a result of the large numbers leaving the state (Whelan *et al.* 1992).

Emigration affected prison policy more directly. As well as reducing the overall population of the state, with an accompanying depressing effect on crime rates, it operated to keep the population in the country's jails artificially low, removing one factor that might have prompted change – that of rising numbers. As one TD later stated, 'the easy way out is across the Channel which saves the Minister from having to double the prison population' (Dáil Debates, vol 183, col 613, 29 June 1960).

Over and above this pragmatic effect of emigration on the crime rate, in a state that could not see its way to provide a basic ability to its citizens to survive when they remained at home, it was unlikely that it would extend greater opportunities to those convicted of crimes and residing in the state's jails.

Isolation and insularity

Girvin and Murray argue that this bleak picture of Irish life during the 1950s 'took place in a political framework that was isolationist, cutting Ireland off from outside influence' (Girvin and Murray 2005: 4), postulating that the political climate of the time was one particularly unreceptive to ideas from abroad and in which there was an intellectual barrenness, though its degree has been disputed (Keogh *et al.* 2004).

The Department of Justice files from the period elicit no indications that the Department was looking elsewhere for inspiration or new ideas. The Department continued to be exceedingly inward-looking and the impression given is that if suggestions for wide-ranging innovation were mooted these would have been received with something akin to embarrassment. It is also difficult to discern where these ideas might have come from. Prison matters are far less apparent in the news media of the 1950s than they had been during the 1940s. The Oireachtas was similarly untroubled by these matters. There is no evidence to suggest that an academic community or any other interested parties attempted to push these issues to the fore. Even the traditional source of interest in prison affairs, regarding internment and IRA activity, during the Border Campaign, could not kindle interest.

It should not be assumed, however, that there was no awareness of developments occurring abroad. Newspapers carried reports from Britain regarding prison reforms occurring there. The Criminal Justice Act 1948, which effected widespread change in penal administration in Britain, was described in the national newspapers (for example, *Irish Independent*, 17 June 1948). Instead, there did not appear to be the tools to connect these developments to ideas for reform in Ireland, with the Department studiously avoiding comparative research.

Political culture and prison policy in the 1950s

The 1950s in particular were a time of general stagnation and neglect in Irish politics and policy-making. Many areas of Irish life received minimal attention, resources or energy from those in a position to influence them, with the most obvious example being the apparent impotence of the political classes to provide enough opportunities for its citizens to remain in Ireland. The overwhelming restraint was financial, though Lee also indicts the state's leaders for a lack of imagination and a generalised absence of policy (Lee 1989: 384). Bew and Patterson describe the state's economic situation as one of '*immobilisme*' (Bew and Patterson 1982: 77). The decade has even been referred to as 'lost' (Keogh *et al.* 2004), suffering from the 'politics of drift' (Keogh 2003: 202), and the Fianna Fáil Cabinet of 1951 to 1954 as one of 'the worst' ever (Lee 1989: 321; Murphy 1979: 3). It was a decade in which Irish people 'never had it so bad' (Puirséil 2007: 193) and one in which Irish society was 'lacking in self-confidence and creativity' (Sexton 1986: 38).

There were certainly not the healthy coffers or the existence of social solidarity in the crucial post-war years that Garland identifies as necessary to implementing penal-welfarist methods and practices (Garland 2001: 49). Intervention by the state in social life was stifled by the socio-economic and cultural situation of the time. Innovation was difficult in light of the comparatively regular changes of government and the fact that each held unsafe majorities, relying on independents for support (Whyte 2003a).

In this climate, the form of prison policy in this period becomes more understandable. Indications that change in a more welfarist direction might take hold in the late 1940s and early 1950s were dashed as the 1950s went on.

Prison reform, not penal reform

In 1958 Paddy McGilligan of Fine Gael, a former Finance Minister, took Minister Traynor to task on the progress of penal reform in Ireland. Traynor, in reply, argued that penal reform had been 'continuous' and gave an example of spring beds being available in Mountjoy. The remainder of this exchange is worth reciting.

> Mr McGilligan: We are to mark that down as a big advance – beds for prisoners in Mountjoy! Is that the extent of the penal reform?

> Mr Traynor: It is prison reform.

> Mr McGilligan: Is that the extent of it? I thought penal reform related to rehabilitation and training. I thought that was what was intended in penal reform. Keeping cells in a cleaner condition or providing better beds is not exactly what the public understand by penal reform. What is generally

understood by the term is reform of the penal system leading to reform of those who undergo imprisonment with the object of making them good citizens or better citizens when they emerge. Certainly, that is what I understand by penal reform. I gather nothing has been done in that respect.

(Dáil Debates, vol 167, col 253, 6 May 1958)

Traynor's part in the exchange is characteristic of prison policy in Ireland in the time-frame under assessment here, and indeed the entire period from the mid-1920s until the later 1950s. 'Prison reform' rather than penal reform was the mainstay of governmental action within the system. Indeed, penal reform seemed almost alien to administrators, with the difference, succinctly stated by Paddy McGilligan, not clearly apparent to the Minister. In such a climate, innovation and experimentation would have been unthinkable. There was a general consensus, with some dissenting voices, that the system should be humane, but it should be relatively untouched by administrative guiding hands.

However, things were about to change in Irish prison policy, as well as Irish political, social and cultural life. The year was 1958 and Seán Lemass had finally become Taoiseach, taking over from de Valera, who had been leader of the Fianna Fáil party since 1927. Traynor announced that a bill was shortly to come before the house that would deal with 'certain limited aspects of the [prison] problem' (Dáil Debates, vol 167, col 234, 6 May 1958), while Charles J. Haughey was about to be appointed parliamentary secretary (a junior ministry) in the Department of Justice. The stasis and lack of innovation of the 1950s was about to come to an end.

5

THE 1960s
'Solo runs' and social change

Introduction

After decades of stagnation, neglect and a focus on 'subversive' prisoners, the period 1958–72 is one of relatively radical change in Irish prison policy. The early period, from 1958 to 1964, witnessed developments in Irish prison policy that were unparalleled in terms of content and speed of implementation than at any time previously. For the first time since the foundation of the state there was a combination of legislative, administrative, philosophical and imaginative change within the system. As Osborough states, during this period 'the forces insistent on action in the tackling of penal questions in the state did finally manage to coalesce. There was the pressure to make changes, and the political will to approve them' (Osborough 1985: 184).

The changes that occurred in this decade were explicitly framed as innovations, changes and novel breaks with the past. During this period a number of important developments occurred in this vein. These included temporary release, the establishment of the Inter-Departmental Committee with the explicit remit of assessing criminal justice and penal policy, the introduction of a new institution for adults, attempts to abolish penal servitude as a sentence, some changes in penal regimes, the expansion of the welfare service and increasing emphasis on probation.

Following years of floating along on various tides of 'events', prison policy began to be taken in hand. Many factors can be identified as cumulatively causative of this change, with the personalities of ministers playing a key role.

The changes to prison policy witnessed during the period were indicative of broader changes in the social, political and cultural assumptions and impulses of those years. All of these combined to create a 'policy window' in which changes were made in the Irish prison system.

A tale of two Ministers for Justice: a break with the past

The period under assessment did not start with many clues of what was to follow. Oscar Traynor, a veteran of Fianna Fáil and a Minister for Justice who had himself spent time behind bars, continued the prevailing attitude towards prisons – to cut costs and express contentment at the low numbers within the system.

However, in 1960 Traynor received some additional help in his Department. Charles J. Haughey, elected to the Dáil in 1957, had been appointed parliamentary secretary to the Department in May of that year; this was his first appointment to office.

The change in the office of the Minister for Justice is a useful motif for the alteration of the Irish political system during these years. Traynor was of the traditional Fianna Fáil type, with a Civil War pedigree and long service. He was 75 years old in 1961, when he retired from the position; he died in 1963. Charles Haughey, on the other hand, was 37, at the starting point of his career and determined to make his way up the political ladder.

Traynor was part of a generation that was the last of its kind. The rise of Lemass to the position of Taoiseach and his subsequent tenure has been widely recognised as marking a significant break with Ireland's past political, economic and social culture (Bew and Patterson 1982; Horgan 1997). In political terms, Lemass is noted for promoting innovation, with his own approach often being decisive and impatient (Carey 2007: 213), and appointing a new 'breed' of politician (Farrell 1971). These were known as the 'men in the mohair suits', shorthand to describe a group of politicians noted for their modernising approach, energy, rejection of past mores and axioms, their wider outlook, and impatience with what they perceived as the outmoded restrictions on action experienced by politicians of the past.

Haughey has been described as the archetype of this set (Dwyer 2005; O'Brien 2002). Though there is no evidence that Haughey and Lemass discussed a vision for the prison system, it can be posited that Haughey's anxiety for innovation would have met with approval.

The Criminal Justice Act 1960

In prison policy terms, the 1960s dawned with the introduction of a Criminal Justice Bill that introduced legislative reforms into the prison system for the first time since 1947. While it ran to only 15 sections, the bill nonetheless indicated a significant alteration in approach.

The bill was mainly concerned with provisions for young offenders, allowing judges to detain 16–21 year olds in remand institutions rather than in prison, and providing for 17–21 year olds to be detained in St Patrick's Institution instead of in prison.

Section 2 of what became the Act was the provision of most application to all prisoners. It gave the Minister for Justice the power to make rules allowing for the temporary release of prisoners from all institutions, for whatever period the Minister saw fit.

The balance in the bill reflected the factors behind its genesis. While the introduction of temporary release was undoubtedly a major change in the history of Irish prison policy, its inclusion in the bill appears to be something of an 'add-on' to provisions aimed mainly at young offenders.

Impulses behind the introduction of the bill

Though the Criminal Justice Act heralded something of a new departure for Irish prison policy, the impetus for the bill came squarely from the previous Taoiseach, de Valera, as far back as 1957. De Valera had met the Catholic Archbishop of Dublin, John Charles McQuaid, in March of 1957 to discuss state provision for young offenders, particularly girls, a matter that had long given rise to concern. There was no centre to which they could be remanded while awaiting trial, except to Mountjoy prison. De Valera requested that the Minister for Justice address the situation (TAO S13290A). At the end of 1958, the Department of Justice prepared a memorandum for government on the proposals for a Criminal Justice Bill with two aims – the provision of temporary release and the power to remand young female offenders in a convent rather than prison.

The impetus for the former development is unclear, and seems to have been very much a departmental innovation. Revealingly, Peter Berry, long-time Secretary at the Department of Justice, suggests that the introduction of temporary release was a civil service-driven development, rather than being attributable to political actions (Berry 1980).

The Department of Justice was concerned that there was then no official provision for the temporary release of a prisoner during the currency of his sentence, though in practice this had been granted to certain prisoners (mainly those sentenced under the Offences Against the State Act 1939) where a close relative died, was ill, or it was felt to be a humanitarian act to grant the temporary release. All the prisoners involved had returned promptly, but if they had not they could not have been compelled to do so, which was a further factor taken into account in promoting action. Significantly, temporary release was advocated as a benefit to long-term prisoners to prepare them for release and possibly employment. There is no evidence that it was introduced as a mechanism to relieve pressures on numbers, which was the case in England and Wales, or indeed for which end temporary release was later used in Ireland also.

The bill as originally drafted by the parliamentary draftsman at the Office of the Attorney General had also contained provision to abolish the divisions between penal servitude, hard labour and the other prison divisions, which were long disused (OAG 2000/224868). Subsequent drafts of the bill dropped these provisions, though there is no evidence of any reasons for this change.

The bill was eventually brought before the Oireachtas in 1960. Given the centrality of the provisions regarding young offenders to the introduction of the bill, the debate on it unsurprisingly focuses on these elements. However, the passing of the Act also gave the Dáil an opportunity to explore conditions pertinent to the prison system during this period and provided an occasion to assess the prevalent conceptions of prison policy.

In introducing the legislation, Traynor reiterated the reasons explored in the departmental memorandum for the introduction of temporary release and not much more was said about adult offenders by the Minister (Dáil Debates, vol 183, col 410, 28 June 1960). However, 1960 also saw the publication of a pamphlet by Captain Peadar Cowan. This pamphlet prompted a wide-ranging debate about the nature of Irish prison policy and its future directions.

Dungeons Deep and the Dáil

Cowan had been a prisoner in Mountjoy for two years in the mid-1950s. *Dungeons Deep* (Cowan 1960) was a monograph on prisons, borstals, reformatories and industrial schools in the Republic of Ireland. His memoir contained a scathing attack on the prison system, detailing demeaning procedures of the communal laundry of prison clothing, primitive sanitary facilities, poor diet and the inherent dehumanising effect of institutionalisation.

This pamphlet had an impact on James Dillon, the leader of Fine Gael, who quoted extensively from it. For his part, the Labour leader agreed that reformation rather than punishment should be the aim of the prison system, arguing that for most first offenders their 'downfall' was due to a condition of mind or body (Dáil Debates, vol 183, col 591, 29 June 1960). Other deputies, such as Declan Costello T.D. of Fine Gael, concentrated on juvenile offending but expressed broadly similar sentiments about the need for rehabilitation, psychological assistance and training.

While this debate marked something of a sea change in the political discussions surrounding Irish criminal justice issues, it was mainly concentrated on young offenders and the operation of St Patrick's Institution. Temporary release received comparatively little attention.

Cowan's pamphlet had, in truth, little bearing on the ultimate content of the Act and was not referred to regarding the substantive elements thereof. Rather, it was used as an exposition of the general conditions of the prison system. In this, it was also of relatively negligible impact, being rebuffed by Traynor. Indeed, Captain Cowan was somewhat ill placed to engender sympathy within government. He was considered something of a political maverick and was most unpopular in the Labour Party where he had commenced his political life. There were further suspicions that he was a 'stooge' for communist elements in Labour and his resignation from that party was viewed as a 'blessed release' (Puirséil 2007: 120). His involvement in founding a socialist Republican organisation called 'Vanguard' was also unlikely to enamour him to the Department of Justice.

An indication of things to come?

Though the Criminal Justice Act 1960 was an important development for prison policy in Ireland, and marked a movement towards welfarist techniques, it was not earth-shattering in its effects nor representative of a paradigm shift in Irish penal thought; rather, it was a straw in the wind indicating potential changes ahead. The fact that ministers, senior civil servants and the Dáil were turning attention to such matters was also a key discontinuity from the previous decade.

The tension between forces of caution and change evident in the late 1950s and the early part of the 1960s, apparent in the cautious language of Traynor and the legislation prompted by departmental examination and action, becomes all the more intriguing when examined with the knowledge of what was later to come for Irish prison policy. Peter Berry revealed in his diaries (Berry 1980) that Oscar Traynor was having 'difficulties' in piloting legislation through the Dáil because of its complexity, his advancing age and, Berry suggested, his increasing deafness. He was also, it was claimed, having problems with the Criminal Justice Bill. In fact, it was in the aftermath of the debate on the bill that the Taoiseach decided to offer Traynor the assistance of a parliamentary secretary, who was, it transpired, Charles J. Haughey.

Charles Haughey takes the reins: a transformed Department of Justice

Traynor retired from politics entirely in 1961, privately citing one of his reasons as the uneasy relationship he had with his parliamentary secretary (Berry 1980). Haughey took over in October of that year. His two-year apprenticeship as parliamentary secretary in the Department of Justice meant that he was well versed in the processes and culture of that Department, and was apparently well

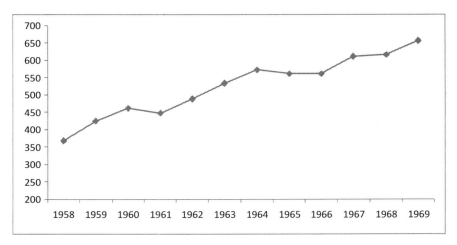

FIGURE 5.1 Average daily prison population 1958–64

respected by the civil servants. With his hands finally on the levers of ministerial power, Haughey approached his task with vigour and energy. As Lee puts it: 'when Lemass appointed ... Charles Haughey, as Minister for Justice, it can only have been in anticipation of significant change in a traditionally conservative department' (Lee 1989: 408).

The Secretary of the Department, Peter Berry, described him as a 'dynamic Minister ... a joy to work with and the longer he stayed the better he got' (Dwyer 2005: 220). Berry went so far as to rate him the ablest Minister of the 14 under whom he had served, arguing that he managed to break the traditional inability of Ministers for Justice to extract money from the Department of Finance.

It is unclear whether he was placed in Justice with the specific intent by Seán Lemass to shake that Department up or simply to provide him with a portfolio. Either way, the results had a serious impact upon Irish prison policy.

It was not just Haughey, however, who created the conditions for change within the Department of Justice. Work was ongoing by civil servants in various areas of law reform and penal policy. Lee argues that Haughey was supported in his law reform efforts by an enthusiastic Assistant Secretary, Roger Hayes (Lee 1989: 408). At the same time, a separate Department of Law Reform was established to aid in this task.

Initially the new Minister was concerned, as all his predecessors had been, with prison matters as they affected and were affected by IRA members. In November 1961 the Special Criminal Court was briefly reactivated in the aftermath of an ambush and death of an RUC constable on the border. Those imprisoned for offences against the state were by this time being kept in segregation from other prisoners and the prison rules had been relaxed for them (Dáil Debates, vol 194, col 376). This fact meant that there was little in the way of protest by such prisoners or on their behalf. There was certainly nothing to compare with that which had occurred previously.

However, this Minister was not content to deal with such matters and allow other prison issues to be neglected. In March 1962 Haughey announced: 'My Department's programme for 1962 includes an examination of the whole penal reform system, a beginning of the revision of the prison statutes and rules and a continuation of the improvements recently sanctioned in the dietary and scale of gratuities paid to prisoners for good conduct and industry' (Dáil Debates, vol 193, col 111, 1 March 1962).

Compared with previous years, under Haughey change began to occur within the Department of Justice at breakneck speed. A programme of law reform was drawn up and all the barriers that had been cited as inhibitors to change no longer appeared to pose any problem, being instead swept away in a tide of effort and movement. Later, both media and academic comment would describe 1962 as a 'turning point' for Irish prison policy, and the evidence suggests that this was a fair reflection (O'Flynn 1971; *Irish Press*, 29 June 1967).

The Inter-Departmental Committee

By September 1962, however, these initially limited proposals for change were expanded upon enormously to become a full Inter-Departmental Committee – The Inter-Departmental Committee on Juvenile Delinquency, the Probation System, the Institutional Treatment of Offenders and their After-Care – which was set up to investigate methods for the prevention of crime and the treatment of offenders. The Committee was a highly active body, leaving behind 18 voluminous files consisting of minutes of meetings, research material and correspondence.

The work of the Committee warrants the conclusion that its work represented a watershed in Irish prison policy. The Committee worked speedily, being most active during an approximately year-long period commencing in September 1962. It surveyed a large amount of material and investigated a wide range of issues over a relatively short period of time. After decades where such matters had been firmly off the agenda, the Inter-Departmental Committee appears to have arrived on the scene and rapidly come to grips with topics long ignored.

Many of its recommendations bear the hallmarks of penal-welfarism and rehabilitationism. Later, Haughey would remark that the Committee's recommendations had 'in the main, as their aim the social rehabilitation of the offender' (Dáil Debates, vol 198, col 124, 27 November 1962).

Significantly, crime and responses to it were not conceived of in party political terms, but were, rather, left to a group of civil servants, detached from such concerns and certainly in an 'elitist' mould, formulating ideas and proposals within the structures of the civil service and its modalities.

The Committee received its warrant of appointment from the Minister on 12 September 1962. It comprised six members from the Departments of Education, Health, and Industry and Commerce along with a secretary, with Peter Berry installed as chairman. The Committee had a remit of examination and recommendation in four main areas: juvenile delinquency, the probation system and the institutional treatment of offenders and their after-care, and to recommend changes in the law and policy as appropriate.

The files do not reveal in any direct way what the official thinking behind the establishment of the Committee was, though the material therefrom does lend credence to the contention that it was an idea considered by the Department of Justice and put into practice by Minister Haughey. When viewed in light of other evidence available from the period, this reason for such a policy change is compelling.

Haughey's role in the establishment of the Committee

In the course of his address to the Fianna Fáil Ard-Fhéis (Party Conference) in 1962, Haughey revealed that the motivation to establish the Committee had come from a resolution submitted to the Fianna Fáil Ard-Fhéis in 1961 by a member of the party, P. W. Mackay of Dún Laoghaire. Mackay had quoted recidivism figures at the meeting, asserting that 60 per cent of prisoners had served previous terms of imprisonment and this 'was a sad reflection on our Christian state' and showed the Irish system of rehabilitation was inadequate (*Irish Times*, 17 January 1962). Haughey stated in response that he promised to carry out an examination of the penal system as soon as possible, and that he was 'anxious that more should be done for the prevention of crime and the rehabilitation of offenders'. In the event, the resolution proposed by Mackay that the prison system should be reassessed was defeated, but Haughey's interest remained.

Shortly after the Committee had been established, Haughey stated in the Dáil:

> I should like to emphasise that I have no intention of making changes for change's sake, but once I am convinced that new methods or intensification of old methods or changes of direction would lead towards an appreciable diminution of crime, or greater rehabilitation of offenders, I will not hesitate to take the necessary steps. I need hardly say also that I shall welcome any proposals that may be made to me by Deputies about any of these matters.
>
> *(Dáil Debates, vol 198, col 125, 27 November 1962)*

To facilitate these suggestions, Haughey recommended all deputies visit the prisons of the state or at least read the annual reports. Such openness was previously unheard of in Irish debates on prison matters.

His own interest in penal reform and an openness to developments from abroad were also apparent:

> As I have already mentioned elsewhere, I have in mind to examine closely the whole field of penal reform. I am aware, in a very general way, of the efforts at penal reform that are going on in Britain, in Denmark, in France and in other countries. This year and last year, I attended conferences of European Ministers of Justice and I was impressed with the evident anxiety on all sides to establish a code of prisoners' rights and to find better methods of dealing with juvenile delinquency. It is a problem of worldwide dimensions, in the solution of which, I hope, this country can play a part.
>
> *(Dáil Debates, vol 198, col 128, 27 November 1962)*

In a passage that would have astonished former Ministers for Justice, Haughey agreed that some recommendations for the practice of penal reform would require recruitment of personnel and structural alterations of the prison system, involving departmental planning and cost, but he declared himself 'sure that when the time comes to look for the money I will have no difficulty in getting the full support of the House' (Dáil Debates, vol 198, col 126, 5 December 1962).

It was into this intellectual and political framework and openness to ideas and desire for reform that the Committee was introduced and conducted its activities. In light of these assessments, Kilcommins *et al.* make the demonstrably correct assertion that the establishment of the Committee can be attributed to the particular modernising zeal displayed by the new Minister (Kilcommins *et al.* 2004: 70).

The inability to separate the Committee from the personality of Haughey is further evidenced by the fact that at times the Committee itself was referred to as 'Haughey Committee' (DDA, Archbishop Walsh files, Government Box 1). Newspaper reports at the time also referred to the 'Haughey plan', which involved three steps – the Juvenile Liaison Scheme (prevention), probation and the prisons (*Evening Herald*, 1 June 1964).

The role of the Department of Justice in the establishment of the Committee

While Haughey's role in the creation of the Inter-Departmental Committee was pivotal, it is not correct to attribute its establishment entirely to a 'solo run' (Kilcommins *et al.* 2004: 70) on his behalf. Civil servants within the Department of Justice were considering fundamental change in Irish prison policy during the same period and the role of Peter Berry, who had assumed the position of Secretary General in 1961, must be acknowledged. The Department of Justice had already drawn up a list of matters for study and made preliminary investigations on particular issues before the formal creation of the inter-departmental body. At one of the Committee's meetings, for example, Peter Berry, chairman of the Committee, stated: 'the Committee's activities had come about as the result of serious rethinking in the Department of Justice on these matters' (unreleased files, JUS 93/182/4). Furthermore, included in the material relating to the Committee's first meeting is a list of matters the Committee 'might consider'. This memorandum seems also to have been a creation of the Department of Justice.

In January 1962 the Department of Justice had already drawn up memoranda for consideration by 'the Committee', which itself indicates that the Inter-Departmental Committee had been contemplated for some months before its creation. One of the proposed areas for discussion was the creation of a corrective training unit within Mountjoy prison, an institution that had the specific object of assisting prisoners to reintegrate to society on release with improved educational and employment skills. The Department of Justice had also already explored the potential of re-establishing the school at Mountjoy and proposed the expansion of the shoe-making industry in the prison, bringing it up to modern standards, and the introduction of training in the techniques of dry cleaning in place of the outmoded tailoring industry (unreleased files, JUS 93/182/4).

Haughey's 'solo run' was therefore patently accepted and facilitated by Department of Justice officials whose appetite for reform appears to have been growing since the implementation of the Criminal Justice Act 1960 and throughout Haughey's tenure as Parliamentary Secretary.

The Committee's 'style' of work: impatience for results

The Committee's establishment denotes the first example of a dedicated study group of the prison system within governmental competence. In light of this, as Kilcommins *et al.* also point out, it is rather frustrating that the work of the Committee was never published in report format (2004: 70). While the lack of a report could be interpreted as a way of avoiding the imposition of transparent benchmarks by which the implementation of the Committee's recommendations could by judged, this interpretation may be overly cynical. Haughey was open with the Dáil on the recommendations of the Committee and agreed, it appears, with all of them; moreover, the Department of Justice had pre-empted several of the Committee's suggestions already.

It seems more likely that the Committee was of a somewhat *ad hoc* nature, perhaps being a product of the speed with which Haughey desired it to move and its rapid and informal establishment. It can only be speculated, but the Department may have been concerned about the danger of setting up a formal committee that would report at a later date, involving a lengthy process and making recommendations maybe years later. Haughey conceived of it as 'a practical working party of experts from which I expect to get results more or less immediately' (quoted in Mansergh 1985: 7).

The Minister for Justice addressed the inaugural meeting of the Committee and laid down his ideas regarding its future work. He stated: 'The Committee, however, should not delay making recommendations until they were in a position to make a comprehensive report. Many side issues might, perhaps, be the subject of interim recommendations' (unreleased files, JUS 93/182/2).

The Minister also suggested that the Committee divide into working parties or subcommittees to deal with particular problems or matters for attention, a suggestion that was immediately acted upon, with the Committee subdividing into three such groups, lending credence to the contention that the Department of Justice had already given significant consideration to its desired areas of examination.

The Committee's members, apart from Berry and the other representatives from Justice, did not have any particularly obvious knowledge of the Irish prison system. While it would have been difficult to source experts of an academic bent, for example, within Ireland, where there were essentially no such individuals, neither was there an attempt to recruit knowledgeable persons from abroad, nor indeed penal administrators such as governors or prison staff. It is therefore hardly surprising that prisoners or ex-prisoners were not even within the Department's radar in this regard.

The Committee's first recommendations on prison policy

Prison policy was one of the first areas tackled by the Committee. In its first meeting, held on 18 September 1962, the Committee decided to recommend to the Department of Justice that two welfare officers should be appointed to the prisons. An after-care society was further recommended for Mountjoy prison, it being hoped that this Committee would work in conjunction with existing prisoners' aid societies. This was explicitly framed as a form of 'social work' in the prisons (unreleased files, JUS 93/182/1).

An in-prison hostel was proposed for Mountjoy, where prisoners going to outside employment while on temporary release could live, segregated entirely from other prisoners and enjoying a more liberal regime. Such prisoners would be freer from supervision than others and assume a progressively greater degree of responsibility for 'their own conduct and improvement' (unreleased files, JUS 93/182/1). The Department of Justice gave an indication of its attitude in this regard, stating that temporary conditional release for this purpose was 'becoming a normal stage of treatment for prisoners undergoing corrective training in Mountjoy prison' (unreleased files, JUS 93/182/1). Overall, the Committee endorsed the greater use of temporary release in order to further the 'social rehabilitation' of the offender (unreleased files, JUS 93/183/16).

One area that was particularly noted for future efforts was that of post-release employment for prisoners. Relatedly, the Committee also sought to examine prison trades and training, with the Department of Justice averring that these were already being extended and plans being explored to introduce self-contained manufacturing processes to the prisons, a form of in-prison contract labour (unreleased files, JUS 93/182/8).

The fact that all of these matters were approved at the very first meeting of the Committee indicates that the Department of Justice had already given significant thought to the matters involved and was clearly influential on the other members of the body. There is no evidence of correspondence ongoing between the representatives of the various departments in advance of this meeting and many of the suggestions appear to be foregone conclusions, being most likely proposed by Berry and approved by those present.

Committee proposals: swift developments

As early as its second meeting, on 2 November 1962, the working parties had reported their preliminary findings after discussions, tours and meetings with prison staff and interested persons. The Medical Working Party proposed the introduction of occupational therapy for prisoners needing psychiatric assistance, the intensification of treatment for offenders in need of psychiatric attention, the establishment in Mountjoy's hospital wing of a psychiatric unit with 20 beds, an increase in the medical orderly staff and the provision of training in mental illness nursing, greater vigilance in the detection of psychological deterioration among prisoners, the provision of the services of a consultant psychiatrist, a proper padded cell and, though it is unclear what the basis for this recommendation was, the segregation of homosexuals from other prisoners.

The Education Working Party concentrated mainly on matters relating to St Patrick's Institution, recommending that consideration be given to the use of temporary release for vocational courses or apprenticeships and the expansion of the prison industries. The members of this group visited borstals and a training school in the north of Ireland, with additional contacts made with the probation service there.

The Employment Working Party was similarly focused on St Patrick's Institution, though it suggested, more broadly, the introduction of training courses for prison officers with selected officers to attend courses at the Prison Staff College, Wakefield Prison, England (unreleased files, JUS 93/182/17). The holding of conferences of prison governors was a further suggestion, aimed at improving staff training and the sharing of information. This working party also advocated temporary release for prisoners to attend vocational schools, interviews with employers, employment or to aid generally in the maintenance of links with home and community. Moreover, it endorsed the establishment of a corrective training unit, the reopening of the school in Mountjoy, the extension of shoe-making, gardening, and the provision of comprehensive background reports from the Gardaí in the case of prisoners serving sentences of two months or over to assist with the selection of 'treatment' best suited to particular cases (unreleased files, JUS 93/182/2).

The third meeting of the Committee was held in January 1963 and this meeting concentrated on the probation system, the industrial and reformatory schools and psychiatric examination of juvenile offenders. Here, the establishment of an after-care society for Mountjoy was recommended, along with the provision of proper dental facilities at that prison.

In an indication of the speed of action during this period, the chairman reported that the Committee's recommendations up until then had been availed of by the Department to make recommendations for reform and, furthermore, the 'Minister for Justice had enthusiastically accepted all the recommendations for improvements and reform and they had either already been implemented or were in course of implementation' (unreleased files, JUS 93/182/4).

By this stage and during the next two meetings, however, the Inter-Departmental Committee turned its attention seriously to the industrial and reformatory school system in Ireland, with members of the Committee paying visits to Artane and Letterfrack industrial schools. Much effort was dedicated to these topics, and significant concerns and criticisms were voiced and relayed to the Department of Education. As a consequence of this shift in focus, prison policy largely slipped from the scene in the subsequent discussions.

Peter Berry expressed his disquiet that the Committee was moving away from the broader elements of its remit and tried to divert the Committee away from the question of physical improvements to the institutions and the prisons and on to the question of after-care for both juveniles and adults released from such institutions. It seems fair to suggest that the Department of Justice hoped that the Committee would lead to the formation of prison policy proper, rather than tinkering with the existing administrative arrangements. It also lends further weight to the contention that the Department of Justice was instrumental in the work and recommendations of the Committee.

Most of the Committee's energy in the area of prison policy had been expended by this stage and no further assessment of that area was conducted.

A research agenda – of sorts

During its work, the Committee was keen to investigate the existing prison system and conduct some investigations of the experience and activities of other jurisdictions. No academic research was commissioned, nor was a wide-ranging appraisal of the entire prison system carried out, but some small-scale investigations were instigated. The Committee requested the governor of Mountjoy prison to examine the 'case histories' of 165 prisoners under his care, with the hope expressed that all prisoners would eventually be surveyed (unreleased files, JUS 93/182/1).

Evidencing a more general commitment to increasing their knowledge of crime and its causes, members of the Committee attended lectures on various sociological topics, with reports circulated among members (unreleased files, JUS 93/182/14). Members of the Committee interviewed and took information from lecturers in sociology on university programmes to train social workers with a view to drawing up the credentials required for probation work.

A list of publications on the prison system was hastily drawn up by the chairman of the Committee for order to be circulated among the members. The items studied provide an intriguing insight into the materials examined by the Committee members and the influences on their discussions and recommendations. The majority of these documents were of British origin, including, consequentially, the 1959 White Paper *Penal Practice in a Changing Society: Aspects of Future Development* (Home Office 1959), which is considered to represent much 'penal-welfarist' philosophy and principle. Newspaper reports on Swedish plans for imprisonment and British and Council of Europe publications on prisons and after-care were also sourced. English efforts in the field of training for prisoners and publications of the Secretariat of the United Nations' Department of Economic and Social Affairs on the topic of the integration of prison labour with the national economy were explored. The research efforts were hardly in-depth or wide-ranging and there is little evidence of exploration of the implications, foundational legitimacy or efficacy in practice of the matters investigated. The work conducted also has a rather haphazard air about it. However, when compared with the attitude to research that had prevailed previously, they were somewhat revolutionary.

The Committee's impact on prison policy

While many of the potentially transformative suggestions came initially from the Department of Justice, some concrete results of the Committee's work were remarkably quick to come to fruition.

The corrective training unit

In 1962 the Minister for Justice approved the recommendation of the Committee to establish a corrective training unit in Mountjoy prison, approval was somewhat academic given that the original proposals had emanated from the Department. This was opened that same year. The Department's thinking behind the introduction of the unit is revealed as follows: 'The establishment of a corrective training unit would be a definite step towards the achievement of one of the primary aims of prison treatment, namely, the rehabilitation of the offender' (unreleased files, JUS 93/182/1).

Education and other developments

The school in Mountjoy was reopened in 1962 after some years of disuse. This was another departmental plan approved by the Committee. The Committee had also recommended the prison garden be cleared and converted into a nursery and general garden to assist prisoners to train in horticulture. This was carried out in the same year.

In 1962 plans were laid to implement the Committee's recommendations regarding the modernisation and expansion of prison trades and industries, the introduction of physical training and the appointment of a welfare officer. Preparations were being made to establish a psychiatric hospital at Mountjoy. General staff training courses dealing with topics such as the prisoner/staff relationship, group counselling and supervision of inmates requiring special medical care were also introduced.

Changes attributable to the Inter-Departmental Committee

Overall, the following results can be attributed to the work of the Committee, either independently or in the form of departmental approval:

- A 20-bed psychiatric ward and the renovation and modernisation of the hospital wing at Mountjoy.
- The introduction of a new padded cell and the repair of an existing one at Mountjoy.
- The renovation of the dentist's surgery at Mountjoy.
- The reopening of the school at Mountjoy.
- The expansion and modernisation of prison trades, particularly regarding shoe-making, dry cleaning and gardening.

- The introduction of some in-service training courses for prison officers.
- The establishment of conferences of prison governors.
- Support for the establishment of the corrective training unit.
- The greater use of 'background reports' of prisoners.
- Recommendations for the reassessment of the probation service, and commitments to providing extra staff.
- A reassessment of the Industrial and Reformatory School sector, perhaps eventually leading to the formation of the Kennedy Commission.

Assessment of the Committee's work and influence

The Committee was a serious body with status within the civil service. A small but illuminating event was the fact that by the end of 1962 it was working from its own headed notepaper (unreleased files, JUS 93/182/6). While it had a significant degree of autonomy and was encouraged to investigate widely, it was clearly operating under a great degree of influence from its chairman, Peter Berry, and the Justice line.

The Committee's recommendations and their relationship to penal-welfarism is a more intricate object of study. Many of its recommendations could certainly be categorised in this vein – a focus on the young offender, attempts to improve prison conditions and after-care along with the general aim of rehabilitation. The Committee's work and discourse bear the hallmarks of such an approach. There is no evidence that the members of the Committee had put a large amount of thought into their conception of the meaning of rehabilitation. Discussion on its legitimacy or indeed its effectiveness is entirely absent, something that is of itself illuminative. It appears that the members simply conceived of their actions as 'the right thing to do', or the 'modern' way.

Abrupt termination of Committee's work – more questions than answers

Given the acceptance of the Committee, indeed its essentially whole-hearted embrace by the Department of Justice and its vigour, efforts and achievement, it is a conundrum as to why it appears to have run aground rather abruptly. The sixth and final meeting of the Committee was held on 2 July 1963, less than a year after its initial creation. This meeting focused a great deal on the probation system, but also evaluated the achievements to date on establishing links with industry.

The next meeting was fixed for 10 September 1963 and substantial effort was invested in its preparation. This meeting appears never to have been held. There is no indication as to why this is so, and the Committee was certainly not disbanded in any formal manner at this time. Later in 1963, for example, the Department of Justice was engaged in drawing up a questionnaire to be sent out to employers to assess their attitude towards taking on ex-prisoners for work, apparently as part of the Inter-Departmental Committee's work (unreleased files,

JUS 93/182/17). In January 1964 the Department drafted a 'memorandum on action' on decisions taken at the sixth meeting and outstanding matters (unreleased files, JUS 93/182/17).

The winding up of the Committee is even more bizarre and unfathomable given the sweeping, innovative and potentially radical proposals under consideration by the Department of Justice regarding the future direction of policy, which have now come to light from the previously unavailable archival material.

Department of Justice plans: radical changes envisaged

It is evident that the Department of Justice in the early 1960s was contemplating far-reaching changes in Irish prison policy. These appear never to have been presented before the Inter-Departmental Committee, again suggesting that the real catalyst for change during these years was the Department.

One such proposal was to investigate the possibility of providing farm work for prisoners on a hitherto unprecedented scale. The Department of Justice mooted the possibility of assessing the abandoned farms in Ireland with a view to providing temporary or permanent housing in abandoned homesteads for groups of prisoners or for single prisoners with their families. It was suggested that the prisoners would be paid at a rate lower than the minimum for such work, with a contribution made by the state. No legal or constitutional objections towards such a scheme were envisaged.

The proposals were discussed using explicitly rehabilitationist language, and characteristically penal-welfarist discourse. In a Department of Justice memorandum on the topic it was stated:

> [F]or the prisoner whose chief trouble is inadequacy, such a scheme might prove helpful in restoring self-confidence, and might even open a new way of life ... There could be no question of supervision by prison officers: the security for good behaviour would be fear of return to conditions of maximum security and loss of privileges (if this does not keep out of trouble a prisoner who is on the way to rehabilitation, he is not likely to keep out of trouble after final release anyhow, and little has been lost).
>
> *(Unreleased files, JUS 93/182/17)*

This was a startling proposal. While it did not get further than tentative outline on paper, the fact that it was even conceived of is a patent indication of the direction it was hoped prison policy would travel. The combination of agricultural productivity, the continued lure of 'the land' for penal administrators and the optimism that trust and assistance could have beneficial results was a potent one with symbolic resonance for policy-makers. The idea that prisoners would receive state aid to run their own farmsteads was radical, visionary and liable to sustained objection and excoriating criticism, yet the Department of Justice was not only willing to contemplate it, it appeared to them a viable and serious proposal.

In light of this assessment, the Department of Justice had in mind a fundamental restructuring of the prison system as it then stood, seeing the conditions of maximum security, requiring large numbers of prison officers, ironwork, keys, routines of counting heads, locking and unlocking and parades as inappropriate to the vast majority in prison. It went even further, stating: 'Rationally, if iron bars, locked doors and constant watchfulness are necessary to keep a person in line even in prison, then he should never be released and conversely, if he is remotely fit to rejoin society he must be able to behave himself without undue supervision' (unreleased files, JUS 93/182/17).

Given such conclusions, the Department proposed the establishment of a 'maximum security' unit for repeat or disruptive prisoners, but that the majority of prisoners be dealt with in conditions of much less stringent security with progressive emphasis on personal responsibility for good conduct, building self-confidence through task-projects, simple at first and then of progressive complexity.

The proposals were self-consciously bifurcatory. The memorandum ran: 'prison should mean two *quite* different things: A means of rebuilding and restoring the failure, and a punishment – severe enough to be an effective deterrent – for the outlaw. At the moment it is not quite either and falls between the stools' (unreleased files, JUS 93/182/17).

Prison policy appeared to be on the cusp of momentous developments which, had they been implemented, would have recast the Irish prison system beyond all recognition. As a general rule, they did not come to pass, though some new projects were undertaken in the following years.

The Department of Justice continued to work in the area with an eye to future Inter-Departmental Committee meetings, but the Committee itself does not appear to have been active. In February 1964 suggestions for a hostel at Mountjoy were explored by Berry with the governor and letters were sent out using the Committee's notepaper into 1964, with a summary of the progress of the Committee being drawn up on 18 December 1964. This seems to be the last correspondence relating to the Committee's work on file, but relevant press clippings from 1965 and 1966 were kept, and the file remained in use during 1966 (unreleased files, JUS 93/182/17).

It can be posited that the reason for the termination of the Inter-Departmental Committee is similar to the reason for its establishment – the presence of Charles Haughey as Minister for Justice. The timing involved lends credence to this contention. Haughey departed for the Department of Agriculture in October 1964. While his successor, Brian Lenihan, did see some of the matters relating to the Committee, his main focus in this regard appears to have been encouraging the Department of Education to take action regarding the institutional treatment of young offenders. Without the guiding hand and enthusiasm of Haughey the *raison d'être* of the Committee and its vigour for action dissipated, and the visionary and remarkable proposals drawn up never progressed beyond the musings of departmental officials.

Much of the remaining endeavour seems to have been carried out solely by the Secretary of the Department of Justice. Interestingly, a colleague of Berry's within the Department of Justice was also demonstrably active in researching criminal justice matters. Handwritten notes, seemingly compiled by the Committee's second secretary, Mr McAllister, who replaced Mr Toal after a number of months, contain a series of musings or reflections on such issues, the shadow of which can be seen in the memorandum produced by the Department of Justice on its proposals for the future. McAllister's writings appear to be a collection of thoughts prompted by readings on prison-related topics and their possible translation into Irish policy. McAllister felt that the papers he had read were 'drifting one towards idea of abolition of the prison system save as preventive detention for hopeless cases and substitution of a much extended probation system covering correctible adults as well as youths' (unreleased files, JUS 93/182/17). Mountjoy, he felt, could be turned into a wholly corrective institute, with Limerick and Portlaoise reserved for those not likely to be 'correctible'. The Department of Justice during these years seems to have been a comparative hot-bed of fresh ideas and innovative thinking.

Innovation in prison policy becomes the aim not anathema

The Inter-Departmental Committee was not the only or indeed main source of ideas or actions during this period. Many of the developments of the period can be attributed to the work of the Department solely, all of which can be considered as part of a general programme of 'penal reform'.

From 1 January 1962 all 'well-conducted and industrious' prisoners were authorised to receive increased gratuities (*Annual Report on Prisons*, 1962). Haughey also adopted a more liberal approach to the granting of temporary release. Change continued apace in 1963. The trainee wing of Mountjoy was extended with plans for extra space and extra rooms 'for professional visits'. Physical renovations were carried out across the penal estate, with work commencing in Limerick prison in 1964. A cabinet-making shop was opened in the men's prison at Mountjoy, a greenhouse was built and courses in physical training were commenced, with plans for a gymnasium. All of these developments were part of the plans for the training unit. Plans were also made to renovate the women's prison at Mountoy.

At Mountjoy, the psychiatric unit was opened with various occupational therapies in operation in that year. The staff of the prison hospital also began courses in medical and psychiatric nursing. A branch of Alcoholics Anonymous was set up in Mountjoy in the same year. In 1964 the two full-time welfare officers recommended by the Inter-Departmental Committee were appointed, one to Mountjoy and one to St Patrick's Institution.

The Mountjoy 'hostel'

In 1964, one of the most significant developments in Irish prison policy occurred. An in-prison hostel was completed at Mountjoy and opened, marking 'an important step forward in the penal reform programme', according to the Department of Justice (*Annual Report on Prisons*, 1965).

The hostel was designed primarily for offenders selected to take advantage of temporary release to work in the community, returning to a less prison-like environment on return each evening. This marked the final element of the proposed pre-release treatment continuum within the training unit at Mountjoy, and was another departmental innovation.

Such was the hope for the system that there were rumours that the hostel was to be named after Kevin Barry (*Irish Times*, 2 October 1964). The degree to which prison policy had changed from 20 years previously reflected in this suggestion was quite remarkable. Calling any part of an institution for ordinary prisoners after a Republican martyr would have been unthinkable in prior decades. In the event, however, the hostel does not appear to have received a name.

An alteration in discourse: treatment and rehabilitation

As well as the tangible changes in Irish prison policy, this period is characterised by a change in the 'symbolism' or tone of policy and the discussions thereon. There is no doubting the drastic alteration in the discourse surrounding prisons, with the language of treatment and 'rehabilitation' as opposed to simple reclamation or reform becoming the dominant feature of statements regarding the objectives of the prison system.

There was, moreover, unquestionably a consensus that the system was being transformed and that this was quite intentional, and also beneficial. The Mountjoy Visiting Committee in 1963 speak of the 'changing' of the prison and the 'new system' (*Annual Report on Prisons*, 1964).

Most of these sentiments emanated directly from the Minister for Justice. Haughey argued that penal reform was justified both in order to create an enlightened, humane and just society and to save the community money (Dáil Debates, vol 206, col 842, 10 December 1963). The question of penal reform was placed squarely in the bracket of social reform. In another speech, this time to Ministers of Justice from the Council of Europe, Haughey justified the use of temporary release in strongly rehabilitationist terms. He argued that it should be used widely in conjunction with supervision to avoid 'the institutionalisation, psychological deterioration and disruption to family and individual life consequent on imprisonment'. It also enabled an offender to be guided and supported '*in his own milieu*' (JUS 2005/12/6, emphasis in original).

Nor was Haughey shy of the newspaper media and gave several interviews on his programme for penal reform, many of which presented him in the style of a crusading mould-breaker, convinced of his purpose and unstinting in his application. In 1963, another 'unthinkable' occurred within Irish prisons when Haughey granted the film production group An Radharc permission to make a documentary about St Patrick's Institution, which was shown on what was then Telefís Éireann, the national broadcaster (An Radharc Archive, Irish Film Archive,

Ref 9), indicating Haughey's pride in his efforts and in which he described temporary release as 'enormously successful'.

An interest in research and international developments

Other factors prevalent during this period marked a change in prison policy, particularly between 1962 and 1964. One such was an increasing interest in research, particularly from abroad on some prison issues.

This greater interest in international experiences of prison and justice matters generally was most clearly reflected in the holding of the Third Conference of the European Ministers of Justice in Dublin in May 1964. This gathered together ministers from the countries comprising the Council of Europe. It appears to be the case that states extended invitations to the body of the Ministers for Justice to host these conferences. Ireland would therefore have made this invitation in 1963, under Charles Haughey as Minister.

The move is indicative of the growing confidence within Irish administration, a desire to showcase itself to European neighbours and, in truth, an appetite for the 'glamour' of European cooperation. The timing of this invitation is also revealing. Around this time, the Council of Europe was itself turning its attention towards criminological matters, with the Criminological Scientific Council founded in 1962 to give technical advice to the Council on creating a 'scientific' programme in the field of crime problems. Its first chairman was Sir Leon Radzinowicz (Anttila 1974).

The opening address to the conference in Dublin by Minister Haughey displayed elements of this growing interest in criminological research and the sharing of best practice and ideas. He stated: 'we in Ireland feel that we have much to gain from the results of criminological research in the larger countries of Europe' (JUS 2005/12/6).

No doubt Haughey wished to present the best possible side of Irish policy-making and its interest in looking elsewhere for inspiration and this should be borne in mind when assessing such statements. He also took the Ministers for Justice on a tour of the corrective training unit and the rest of Mountjoy prison.

The products of this change in approach were as stylistic as meaningful, involving the self-conscious presentation of both Minister and Department as 'modern', outward-looking, keen on international engagement. Those involved were, at this time, very keen to court this image and such desires and impulses represent some of the greatest examples of the discontinuities with the past evident in the early 1960s.

Haughey moves on

From the end of 1964 it was no longer Charles Haughey's role to oversee these developments. After a rushed Cabinet reshuffle he was replaced by another recent entrant to the Dáil, Brian Lenihan, also part of the new generation appointed by Seán Lemass.

Right at the end of Haughey's tenure, the prison system was subject to some of the greatest media coverage it had experienced at any peaceful time in Ireland. Most of it was also astonishingly favourable towards both the Minister and his plans for the prison system. In a review of the changes that had occurred in Mountjoy, the *Sunday Independent* (4 June 1964) reported: 'many of the changes may seem startling, even revolutionary' and, remarkably, 'some of them are in fact the implementation, consciously or not, of the recommendations of the Gladstone Committee in Britain nearly 70 years earlier.' The *Evening Herald* (1 June 1964) stated its assessment thus: 'It is early yet to make a full appraisal of the eventual results of the "Haughey Plan" but even the sternest critics have to admit that the results in terms of men returned to normal lives in society are impressive for such a sweeping departure from traditional ideas.'

These statements are extraordinary. Not only it is startling with hindsight to see such warm praise for work in the area of prison reform in the press, the fact that praise was directed towards elements of such work that can be categorised as 'progressive' and liberalising is equally exceptional.

These reports represent the zenith of interest and even excitement about the prison system in the national press during the 1960s. After the departure of Haughey, prison policy assumed, in comparison to the previous years, a less frenetic tone and also a less optimistic, fervent and self-congratulatory appearance.

Lenihan as Minister for Justice: a continuity in discourse

Lenihan carried through much of the legislative programme that had been started by his predecessor and implemented some of the existing plans in the penal field. The After-Care Committee for Mountjoy prison was instigated at the end of 1965, for example. Composed of a number of businessmen, it was designed to assist prisoners to obtain employment and accommodation on discharge from prison. It also had an advisory role regarding the organisation of prison labour and industries and consulted with existing prisoner welfare organisations.

Lenihan's tenure marks a time of consolidation of the measures that had been planned under Haughey. While subsequent years were less dramatic in terms of pace, the Department and its new Minister did not reverse the tenets or practices introduced by Haughey. Lenihan's own commitment, at least on a rhetorical level, to rehabilitation was also clear. The training unit and temporary release were warmly praised by the Minister on his arrival into office. He was proud of what he saw as a shift in Irish prison policy, inviting deputies to 'come and see for themselves the radical changes that have been taking place in recent years' (Dáil Debates, vol 225, col 1569, 24 November 1966).

A slowing of pace

While rehabilitation was by now the declared aim of the system and there was little disquiet about this or about the improvement in conditions within the prisons, Lenihan's tenure after 1965 bears little more fruit in the way of penal developments, and despite holding the portfolio for four years there is far less evidence of a Lenihan legacy on Irish prison policy comparable to that of Haughey.

Mention of the prison system was also less frequent within Oireachtas debates, with the exception of the imprisonment of members of the National Farmers' Association in 1967 (Dáil Debates, vol 226, cols 2137–40, 1 March 1967). The annual reports, which had almost bristled with excitement a few years before, assumed a more settled shape and the prison system fell out of the spotlight. In fact, the reports for 1967, 1968 and 1969 were not published until the middle of 1970. The Prisoner After-Care Committee, which was lauded for its efforts in finding work for prisoners upon release, became inactive in February 1967, after holding 11 meetings and finding employment for six prisoners. It was not re-established.

Signs of trouble ahead

It is important to note some straws in the wind that began to appear in the late 1960s pointing to future problems ahead. From 1965 the average daily prison population continued to increase steadily. This was attributable partly to an increase in long-term sentences and partly to increasing population figures.

The crime rate began to increase from 1966 after fluctuating year on year throughout the early part of the decade. In 1967 the volume of indictable crimes exceeded the 20,000 mark for the first time. Lenihan began to use the phrase 'war on crime' in official discourse to describe the increased powers proposed for Gardaí under a Criminal Justice Bill introduced in 1967, though this language was not, as will be seen, representative of the discourse of penal policy generally.

The first reference in Oireachtas debates to an increase in drug usage and its effect on crime appeared in 1967 (Dáil Debates, vol 230, col 1545, 21 October 1967). In that year it was also felt necessary to introduce legislation to deal with flick knives through the provisions of the Criminal Justice Bill 1967. Prison officers began to register grievances about pay and conditions at the end of 1969. On New Year's Eve 1969 a riot took place in Mountjoy and Portlaoise prisons, the first such significant incident of a kind which, as will be seen, began to occur with greater frequency in the following years (*Irish Times*, 23 June 1970).

Another new Minister for Justice: Micheál Ó Moráin

1968 saw another change that affected the Irish prison system. In this year Jack Lynch, who had succeeded Seán Lemass to both leader of Fianna Fáil and Taoiseach in 1966, appointed Micheál Ó Moráin as Minister for Justice.

A number of contradictory trends can be discerned during his period in charge of the prison system. First of all, the remaining energy and drive in penal reform that had survived during Lenihan's tenure seemed to dissipate entirely under Ó Moráin.

Dissonance between Minister and Department

The Minister's speeches in the Dáil from this time are puzzling. It appears that the elements that were most likely drafted by Department of Justice officials represent a continuing commitment to the tenets of reform of the system and a move towards rehabilitation. However, in Ó Moráin's more unguarded moments, his own approach seems to be somewhat harsher, deliberately provocative, and even anti-intellectual at times. This is an interesting indication that the Department was in fact more progressive and active than the Minister.

There is evidence that Peter Berry of the Department and Ó Moráin had very different outlooks on law reform and similar matters. Relations between Minister and his Secretary were not ideal and in many ways the Department was getting on with its work without the input or interference of the Minister. The diaries of Peter Berry suggest, politely, that the Minister was afflicted by much 'ill-health' and found it gravely difficult to function in the Department (Arnold 2001; Berry 1980: 52; Puirséil 2007), while O'Halpin describes the Minister as 'ailing and ineffectual' (O'Halpin 1999a: 309).

The Department by 1968 was still working on what it considered to be 'penal reform' and 'criminological and penological advances' (JUS 2002/2/147). In 1968, the Department outlined its 'long-term' policy, a concept that would have been resisted just ten years previously. This envisaged the establishment of probation hostels, run by voluntary organisations, the provision of hostels outside prisons for 'working prisoners' and a review of juvenile detention (JUS 2002/2/147). A report was commissioned within the Department in 1969 on the probation service and prisoner after-care. Much work was going on behind the scenes, though fewer eye-catching developments were announced.

Rehabilitation in theory: recycling ideas and raised expectations

Most of the ideas being put forward at the end of the 1960s were, however, essentially recycled from the earlier part of the decade. There was an ongoing rhetorical commitment to rehabilitation and regular reassertions of the government's dedication to penal reform, but a definite stalling of progress in practice. Expectations for the prison system and the beneficial impact it could have on prisoners had been raised in the optimistic days under Haughey. This tension and the frustration it engendered are also significant features of this period.

The debate on the Estimates for the Department of Justice in 1969 exemplifies these themes quite well. One of the key features to emerge from an analysis of the Dáil reports is the consensus among all sides of the Dáil that rehabilitation should be a key aim of the prison system. No voices of dissent were raised on the desirability of rehabilitation, with the only criticisms being that the Department wasn't doing enough to rid the system of its Victorian elements and a disquiet that the public wasn't as accepting of ex-prisoners as could be hoped (Dáil Debates, vol 242, col 140, 21 November 1969). The Minister was subject to a barrage of points about penal reform and the application of rehabilitative thinking. Frustration was also evident at the slow movement towards greater training in the disciplines of criminology and penology for staff and members of visiting committees alike (Dáil Debates, vol 242, col 1483, 20 November 1969). The official response was to defend the government's record on these matters and to sound some words of caution.

The optimism and unabashed zeal with which commitments to rehabilitation were expressed in the earlier part of the decade now gave way to greater qualification, restraint and caution. The Minister argued, for example, 'prisons exist for deterrent purposes as well as to rehabilitate prisoners' (Dáil Debates, vol 243, col 1204, 20 November 1969).

Academic and media comment

That said, the language of rehabilitationism had become essentially hegemonic and was shared across all elements of the political spectrum and beyond as the decade progressed. As well as being prevalent within official circles, these sentiments and sensibilities were apparent in academic and media comment on the prison system.

The legal periodical the *Irish Jurist* carried an article on the topic of punishment and responsibility, with particular emphasis on the insights to be gained from psychiatric and social scientific advances in 1966 (Bazelon 1966). In the same year, the *Dublin University Law Review* carried two articles along similar themes. Later, in 1971, the *Irish Law Times* published comments made in the Dáil by Dr Noël Browne under the title 'Court Penological Practice', which lambasted the reluctance of judges to engage with social science. In the same year Paddy Hillyard (later Professor) made a general plea for increased knowledge of the techniques of social research and investigation on the part of judges who undertake social inquiries (Hillyard 1971). Prisoner after-care was the subject of an article by Mary C. O'Flynn in the 1971 volume of the *Irish Jurist*.

These were, of course, only a handful articles carried in three legal journals and they do not, even collectively, represent a transformation of the Irish academic community or, indeed, the creation of an Irish criminological community. However, their inclusion in such volumes demonstrates that Irish intellectual, and particularly legal, circles were aware of the tenets of rehabilitationism and the potential influence of the social and life sciences on the criminal process as well as the discipline of 'criminology'.

The Irish Society of Criminology

In 1971 the Irish Society of Criminology was founded. This was the first of its kind in the history of the state. In its constitution its aim was stated as: 'to encourage discussion and research of criminological matters in Ireland'. Four meetings were to be held every year and a biannual publication describing current criminological and penological research and developments in Irish penal systems was planned.

The society was the product of the coalition of a number of young academics, an undoubtedly but small 'critical mass' of young, inquiring intellectuals who felt that an appetite for such subjects was now present in the state. Some were graduates of the social science programmes that were becoming more common in Ireland during those years.

The establishment of the Society is revealing of the growing awareness of criminology and an awakening of interest in crime in Ireland. Equally as informative is the reaction of the Department of Justice to its establishment. While the Department of Justice had given an initial indication of support by making efforts to obtain a speaker for a conference, Dick Crowe of the Department reacted severely to a paper delivered by Peter Shanley, a law graduate with an interest in criminology. The paper was reported on by *The Irish Press*, including the criticisms of the system of rehabilitation. This coverage appears to have upset the civil servants significantly. Crowe described Shanley as 'a bit of a nuisance' and he 'avoided him like the plague' on the sole basis that he would often 'corner' Crowe with questions about the Irish penal system (JUS 2002/2/169).

The Minister for Justice directed that no member of the Department should join the Irish Society for Criminology as it would compromise their 'detachment' in the discharge of their duties, but did nominate Martin Tansey to address their conference on the subject of 'Whither Probation' (JUS 2002/2/169).

Research and the Department of Justice

The Department was evidently somewhat suspicious and hesitant regarding research that it could not control. A letter was sent by Dr (now Professor) Roger Hood of the University of Cambridge on behalf of Peter Shanley to An Garda Síochána in 1970 seeking access to observe Garda work with juvenile offenders. The Gardaí were receptive, but the Department of Justice gave a cautious consent, stating there that were no perceived difficulties 'as long as there is not an influx of researchers' (JUS 2002/2/169).

As will be seen in the following chapter, the Department's attitude can be accounted for to some extent by the Department's growing defensiveness and insularity, which was prompted by concerns about a subversive threat to the state evident in the early 1970s and particularised threats to members of the Department. As such, the early 1970s was not a climate in which the Department was likely to be receptive to outside investigation. However, this alone cannot explain the unwelcoming stance that was adopted. It should be pointed out that the Department of Justice was not unique in this behaviour. The British Home Office was also prone to secrecy and exclusion of the press and others, particularly in the 1950s. Ryan demonstrates that permission was rarely given to the press to write about the penal system and those that did were kept on a tight rein, such that 'if they dared to criticize, then there was usually an almighty row as the metropolitan elite closed ranks against what it identified as "ill-informed" outsiders' (Ryan 2003: 27). Fears of 'outsiders' beyond the control of the Department of Justice may also account for the particular relationship that developed here.

This is puzzling, as in the previous few years the Department had looked closely at research produced in England and by the Council of Europe in the search for ideas. Even in that period, however, the Department, particularly in the person of Peter Berry, had been cautious about the need for an Irish academic research community, preferring to make its own assessment of penal matters. Berry, furthermore, seemed to prefer to retain and maintain departmental and to some extent personal control over matters. This extant position and the particular years in which the Irish Society of Criminology was formed combined to deprive the Society of any influence.

During the Haughey years attempts were made to at least give the appearance of a serious effort to keep up to date with European developments and to attend conferences in this vein. This element of penal policy also appears to have petered out by the 1970s. For example, in 1972 a conference of prison directors from the countries that comprised the Council of Europe met in Paris with the aim of reviewing the European Prison Rules and to investigate the extent to which the United Nations Standard Minimum Rules for the treatment of prisoners were being applied in such countries. Ireland did not send a representative, despite being a member of the Council.

Social investigation: media portrayal of prison policy

Within the academic community, 'rehabilitation' and its precepts had permeated much of its output on the criminal justice system and was, by now, the accepted benchmark by which governmental action was judged.

The period under assessment is also notable for growing coverage of criminal justice and penal matters within the popular media. This is partially attributable to the fact that there was simply more to report on than in previous years, but is also connected to the greater diversity in the media, with the introduction of new newspapers such as the *Evening Herald* and the advent of television (Cathcart and Muldoon 2003). Documentary-makers utilised the prison environment for material for 'social investigation' style programmes, which were also used as a platform by Ministers for Justice to put forward their view of such matters as well as a means of holding ministers to account for their actions (Horgan 2004; Keogh 2003).

Social investigation was facilitated by the increasing expansion of social science and social work courses at universities, with degree courses being offered by

University College Dublin in 1954, Trinity College Dublin in 1962, and University College Cork in 1965, with postgraduate courses following later. Sociology in Ireland made strides during this decade, becoming independent of the Catholic influences that had long characterised its work thereto. More academics were recruited and there was a growing presence of the discipline within Irish third-level institutions (Tovey and Share 2003).

Most newspaper coverage, particularly in the period 1964–69, refers to the idea that the prison system had undergone extensive modernisation and the majority were strongly in favour of this change. In 1964 the *Irish Independent* carried a very favourable report on the opening of the prison hostel in Mountjoy, calling it 'one of the most encouraging steps forward in prison reform and rehabilitation ever taken in this country' (10 October 1964). In 1967 the *Irish Press* carried a feature piece on 'Our Prisons Today' which left the reader in no doubt that there had been a radical transformation in the prison system, arguing that 'the emphasis has now passed from punishing men to attempting to cure them of the disease of crime' (29 June 1967).

In the latter part of the 1960s, the media coverage of the prison system reflected a growing unease about crime and a frustration with the prison system and its perceived inadequacies. Most of the commentary referred, however, to the slowness of implementation of rehabilitative techniques rather than questioning the underlying effectiveness of those methods. For example, one piece in the *Irish Times* referred to the prison system as 'inadequate', with this assessment based on the fact that all the prisons in the state were closed with the exception of Shanganagh (discussed in Chapter 6), and there was no special categorisation within the prisons nor separation between remand and convicted prisoners (21 May 1970).

Rehabilitation in practice: symbolism in policy versus execution in reality

While rehabilitation had become the declared aim of the system during the 1960s, it cannot be said with the same degree of conviction that rehabilitation was the outcome of that system. It is difficult to assess the true impact of the changes mooted at departmental level within the state's institutions. For a start, there was no empirical analysis conducted by which this could be measured. Of more theoretical significance, however, is an assessment of whether the rhetorical commitment to rehabilitation ever made it from the realm of policy statement to the prison cell.

It is patently the case that the optimism and energy of the early 1960s were not matched by practical implementation in the latter part of that decade. For example, plans were laid to build a new women's prison, but these did not come to fruition for several decades afterwards. Educational progress was talked up, but it appears that the educational staff in the state's prisons continued to have no specific qualifications to deal with prisoners' needs. Moreover, the influences of the social sciences had yet to make a significant breakthrough in official practice, with only one member of a visiting committee out of 48 such members having a qualification in social work. Prison staff continued to lack training in many areas. Provision for after-care and employment remained inadequate. There was, moreover, still no attempt to undertake a serious assessment of penal methods in Ireland.

The efforts that were made were concentrated on Dublin prisons, and, in truth, essentially within the training unit attached to Mountjoy prison. The prison industries outside of the training unit remained relatively unchanged over the course of the decade, with farm work remaining the main activity at Portlaoise. In 1969 prisoners were still engaged in mat-making and wood-cutting, with a large number working on the ordinary service of the prisons on tasks such as cleaning, washing and cooking (JUS 2005/135/4).

Slopping out remained a feature, and while renovations did occur in most institutions, structurally most of the prisons were essentially the same as they had been when the Free State had taken over in 1922. Lock-up was still for fourteen and a half hours per day.

The most significant factor that must be assessed when investigating the true extent of the avowed commitment to the tenets of rehabilitation is the fact that the institution of imprisonment itself endured throughout this period. Alternative sanctions continued to be few and far between and the probation service, in particular, was subject to a great deal of departmental lethargy and delay.

While 'progress' was made in Irish prison policy and practice the like of which had not been seen at any time during the history of the state, this was most effectively implemented at the level of policy 'style' rather than within the practice of imprisonment.

Female prisoners: particular neglect exposed

Subject to particular neglect were the state's women prisoners. Plans to construct a new prison to replace the outmoded women's prison at Mountjoy, located in the basement of St Patrick's Institution, were placed on the longest of long fingers throughout the entire period under analysis. Furthermore, no female welfare officer was attached to any prison in Ireland during this same period, nor were any regimes innovated with female needs specifically in mind. The numbers of women in prison were extraordinarily low during the 1960s, being measured in the tens rather than the hundreds. Prison was not the place where women were detained in Ireland; they were mainly confined in other institutions such as the Magdalene laundries, mother and baby homes and other similar institutions.

Throughout the late 1960s and early 1970s greater light was cast on the imprisonment of females with several opinion pieces criticising their treatment by the state. The conditions of the female prisoners piqued the interest of a growing number of female journalists who were self-consciously committed to social investigation and criticism. In 1971 Nell McCafferty wrote a scathing article on this topic, arguing that the absence of any official help or advice to women prisoners demonstrated a desire of the state to punish rather than rehabilitate women, silently locking them away from society (*Irish Times*, 4 May 1971).

The conditions in the female prison at Mountjoy were exposed further in January 1972 in a collection of three articles written by Mary Maher in the 'Women First' pages of the *Irish Times*. These were based on her interviews with two women who had been imprisoned there for offences arising out of an anti-Vietnam war protest in Dublin and a number of other ex-prisoners. She was highly critical of the conditions in the female prison, castigating the food, hygiene, the visiting committee system and medical treatment, further alleging that corporal punishment was a regular feature of prison life (14 January 1971).

Prisoners' rights groups and their impact

Given this growing frustration and visibility of prisoners' views in the media, it is surprising that it does not appear that any groups were established to agitate for prisoners' rights during this period. This is partly a reflection of the absence of subversive prisoners from the system in the 1960s and is another indication that the impetus for change in prison policy in these years came firmly from within government. Civil society, by contrast, did not appear greatly interested in penal affairs. Those efforts that were made from within the voluntary sector were concentrated in the visiting committees, after-care committees and, most notably, in the formation of PACE (Prisoners' Aid through Community Effort), a voluntary organisation that set up a hostel for homeless ex-prisoners.

One group did try to get off the ground. In 1968 it was reported that a number of people in Offaly were forming an Irish League for Penal Reform, and had already studied conditions in Mountjoy and at the Daingean Reformatory. Expressions of interest and support were sought from prison and probation officers, social workers or anyone with experience for such institutions (*Irish Press*, 28 October 1968). The Department of Justice officials were at this time hopeful of such interest, with Peter Berry writing in an internal document: 'we should be glad to hear from them and to hear how they speak with knowledge (sic)' (JUS 2002/2/106). This organisation seems to have struck the Department as far less offensive or troublesome than the academic efforts outlined above. However, there is no indication that this group ever functioned in a serious manner, nor that any such group had an impact on the policy-making process either in terms of presentation of research or the agitation for change during the 1960s.

The Criminal Justice Bill 1967

Prison policy in the late 1960s was constituted by ongoing official commitments to the aim of rehabilitation and an unabashed enthusiasm for the language of such an approach. However, the reality of these statements was far less evident. These contradictions and the ideological flux in policy during these years are manifested very clearly in the ill-fated Criminal Justice Bill, introduced first in 1967 though elements of it were apparently being planned for as far back as 1965 (JUS 2003/5/53).

This bill proposed serious changes to a number of areas of criminal justice administration including the law of bail, with the aim being to restrict its availability in a number of instances. The bill proposed to continue the programme of law reform and modernisation of legal rules that had begun in the earlier part of the decade. The bill would also have removed a vast array of archaic statutes from the Irish statute book. It covered an enormous amount of criminal law, evidence and procedure, and the provisions that ultimately led to its downfall were comparatively minor elements of the proposals. Strikingly, the bill sought to allow the government to transfer individuals into military custody should the need arise.

The bill therefore combined elements of modernisation, a restatement of the criminal law and criminal procedure, clampdowns on 'liberal' bail regimes and a remarkable change to prison policy. It was somewhat symbolic of the tensions in criminal justice around this period. Given its scope and content, O'Malley is quite right to call it a 'remarkable piece of legislation' (O'Malley 2006: 32).

The bill was never passed, however, and many of its much-needed provisions remained in legislative permafrost for decades afterwards, but the philosophy, or perhaps more accurately philosophies, it exemplified are of major significance in any analysis of prison policy from this period.

Military custody contemplated

The most noteworthy sections of the bill from the point of view of prison policy proper was the power under section 45 that would have allowed for transfers of ordinary prisoners to military custody. Such a transfer would be carried out if the Minister certified that he was satisfied that the continued presence of the person concerned was likely to be detrimental to the security of or the good order in the prisons.

This was framed within a context of fears that widespread demonstrations and mass arrests could put pressure on the prison system. From the latter half of the 1960s the growing unrest in the north of Ireland was beginning to elicit concern. Moreover, social protest of other forms was also prevalent, with anti-Vietnam, anti-apartheid and pro-women's rights movements being just a selection of groups involved in agitation during this period (Foster 2007; Whyte 2003b). The government's reaction was to move legislation to introduce wide powers to suppress such agitation.

The Minister for Justice was of the opinion that should a large and sudden influx of such individuals be committed to Ireland's prisons the system would be unable to cope, and, significantly, rehabilitation programmes would have to be abandoned. This section was therefore an interesting forerunner to provisions that, as will be detailed in the following chapter, would later be enacted in the form of the Prisons Act 1972.

Reaction to the bill

The bill received an extremely hostile response from both the opposition and various academic commentators and interest groups, including the recently formed Irish Council for Civil Liberties and the Association of Irish Jurists, the chair of which was Roderick O'Hanlon, later judge of the Supreme Court (OAG 2003/4/001). The chorus of dissent formed a quintessential 'issue network' as explored by Cope (2001). The renowned jurist, scholar and parliamentarian J. M. Kelly was trenchant in his criticism, arguing that the bill was placed too firmly on the side of crime control over procedural fairness (*Irish Times*, 30 July 1968). Internal dissent within the Fianna Fáil party was also apparent (Whyte 2003b). Particular objection was made to the proposals regarding the restrictions on assembly, whereby public demonstrations could be outlawed.

Downfall of the bill – but an indication of things to come?

In the event, it was the proposals in sections 30 and 31, which rendered certain public demonstrations illegal, that were to prove the bill's downfall. The harsh approach adopted towards political protest and the expression of dissent by the Minister for Justice was defeated through opposition from within the Dáil and a media and academic outcry. In practical terms, its death knell was sounded by the general election of 1969, but there was no appetite to reintroduce it subsequently. This was also a product of the eclipsing of the concerns that led to its introduction by the growth of far larger and more serious problems that were to face the administration of justice. The provisions on military custody were introduced in a later enactment, as will be seen in the following chapter.

Ireland in the early 1960s: a time of change

In terms of action in the area of prison policy, the early part of the 1960s was remarkably different from that which had gone before. A number of practical factors allowed for the changes involved to be introduced, but the broader social and political contexts were also receptive to such change.

The comparative peace of the 1960s allowed intellectual space to the Department of Justice, which no longer had to lurch from one threat to the state to another, to devote its attention to 'ordinary imprisonment' for the first time. Yet this had been equally true of the 1950s, but that period was one of utter stagnation in terms of prison policy.

Many of the developments of the period can also be traced directly to Haughey's own work and his political ambitions. However, Haughey's actions were part of a broader movement in Irish politics during these years. This was characterised by an impatience to make changes, to do things differently and to make progress.

It is noteworthy, however, that the direction of policy was in the rehabilitationist vein. Haughey's 'solo runs' need not necessarily have been such. A Minister of his energy and capacity could have attempted changes in the prison system of an entirely different nature. The fact that he chose to invest time and resources in a rehabilitationist fashion is rooted in the social assumptions and changes of these years. It seems that policy-makers could not conceive of another, perhaps punitive, way forward. These 'unthought thoughts' (Tonry 2001b) were themselves significant.

The changes in Irish political, social and economic life during the late 1950s and 1960s have been described by a range of commentators as a 'watershed' (Lyons 1973: 582), 'the best of decades' (Tobin 1984), even 'a golden dawn', with the government that held power from 1961 to 1965 adjudged even to be 'one of the best in the history of the state' (Murphy 1979: 4–5), presiding over the lifting of the 'pall of gloom' (Lee 1979: 17) or 'smog of depression' (Lee 1989: 152) that had enveloped the 1950s, breaking the connection between the 'rural' cultural and social norms of the previous years (Foster 1990: 569), effecting 'almost revolutionary' change (Coakley 2004a: 42).

Keogh refers to the 'rising tide' of the 1960s as one that created a 'certain sense of spring in the air', a time of 'radical change and apparent radical change' (Keogh 2005: 250–1). A fair assessment of this period is as follows: 'change rather than continuity appears ... as the dominant motif running through the 1960s' (Lee 1979: 173). A number of constituent elements of this change are noteworthy.

Economic outlook

The late 1950s and first half of the 1960s is widely regarded as a time when the economic and social policy of the state was transformed. The year 1958 was designated by Lemass as the 'year of opportunity', with Lemass in particular keenly focused on tackling the malaise of emigration. In the same year, T. K. Whitaker, the most able civil servant of his generation and a man of exceptional talents, drew up the famous document *Economic Development*, which proposed an integrated programme of national development over a five- to ten-year time-frame and became the White Paper, *Programme for Economic Expansion* (Finance 1958).

This programme has been heralded as a watershed in Irish economic history, involving the dismantling of the protectionism that had been a feature of Irish economic policy for decades. As well as the practical economic changes it prompted, as Bradley (1988) notes, the First Programme had a 'psychological' aspect; he argues that it was to act as a mechanism for decisive political action and an encouragement to innovation.

It is also interesting to note that *Economic Development* has been likened to the Beveridge Report in the sense that it marked a fundamental change of direction in Irish political culture and a shouting of 'stop' regarding the social and economic conditions to which the state had grown accustomed (Lee 1989: 373). While there is debate (Bew and Patterson 1982) over the programme's features and effects regarding social investment and expansion, the report is widely considered as an important first step towards greater planning by the state in the economy and in the creation of inward investment from overseas firms (Foster 1990: 579).

During the 1960s the state's economic growth was faster than at any prior period. After the first balancing of the state's budget for ten years in 1959 (Keogh 2005: 253; Whyte 2003b), there was significant expansion in industrial production (Kennedy 1986). Living standards rose by 50 per cent during the decade and the population grew by over 100,000 between 1961 and 1970 (Nolan 1984; Walsh 1979). Emigration rates fell and by the early 1970s net migration became a feature of Irish demographics – and a major transformation from the previous decade (Ferriter 2004: 542). Overall, the contentment with the *status quo* of the 1950s was replaced in the 1960s by impatience and a challenge to the forces of resistance that had stultified change previously.

Social policy

While *Economic Development* did not advocate the expansion of social spending, political developments during the period prompted much greater discussion of and action in this field. The early 1960s saw a change in the discourse of social policy. Both the governing Fianna Fáil party and the opposition appeared to share a greater commitment to social improvements and began to speak the language of greater social compassion in the 1960s. This became most apparent towards the end of the decade, but elements of the change had already become obvious earlier.

The state's role in the provision of welfare also began to change. While the Irish 'welfare state' has proven notoriously difficult to characterise (Kilcommins *et al.* 2004: chapter 7), the developments that did occur in this vein have been typified by their lateness, particularly when compared with Britain (Cousins 1997, 2005; McCashin 2004). Most agree, however, that the Irish 'welfare state' began to emerge only from the early 1960s, with transformations in social provision, health policy and social work key elements of this change (Barrington 1987; Skehill 2003). Fanning argues, for example, that 'the emergence of a distinct post-war era [of welfare] could be dated from as early as 1958 ... it could also be dated from the mid-1960s when political parties broke with the tradition of viewing all state intervention as an outsider's intrusion into the family and the voluntary sector' (Fanning 2003: 10). Around this time, an old age contributory pension was introduced and children's allowances were extended to first-born children (Kennedy 1986).

Carey argues that while significant developments in that field did not occur in Ireland until the late 1960s, a change of attitude was prevalent from the early 1960s and even before, with social insurance becoming 'increasingly viewed as the most appropriate mode of provision for most contingencies' (Carey 2007: 218). With hindsight, such changes were modest and *ad hoc*. However, they represented a change in thinking about the proper role of the state in social provision and indicated a new direction for such policy. Importantly, debate on these matters was also becoming more apparent.

State involvement in the provision of social services grew, particularly from 1962, taking up a larger proportion of GDP than ever before (Rottman and O'Connell 1982;Timonen 2002). Health (Barrington 1987), education (Coolahan 1981; Hyland 1997) and housing (Curry 2003) were other areas that underwent significant change, having been subject to neglect and stagnation for many years. All were conceived of as ripe for expansion and their potential to improve the lives of Irish citizens was a key consideration. As O'Connell and Rottman note, 'the progressive enhancement of social rights' was a basic trend running through post-1960 Ireland (O'Connell and Rottman 1992: 205).

Sheehan dates a shift in the education system to 1963 (Sheehan 1979: 68), with White (2001) noting change from 1958, averring that the Department of Education became open to new ideas from that time.

Interestingly, the legal system was revolutionised by a developing judicial activism, transforming the conception of the Constitution and establishing a corpus of constitutional rights law and a burgeoning body of cases dealing with fundamental rights protection. Kelly attributes much of this transformation to a generational change within the legal profession (Kelly 1980). This transition to a new generation was felt across the political, administrative and journalistic sectors.

Public administration

Another key component of this period was the changed role and self-conception of civil servants. These individuals gained an increasing influence over public policy, and 'planning', though it had some negative connotations in the Irish context, became an increasing feature of Irish administrative life.

Walsh notes that the increasing role for the state in the economy in the 1960s and 1970s was accompanied by an increasing role for the public sector in Irish life and that the expansionary tendencies in education, health and housing required a larger civil service (Walsh 1986). Barrington (1980) and Dooney (1976) agree that the civil service underwent a significant expansion in terms of numbers and role in the 1960s in particular due to the increasing workload for the state produced thereby. The approach of public servants to their task and the foregrounding of their expertise in policy formation as envisaged by Whitaker were also instrumental in developing the importance of the role of administrators (Lalor 2003). Chubb suggests, moreover, that in the 1960s the 'anti-intellectualism' that had characterised both Irish politics and administration until then was challenged through a growing interest in investigation and research (Chubb 1982). The Institute of Public Administration was founded in 1957. This body had the primary aim of encouraging and discussing the 'science' of public administration in Ireland.

Barrington (1982) posits that the civil service generally underwent a significant improvement in the period from the late 1950s to the late 1970s, resulting in ten years of high-quality public service performance. Lalor (1996) similarly argues that the civil service moved away from its traditionally perceived virtues of preventing expenditure and acting negatively towards proposed innovation during this period. As well as the Inter-Departmental Committee noted above, other commissions and investigative bodies included the Commission on Higher Education (1960), the Commission on Itinerancy (1963) and the Commission of Inquiry on Mental Handicap (1965).

1960s Ireland and 'modernisation'

The areas analysed above represent just a few of the sectors of Irish social, political and economic life that were transformed during this decade. The 1960s is considered to have brought about change across many areas of Irish society, from legal reform to popular culture (Keogh 2005; McCormack 1999; O'Brien 1990; Waters 1991) to the Catholic Church (Convey 1994; Whyte 1980) to economics, sport (de Búrca 2000), social policy, and political culture. These areas of change were impacted upon by an overall increase in influences from abroad and outward perspectives impacting upon Irish endeavour. All these developments can be considered as elements of Ireland's 'modernisation' which commenced around this time. In many respects optimism is a characteristic common to all these changes, with an impatience for change, progress and movement of any kind evident across these various spheres. Many of those with an influence on the policy-making process appeared to be in a hurry to drag, as they saw it, Ireland out of its 1950s' torpor and neglect.

This concept of modernisation also characterises prison policy during these years. Rather than adhering to a particular philosophy, such as that of penal-welfarism or punitivism or liberalism, those instrumental in the formation of prison policy were more concerned with 'improving' matters generally, applying an enlightened approach to the treatment of prisoners. It was an attachment to the principle of 'improvement', updating, or modernising, which was felt at the time to be found in the discourse of rehabilitation and a humane approach to punishment.

The genesis of the change in Irish prison policy was therefore a confluence both of dynamic individuals at political and administrative level, and of an economic and social context that was far more open to change. The 'solo runs' of Haughey and his civil servants were vital, but their direction towards rehabilitation and their ease of implementation were closely allied to the broader changes in Irish society. Real movement was the result, including some comparatively radical innovations. The ripples of these changes were felt in the following years, though the scale and speed of change witnessed in the early 1960s was not seen again until the 1990s.

The late 1960s: consolidation, a change of pace and conflicts

Throughout the latter part of the 1960s, many of the elements that marked out Irish prison policy in the early 1960s from the previous decades continued to exist. The commitment, however loose, to 'rehabilitation' remained, but the pace of change was far slower than before. What appeared to be significant contradictions – such as the proposed introduction of military custody – also appeared.

In many ways, this scene was reflective of the Irish political and social landscape during this period. The key 'ideas' of the early 1960s went unchallenged, but their implementation was often less hurried and dramatic. Consolidation, rather than change, characterised these areas.

A 'shift to the left'? Maintaining social change

As had been the case earlier, political change, interest in social affairs, a growing confidence that the state could and should provide social services for its residents were all features of the latter part of the decade. The shift 'to the left' (Puirséil 2007: 230) in Irish politics continued when Fine Gael's Declan Costello TD published a policy document, *The Just Society*, based largely on Catholic social teaching and which lauded social provision and social protection as worthy political aims. This remarkable document was promoted by that party's own 'young cubs' and became the basis of the party's electoral document in 1965. Formally, at any rate, had they been implemented, the proposals would have put the party to the left of Fianna Fáil.

Puirséil (2005) demonstrates that the main parties attempted to leapfrog each other to give the impression of being furthest to the left. The Labour Party published *The New Republic* in 1968, which set out that party's vision for Ireland's future, and declared, famously, that 'the seventies will be socialist', reflecting a much greater confidence in left ideals than had thereto been apparent. The party's membership increased significantly, particularly in Dublin, and its ranks were swelled by the addition of young, urban intellectuals much less afraid of the label 'socialist' (Whyte 2003b). Sinn Féin also became involved in social agitation, particularly regarding the provision of housing.

The 1965 general election saw the opposition parties concentrate their attacks on the government's social policy, with parties engaged in emphasising their commitment to social spending and the reform of social welfare programmes, and the budget of that year was pronounced a 'social services budget' (O'Connell and Rottman 1992). An occupational injuries scheme was introduced in 1967 to make it less burdensome on workers to claim compensation for work–related accidents. In the same year a free travel scheme was introduced for pensioners. In 1968 the maximum duration of unemployment benefit was extended from 156 to 312 days. A Department of Labour was established in 1966 and a scheme of redundancy payments introduced in 1967 and 1969 (Kennedy 1975). Children's allowances were increased in the Budget of 1969 and the election of that year was full of promises of greater spending on social welfare payments (Kennedy *et al.* 1988).

Spending on education rose significantly in the latter part of the decade, which saw the iconic introduction of free second-level schooling for all by Donogh

O'Malley, Minister for Education, in 1966 (Sheehan 1979). The government put significant investment into University College Dublin's new campus at Belfield, south County Dublin, and established the non-university, technologically focused regional technical college system in the early 1970s, having planned for it since 1963 (Curry 2003: 97). The Higher Education Authority, founded to administer the by then expanded third-level sector, was set up in 1968 (Osborne 1996).

More broadly, the liberalisation of Irish cultural life was given a significant boost by Brian Lenihan's decision to relax the censorship laws in 1965 (Whyte 1980: 343). Tax exemptions for artists were granted in 1969 (Lee 1989: 466). The interest in social affairs and the improvement of public administration was maintained. The media generally began to diversify and modernise during this period. Irish radio, for example, began to broadcast throughout the day only from 1966.

Within civil service structures, an increasing number of publications reflected this mounting concern with analysis of matters of public administration and a greater professionalisation of the area. *The Economic and Social Review*, for example, was founded in 1969 and the Economic Research Institute, which later became the Economic and Social Research Institute, was established in 1966.

State-sponsored investigations into long-neglected areas of Irish life continued to be popular, such as the Commission of Inquiry into Mental Illness (1966), the Inter-Departmental Committee on Alcoholism (1968), the Care of the Aged (1968) and the First Commission on the Status of Women (1970). The Kennedy Report of 1970 is a patent example of such a trend. It appraised the reformatory and industrial school system and concluded that it was in need of significant reform.

The mid and late 1960s, therefore, display a significant level of continuity with the earlier part of the decade. The altered approach across economic and social policy was maintained and the commitment to 'modernisation' noted in the previous chapter endured. Within Irish politics, modernisation remained a patent goal and the improvement of social provision a clear aim.

The political scene: little change

Although there was significant action in the area of social welfare – and definite expansionary tendencies therein – this did not signal a fundamental transformation of the Irish political landscape. The three main parties, for example, consolidated their positions at the expense of smaller alternative parties, and pragmatic reaction to what was perceived as popular concern was apparently the main guide to action. Fine Gael developed something of a left wing, but its leader and many of its activists were neither convinced nor converted (Patterson 2006: 264). As Lee argues, 'both Fianna Fáil and Fine Gael would remain essentially coalitions of interest groups spanning the narrow Irish ideological spectrum' (Lee 1979: 176). This flexibility in approach, or populist tendencies, denuded Irish politics of 'ideologies' of any description and no fundamental cleavage on economic or social philosophies between the parties became apparent. Murphy makes a similar point when he argues:

> Fianna Fáil had little difficulty in adapting itself, chameleon-like to the changing scene in the 1960s. It made sufficient concessions, as in the sphere of education, to take the sharp edge off the hunger for greater justice and equality in Irish society, but went no further than that … it stayed a page ahead of the class.
>
> *(Murphy 1979: 9)*

The Labour Party looked to be on course for significant gains in the 1969 general election, being buoyed by a climate apparently more favourable to it. However, its performance was a source of major disappointment to the party, and it did not make a breakthrough. A combination of continuing conservatism within the electorate and the stoking of a mini 'red scare' are reasons proffered for this failure (Puirséil 2007: 264–8). The party actually lost four seats.

A slowing of pace in government

The early 1960s had been a time of major political drive. By contrast, the later part of the decade brought less in the way of forceful, vigorous leadership. Ministers Lenihan and Ó Móráin were noticeably less energetic on prison policy matters than their predecessor, Charles Haughey.

While this levelling off of output may have been at least partially a product of individual personalities within a single Department, the ebbing away of the dynamism of the early 1960s in Justice also reflected developments in Irish political culture more broadly towards the end of the 1960s. McCarthy argues that after the retirement of Lemass, 'the vigour and drive seemed to go out of government' (McCarthy 1973: 22). Lee argues that Jack Lynch, the subsequent Taoiseach, was less forceful in his approach, allowing policy to 'emerge' instead of proactively encouraging its propagation (Lee 1989: 409). Murphy goes further, suggesting: 'Lynch had no clear-cut political philosophy and lacked Lemass's vigorous and innovative temperament. It does not seem unfair to say that he personified the party's development as it moved into the late 1960s, standing for nothing in particular except a kind of affable consensus' (Murphy 1979: 6). While this assessment may be somewhat harsh, it is the case that far less of the impatience and pressure for action that had characterised the early 1960s remained later in that decade (Patterson 2006: 169; Puirséil 2005: 26).

The Department of Justice also appeared to take a more reticent and conservative approach and to become less confident in what it could achieve in the prisons. This was a change in view shared across Irish politics at the time. The atmosphere and developments of the 1960s had operated to raise expectations about the government's capacities to increase living standards and improve social provision among the public.

This was most apparent in Ireland's endeavours in economic planning. While the actions attendant on *Economic Development* in 1958 were hailed as a success, the later programmes were far less triumphant. The Second Programme for Economic Expansion was abandoned early, its targets having been unfulfilled, and the Third envisaged a far higher rate of economic growth than that which occurred and similarly overestimated the levels of employment creation. Planning, it became apparent, also operated to raise expectations and leave planners vulnerable when targets were missed and thus fell from favour (Ó Gráda 1997: 76).

Prison policy: hopes of the past, fears for the future

The impulse towards modernisation established in the early 1960s stood alongside slow implementation of reform and an increasing cautiousness towards the close of the decade. In addition to this, the signals from the Criminal Justice Act 1967 were that, should the need arise, the Irish state was prepared to contemplate the abrogation of many civil liberties and the use of the prison system to contain disorder. As such, the period also prefigured the sometimes febrile developments that would take place in the following two years, and beyond.

Prison policy at the end of the 1960s stood almost Janus-like between the transformations of the past and the difficulties of the future. The way in which these strands interacted and progressed is related in the following chapter.

6

THE 1970s
Subversion, suspicion and tension

Introduction

During the 1970s a period of crisis management in prison policy developed. At the same time there were continued movements towards a more rehabilitationist approach to imprisonment. There were obvious differences in policy content and style during the period, with two sets of assumptions, objectives and concerns evident and prison policy becoming intertwined with security policy once more. This chapter assesses the developments in both areas, as well as other factors that impacted upon the direction of Irish prison policy during the 1970s.

Rehabilitation in the 1970s: an official aim

Micheál Ó Moráin left the Cabinet at the request of Taoiseach Jack Lynch in bizarre circumstances. He tendered his resignation from his hospital bed in the midst of the arms crisis, whereby Lynch had become aware of an alleged plot by senior government ministers to import arms to assist Northern Republicans. Lynch sacked two ministers implicated, Charles Haughey and Neil Blayney. Another minister resigned in solidarity. Those alleged to have been involved were prosecuted and all were acquitted. It seems that the Minister for Justice was asked to resign because of lapses in duty and inattention to matters within his brief (Ferriter 2004: 688; O'Brien 2000). Brian Lenihan took the reins at Justice temporarily before a new entrant to government and the Dáil, even younger than Haughey when he had first taken ministerial office, rose to the helm. This was Desmond or 'Dessie' O'Malley who was Minister for Justice from April 1970 until 1973, when the Fianna Fáil government fell. At 31, he was the youngest Minister for Justice since Kevin O'Higgins.

O'Malley's tenure on the 'ordinary' prison front appears to have conformed more to the Department of Justice's ethos than that of his predecessor Ó Moráin. Work had been continuing within the Department in the area of penal reform, which while slow was moving in a direction that was reflexively 'modern' and exhibiting some penal-welfarist characteristics. The culmination of the Department's approach to these matters was the Prisons Bill 1970, becoming the Prisons Act of the same year. While all the groundwork had been completed before he assumed office, it was O'Malley who piloted it through the Dáil. Though this was his first legislative act involving the prison system, as will be seen, it was O'Malley's work on the issue of the imprisonment of Republicans for which he was most remembered, and for which he was compared with Gerry Boland.

The Prisons Act 1970

The Prisons Act 1970 was the first legislative intervention for decades that dealt specifically with the prison system. For the first time the objectives of imprisonment were laid down by the Oireachtas. The Act was notable for the statement that rehabilitation was an aim of the penal system, and for the statutory recognition of the already existent Shanganagh Castle for young prisoners, which had been opened in 1968. Shanganagh was the product of a growing interest among the Department of Justice in the system for dealing with juveniles and the increasing pressure on the only institution for those sentenced to imprisonment by the courts, St Patrick's Institution. It was an open centre, in keeping with the Department's thinking on penal policy at that time.

The introduction of Shanganagh Castle was in fact the immediate impetus behind the introduction of the Prisons Bill, with the other elements being included as appendages to this purpose (OAG 2000/22/7093), a point recognised by O'Malley in introducing the second stage of the bill in the Dáil. He stated: 'the main object of the Bill is to give formal legal sanction to the "open" centre at Shanganagh' (Dáil Debates, vol 247, col 94, 26 May 1970).

The very pressing and practical problems of severe overcrowding at St Patrick's Institution for juveniles meant Shanganagh had become an indispensable potential 'overflow' for the juvenile detention system. In the drafts of the bill and memoranda to government, these two factors were those emphasised, rather than any broader desire to assist in rehabilitation *per se* (OAG 2002/22/7093).

Rehabilitation as an aim of the prison system

The nature of Shanganagh Castle, with the emphasis on trust, training, grading and informality, accounts for the new nomenclature that the bill introduced. Section 2 of the bill enabled the Minister to establish places of a similar nature that were to have the object of promoting the rehabilitation of offenders. The Act's purpose was declared in the preamble and explanatory memoranda to be: 'to enable the Minister for Justice, for the purpose of promoting the rehabilitation of offenders, to provide places other than prisons for the detention of persons who have been sentenced to penal servitude or imprisonment or to detention in Saint Patrick's Institution'.

Rehabilitation had become a declared and official aim of the Irish prison system. This was a momentous change in Irish prison policy. Not only is it significant in terms of the signal that was being sent out by Irish penal administrators, it is the first time that an official policy statement of any sort was made regarding the aims of prison life.

The entry of rehabilitation into official discourse and its status as an accepted aim of the prison system had further effects. The terminology of 'prison' was altered by the introduction of the softer 'place of detention'.

While the Prisons Act 1970 was a most consequential break from the past, at the same time significant cautiousness remained among policy-makers. Though the bill allowed the Minister to establish other places along the lines of Shanganagh, there were no plans to introduce such institutions 'in the immediate future' (Dáil Debates, vol 247, col 97, 26 May 1970). Furthermore, there is no evidence that the penal administrators or legislators had unpicked the notion of rehabilitation to any large degree, being committed to it as a general principle and, it seems, not thinking too much more about it.

Consensus on the purposes of imprisonment

In the Dáil, O'Malley stated a number of principles about which he felt there was 'general agreement'. First, he stated that there was 'no easy or generalised solution to the problem of rehabilitating offenders'. Second, the causes of crime were environmental conditions such as educational disadvantage, emotional disturbance and 'social inadequacy' and the environment of an institution was 'basically unsuitable for encouraging individuals to become adequate and responsible members of normal society', citing the artificiality of the environment and the high degree of uniformity of the penal regime which militated against the development of responsibility and character (Dáil Debates, vol 247, cols 100–1, 26 May 1970).

Consensus, caution and change in prison policy

During the 1970s in Ireland there was an evident 'non-partisan' approach to prison policy and a consensus that prison should not be harsh or punitive in intention or effect. This was reflected in both the houses of the Oireachtas, among the judiciary and the available public and academic discourse on such topics.

A contemporary report from the *Irish Independent* argued, for example, that the debate on the 1970 bill was 'conducted in an atmosphere of sweetness and light' (28 May 1970) and the Prisons Act 1970 was passed with no dissent about its declarations regarding rehabilitation or its desirability, nor any reluctance about plans to improve prison conditions and to assist offenders.

That said, a strong element of circumspection about the ability of attempts by the Department of Justice to eradicate crime and prevent reoffending is also evident in O'Malley's comments. The grand statements made by Haughey in the early 1960s were now being heavily qualified. As O'Malley stated: 'if the results from time to time appear disappointing and meagre, this is not necessarily due to any fault in our particular methods. It is the lot of prison administrations everywhere and we can only do our best' (Dáil Debates, vol 247, col 110, 26 May 1970). A later Minister, Fine Gael's Patrick Cooney, stated similarly, 'no person, no institution and no system can rehabilitate anybody' (Dáil Debates, vol 270, col 510, 12 February 1974).

While there was caution in statements, the Department of Justice in fact moved more quickly during the early 1970s than in the previous six years, with a number of developments announced, indicating that the previous Minister may well have been an obstacle to action. Many of these new developments can be considered somewhat penal-welfarist in tone and content.

The usual administrative techniques were employed at a local level within the prisons. Renovations continued and the prison diet was varied (Dáil Debates, vol 247, col 94, 26 May 1970). To improve employment prospects for prisoners, training classes in painting and decorating, glazing, car repairs, rug-making and slipper-making were introduced to the training unit and discussions were held with AnCo (the industrial training authority) to provide industrial employment training, such as in semi-skilled metalwork. In 1972 motor mechanics and modern printing techniques were introduced to Mountjoy. A most important development was the plan laid down in 1972 to establish a new corrective training unit, within the Mountjoy prison complex, but physically separate from the other buildings, to replace the existing training unit. This was completed in 1976. The appointment of a psychologist to assess the job aptitudes of prisoners was announced and, finally, welfare officers were appointed to Shanganagh, Portlaoise and Limerick (Dáil Debates, vol 247, cols 102–5, 26 May 1970). Twenty further welfare officers were sought by the Department of Justice in December 1972 (JUS 2002/2/150). The positions of coordinator of education and a coordinator of employment were created in 1974 (Dáil Debates, vol 270, col 530, 12 February 1974).

In a Dáil debate in 1972 the Minister expressed his intention to get rid of the traditional industries in the prisons, arguing: 'I make no apology for having done that because I regard the rehabilitation of those men as my primary task', to the expressed agreement of the deputies in the Dáil (Dáil Debates, vol 260, col 179, 24 May 1972).

One explicit endorsement of rehabilitationism within the prisons comes from a revealing advertisement seeking the recruitment to the prison service in 1970. The advertisement was headed 'If you like to help others' and went on to say that 'with the increasing emphasis on the rehabilitation of prisoners, work in which the Prison Officer plays an important part ... can be very rewarding' (*Irish Times*, 26 June 1970).

'Penal-welfarist' developments?

The developments related above reflect a continuity of approach from the previous decade. The language of penal-welfarism remained present, and plans were laid down for future reforms, with training and treatment on the Department's agenda, and the official sanction of rehabilitation apparent. Given this assessment, Kilcommins *et al.* are correct in their evaluation of Irish prison policy during this part of the 1970s. They argue: 'as belief in rehabilitation waned elsewhere, it began to be formally embraced in a modest way by the Irish Department of Justice' (Kilcommins *et al.* 2004: 53).

One of the great unknowns of Irish prison policy is where this might have led or how it would have developed. On the one hand, the ostensible commitment to the aim of rehabilitation was sincere and shared throughout the various sectors with influence over prison and criminal justice policy. On the other, however, the depth of this commitment and its implementation in reality is less certain.

Increase in crime rates and prison populations

The climate in which rehabilitation was cautiously propagated suffered a number of shocks just as the first shoots were beginning to be visible at an official level. This altered landscape encompassed rapidly increasing prisoner numbers, problems with overcrowding within the system, tensions, drug use and disturbances within the system. Finally, the 'Troubles' in the North had a patent effect on the prisons and policy-makers.

In 1970, over 30,000 indictable crimes were recorded by the Gardaí, double the number recorded in 1960 (Kilcommins *et al.* 2004: 67). The prison population also began to increase steadily, undergoing rapid expansion in the early part of the 1970s. This appeared to have taken the Department of Justice by some surprise, with constant underestimations being prepared for the average daily prisoner population.

In 1972, the average daily prison population breached 1,000 for the first time since the Civil War years. A similar situation had already occurred in England and Wales (Newburn 2003: 20), and, like there, the pressure of numbers put a major strain on the system, though as yet this did not cause serious questions to be asked about the purposes or effectiveness of the techniques used or planned in Ireland.

It is surprising that increased prisoner numbers were apparently not prepared or planned for as the crime rate in Ireland began to increase after 1964, a year described as a 'watershed' by Rottman (1980: 144).

It can only be speculated that the Department of Justice was not overly concerned by these matters, or simply neglected to make projections or plan, receiving no direction from its Minister during the late 1960s. It is also noteworthy that the increasing crime rate itself was not subject to a huge outcry, nor did it cause a re-evaluation of the proper purposes of imprisonment or the use of the prison. Similarly, recidivism rates were essentially never measured or discussed.

That said, these increases in prisoner numbers had an obviously detrimental effect on the prison system (O'Donnell 2004a: 253) and the material conditions therein. After years of operation at well below capacity, all the prisons in the state began to experience overcrowding for the first time in decades. This fact alone should put paid to any notion that Irish prison policy was moving inexorably towards more progressive, humane or liberal conditions once the language of rehabilitation had been embraced.

In Limerick it was reported in 1970 that it was becoming difficult to maintain the population at under 100, the maximum operational capacity (*Annual Report on Prisons*, 1971). In 1971 the visiting committee with responsibility for Mountjoy expressed concern at the increase in the prison population (*Annual Report on Prisons*, 1971). In 1972 Brady reported that it had become 'not uncommon' for prisoners to be released before the expiration of their sentence in order to make a cell available for new prisoners or more serious offenders (*Irish Times*, 27 January 1972).

New institutions: a reactive approach

After a period of some inertia, by 1972 the Department of Justice appeared to be determined to tackle this problem. Significantly, the response to the increasing prisoner numbers was institutional – to construct or otherwise commission more prison spaces. Remarkably, after decades where retrenchment in the penal estate had been characteristic of prison policy, a number of new institutions were requisitioned over a very short period of time.

As an interim measure, the Department began to seek an existing institution in the state's possession that could be readily and speedily converted into a prison. The declared aim of this move was to improve conditions, with no indication that its purpose was to create more space for punitive practices (Dáil Debates, vol 259, col 2372, 23 March 1972). In fact, it appears that these measures were entirely driven by the developing crisis of numbers within the system, with no

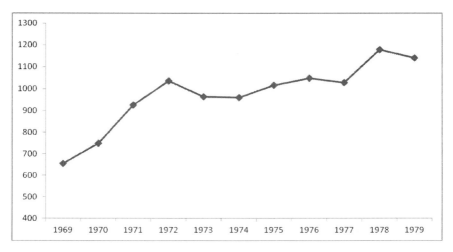

FIGURE 6.1 Average daily prison population 1969–79

further thought given to other purposes or, indeed, the long-term implications of the actions taken. The sluggishness in planning and action of the late 1960s had left the Department of Justice ill placed to deal with the increasing numbers entering the Irish prison system and forced it to act with greater speed than had been the case for many years.

The problems posed by increased numbers at Portlaoise were to be remedied by offering tenders for the reconstruction of a wing of the old county prison, which had long been in disuse. Two of the four wings of the men's prison at Mountjoy were also planned to be vacated after the opening of the training unit, which was due to open in 1973 (but did not in fact happen until 1976) and which would be able to hold 100 prisoners. The women's prison, which had been (and was later also to be) placed on the longest of long fingers, had reached a stage where a site was purchased at Kilbarrack, County Dublin from the Dublin Corporation (*Irish Times*, 29 June 1972).

A further 'solution' was seen to be the requisitioning of the old military detention barracks at Cork for civil purposes in January 1972 (*Irish Times*, 9 February 1972). This was an ironic twist of history, where military detention sites now had to be employed for an excess of ordinary prisoners.

For reasons explored in following sections, the situation became more difficult and pressing after May 1972. From then, several institutions were acquired or considered by the Department of Justice. No new institutions were built during the period, however, with the Department of Justice content to convert existing structures used for other purposes. Loughan House, County Cavan, capable of holding up to 50 individuals, was purchased to become a semi-open institution for males between the ages of 16 and 23. Its potential use was officially not confined to such individuals and the government was cognisant of the possibility that it would be required for both various categories, and increased numbers of prisoners (Dáil Debates, vol 264, col 968, 5 December 1972). Indeed, this happened in 1978 when it became a secure centre for boys aged 12–16 and later again for adult male prisoners. Shelton Abbey, a building that the Department of Lands no longer required, was acquired by the Department of Justice, with hopes that it would hold similar numbers (Dáil Debates, vol 262, col 1691, 13 July 1972). In 1973 it became an open prison for adults over the age of 21. Though these institutions were framed in the language of rehabilitationism, in the immediate context of 1972 it was the extra accommodation provided that was the main attraction for penal administrators. Indeed, as the decade progressed it became clear that there were no plans for further open centres (Dáil Debates, vol 302, col 1183, 13 December 1977).

The Department was also canvassing the possibility of acquiring land at Dunsink, County Waterford, to build a new prison, though this did not in the end come to pass (JUS 2002/2/66). While the expansion of the penal state relieved the worst effects of the pressure on the prisons, Mountjoy, Cork and Portlaoise all operated close to capacity in the 1970s (Dáil Debates, vol 312, col 1150, 8 March 1979), though doubling up was not yet a feature of prison life.

The 'Troubles'

The outbreak of serious violence in Northern Ireland and its overspill into the Republic was another major influence on the prison system during the early 1970s. From around June 1969, the potential for problems arising out of the Northern Troubles began seriously to preoccupy the Department of Justice, with officials receiving intelligence on the operations of the IRA (Berry 1980). Further concern was expressed when this organisation later split into Provisional and Official factions.

The murder of a Garda, Brian Fallon, during an armed bank robbery by the splinter Republican group Saor Éire, was one incident that caused outrage, though this was directed towards 'subversive' elements rather than crime matters generally. Indeed the murder of Garda Fallon took place a short time before the reading of the Prisons Bill 1970 before the Dáil. No political capital was made out of the tragic event by either side in the debates about prison policy generally, nor did it result in any statement challenging the new consensus on rehabilitation or the legitimacy of attempts to improve the lot of the prisoner. However, the response to the murder of Garda Fallon signalled that a different type of approach towards prisoners with Republican aims was contemplated.

A 'new' type of prisoner

Those convicted for offences relating to IRA actions, and significantly for the first time in the history of the state, increasing numbers of prisoners on remand awaiting trial for such activities, entered the system from late 1969. The increasing numbers and different character of prisoners serving sentences for these types of offences began to cause problems within the prison system.

The imposition of security and order was rendered particularly difficult given the nature and self-conception of the prisoners involved, who by 1972 had reached a 'critical mass' in Mountjoy and Portlaoise prison in particular (Mulcahy 2002: 290). An interview with a prison officer quoted by Mulcahy, describes such prisoners as increasingly 'disciplined, dangerous and you knew they might be thinking about escape, and of course they had support on the outside' (Mulcahy 2002: 290). As Osborough sums it up, they were to 'present an array of daunting problems: difficult to house, awkward to handle, not simple to occupy, not cheap to guard' (Osborough 1985: 187).

Political status, disruption and protest

The Republican prisoners who were remanded and imprisoned for offences arising out of the Troubles, like hundreds of those who had gone before, sought political treatment within the prison system through a combination of internal disruption and outside support in the pursuit of 'political' or prisoner-of-war status and its attendant privileges. One prisoner who was incarcerated in Portlaoise prison in the 1970s stated his feelings thus: 'I had great difficulty yielding in any way to the prison authorities. Gaolers were to be despised and that was the norm. No discourse with any member of the prison administration right from the governor down to the ordinary screw, none!' (Wynne 2001: 39).

The disturbances that occurred inside and outside prisons throughout 1971 and the early part of 1972 were relatively minor and could be contained by the authorities. One event in this vein, however, had a colossal impact on prison policy during this period and precipitated the second Prisons Act in two years, though one with very different aims from the Act of 1970.

Riot in Mountjoy

A riot took place in Mountjoy prison on the night of 18–19 May 1972. This was organised by Republican prisoners and lasted almost six hours, during which several prison officers were held hostage and an enormous amount of damage was caused. Remarkably, the prisoners gave a running commentary on their demands and the 'progress' of the riot to assembled news reporters outside the walls (*Irish Times*, 19 May 1972). The particular demands of the prisoners were reported as being the release of a prisoner on remand to get married, the improvement of prison food and the expedition of arrangements for the trials of remand prisoners.

All the panes of glass in the prison were broken, as were toilet bowls and wash hand basins. Cell doors were destroyed and furniture and bedding wrecked. The new dental surgery in the prison was destroyed and all the records of the prisoners in the corrective training unit were annihilated. The roof was affected and running water caused much damage. At its conclusion, the prison accommodation in Mountjoy had been reduced to 76 per cent of its previous capacity. The riot was ended after an ultimatum was issued to prisoners that if they did not desist, troops would be introduced. Negotiations between spokesmen for the prisoners and senior Gardaí followed, with the prisoners then returning to their cells.

Within two days of the riot almost 200 prisoners, a mixture of 'ordinary' and 'political' prisoners, were transferred to the Curragh military prison and other places of detention including Portlaoise prison and the former military barracks at Cork. At a press conference, O'Malley rejected any claim to the status of political prisoner made by the prisoners and their supporters stating that he thought that 'it had never been accepted in the history of the State, that there was any such thing as a political prisoner. The people who described themselves as such were either charged with or convicted or ordinary criminal offences' (*Irish Times*, 20 May 1973).

The Curragh revived

The transfer to other civil prisons was an expected response to the sudden loss of substantial numbers of cells in an already overcrowded prison. However, most controversial was the use by the Department of Justice of the Curragh military prison, an institution under the control of the Minister of Defence, to house around 40 prisoners. This was patently legally and politically sensitive given the resonance that the Curragh had for Republicans during the Civil War, the Emergency and the Border Campaign.

The use of the Curragh as a form of military detention was avowedly a temporary measure. It was originally hoped that the military prison could have been transferred to civilian use. However, the Minister for Justice declared later that there were not adequate staffing levels in the civilian service to take over the running of the prison and that there were 'serious objections' to the maintenance of a civil prison within a military complex (Dáil Debates, vol 261, col 78, 23 May 1972). In addition, it was argued that the destruction wrought in Mountjoy would take some months to rectify and pressure would continue on the existing establishments. Another reason given for the more permanent use of military custody was the particular type of prisoner involved – those who were prepared to go to serious lengths to cause disruption. These assessments, according to the Department, necessitated the employment of military custody in the longer term.

The Prisons Act 1972

The response of the government to these pressing problems of accommodation and security was to introduce a form of emergency legislation to regularise the situation created by the use of the Curragh and to thereby allow for the legal transfer of civilian prisoners to military custody. This was the Prisons Bill 1972 which became the Prisons Act of the same year.

Under the Prisons Bill, if the Oireachtas declared that there were exceptional circumstances that warranted the introduction of military custody, the provisions of the Bill would take effect. This would be so if the Oireachtas felt that the ordinary prison system was inadequate to deal with prisoners in terms of accommodation and staff.

While these very pragmatic reasons required the speedy implementation of remedial and drastic measures, it was suggested at the time that O'Malley and his Department were using the ready excuse of the riot to introduce measures that he had long contemplated. In his diaries, Peter Berry states that prior to the riot he was instructed to prepare the necessary documents to reactivate Part II of the Offences Against the State (Amendment) Act 1940 to allow for internment of certain members of Saor Éire. He also makes the startling revelation that the government wished to press forward with such a course for electoral gain in a by-election in Donegal, against security and departmental advice (Berry 1980). Analysis of the available relevant materials has not substantiated this claim. In fact, the parliamentary draftsman received the shortest of notice to draw up the proposed legislation, receiving verbal instructions from the Minister for Justice on 22 May, with the bill becoming law on 24 May (OAG, 2003/5/174).

Officially, the necessity for the bill was put in the most stark terms. The Taoiseach introduced the first stage of the bill on the basis that 'the prison system is now in serious jeopardy' and the speedy implementation of the proposed legislation was required to preserve public order and democracy (Dáil Debates, vol 261, col 39, 23 May 1972).

Interestingly, while this change of heart was clearly prompted by the immediate events of the riot, there is a strong case to be made that the Prisons Act 1972 was part of a general hardening of attitude towards Republican activity exhibited by Jack Lynch, and shared by Des O'Malley, from around this time (Arnold 2001: 166). The arms crisis of 1970 and events unfolding north of the border had 'caused divisions in the government' (Whyte 2003c: 319) between those who wanted the government of the Republic to intervene in the situation and those who advocated a more restrained approach. O'Donnell argues that Fianna Fáil was left in 'chaos' (O'Donnell 2007: 68), with Lynch attempting to preside over a Cabinet composed of 'hawks and doves' on the position of the Republic on the North (Ferriter 2004: 688). O'Brien argues that the arms crisis prompted the greater prominence of Ministers with a publicly 'hawkish line' and discredited those with associations with Republican violence, or as he puts it: 'the Republican card was now operating at a discount' (O'Brien 2000: xii). Overall, Lee considers Lynch's primary concern during the 1970s to be the maintenance of peace in the Republic and that the public was unlikely to demur in a climate of violence (Lee 1989: 480).

Lynch had previously been accused of ambivalence in his attitude to the Northern question (O'Donnell 2007), and his leadership had, more generally, been plagued by accusations that he wavered over tough decisions and hesitated to move against Ministers openly defying his authority. As Keogh argues, Lynch had taken 'a battering' within his own party during the early 1970s (Keogh 2005: 316). It may be the case that the Prisons Bill 1972 represented an opportunity for Lynch to again put these claims to rest, to demonstrate his victory on Northern policy within his party, or at least forced him and his Minister for Justice to take swift and decisive action.

The Prisons Bill had the further justification put forward by the Minister for Justice that 'security of Republican prisoners and rehabilitation of ordinary prisoners are incompatible' (*Irish Times*, 26 May 1972). The Minister appeared entirely depressed and disillusioned by the effects of the riot on rehabilitative practices, stating that 'all our efforts at rehabilitation and retraining have been set at naught' (Dáil Debates, vol 261, col 179, 23 May 1972). This was a common motif in the official discourse about the events of the riot and an oft-cited justification for the introduction of military custody.

Opposition to the Prisons Bill was split in a number of factions, with Fine Gael supporting the bill and Labour internally divided on it (*Irish Times*, 25 May 1972). Fine Gael agreed to support it 'for the sake of the stability of the state' (Dáil Debates, vol 261, col 85, 23 May 1972) on the basis that it be subject to a 'sunset clause', with its operation lasting only for as long as it took to restore

Mountjoy. This party's objections, so vociferously stated in the debates on the Criminal Justice Bill 1967, evaporated in light of the iconic events of the prison riot.

Security and rehabilitation: incompatible aims or evidence of the emperor's lack of clothes?

While the riot in Mountjoy gave the government the opportunity to introduce military custody, it also provided the chance to bring about significant change within the prison system. In effect, it offered an opportunity to fundamentally restructure Mountjoy prison, or indeed create an entirely new set of plans for the institutional treatment of offenders. In addition, the riot did not prompt a large-scale inquiry into its causes or the conditions in Irish prisons, unlike that conducted by Lord Woolf into the Strangeways riot in the United Kingdom (Carrabine 2004), nor an official investigation into security procedures in the state's prisons such as that carried out under Lord Mountbatten in response to a series of high-profile escapes (Ryan 1983).

In the event, and without any commitments to review the operation of Mountjoy generally, the Prisons Bill was passed by 114 votes to 8. It was signed by the President (Eamon de Valera) on 26 May 1972. On this date another development occurred that would later have significant impacts on Irish criminal justice and prison policy. The Special Criminal Court, which remains in operation today, was reactivated on the basis that the ordinary courts were considered incapable of securing the preservation of peace and public order.

Prison policy and Republican prisoners

Conditions in the Curragh and other prisons

In Portlaoise, regular strip-searching, the denial of visits and the lack of free association were features of daily life. Visits took place through a metal grille. Close confinement was imposed as a punishment for breaches of prison discipline (Dáil Debates, vol 298, col 1320, 21 April 1977). Within Mountjoy, the Base area of the prison was used to hold disruptive prisoners, who were strip-searched once a week (Dáil Debates, vol 309, col 1557, 22 November 1978). The Curragh held around 40 prisoners, initially comprising a mix of 'political' and 'ordinary' prisoners, mainly those considered to be disruptive. These prisoners were held in a two-storey block in which segregation of prisoners in wings, blocks or exercise areas was not possible due to the size and construction of the building (TAO 2004/21/140).

The conditions in which these prisoners were held were the subject of much criticism and were certainly strained, tense and difficult. The Curragh was placed under the oversight of a visiting committee from September 1972 and this group expressed its opinion yearly that 'the Military Detention Barracks is not at all suitable for prisoners serving long sentences' (Curragh Visiting Committee, 1973). The Curragh remained in use, however, until 1983, and was also re-employed later.

In 1972 the Prisons Act (Military Custody) Regulations were promulgated. However, the case of *Cahill v Governor of the Military Detention Barracks, Curragh Camp* [1980] ILRM 191 established a number of breaches of the Regulations 1972. The court also assessed allegations of ill-treatment at the hands of prison staff, but these were not made out. The case furthermore brought to light the protests ongoing within the barracks, whereby staff would remove all the contents of cells in the name of security precautions and a recurring 'dirty protest' during which prisoners would be hosed down if they did not leave their cells for cleaning.

Prisoner protest

As Tomlinson states, the early 1970s were 'very troubled years in the South's prisons, with regular riots and pitched battles with prison staff, hunger strikes, escape attempts and the build up of a well organised group of political prisoners' (Tomlinson 1995: 209). After the passing of the Prisons Act 1972 tensions remained high within the state's places of detention.

In October 1972 seven prisoners managed to tunnel out of the Curragh in a remarkable and dramatic break-out. The prisoners, some of whom had been on hunger strike, had constructed a tunnel beneath a cell and scaled the walls with a rope, overpowering an unarmed military policeman in the process (*Irish Press*, 30 October 1972). A sit-down protest was undertaken by the prisoners in Portlaoise at the quality of the food, a lack of recreational facilities and the bad condition of some of the cells. It was feared that this would spark off a riot along the lines of that in Mountjoy, which had prompted the introduction of the Prisons Act 1972. Other protests occurred periodically in that prison during the decade (see, for example, Dáil Debates, vol 277, col 524, 16 January 1975).

Most striking and iconic was the escape of three IRA prisoners from Mountjoy using a hijacked helicopter, which sparked a major manhunt and much political tumult and embarrassment as well as lively public interest (Dáil Debates, vol 268, col 1114, 1 November 1973). A further escape by the Littlejohns, who had worked as British agents, from Mountjoy in March 1974 added to this sense of concern and political embarrassment about prison security. Other escape attempts occurred throughout the decade, with a large break-out attempted from Portlaoise in 1975 (Dáil Debates, vol 297, col 747, 19 March 1975).

These matters gave rise to periodic calls for the government or the Minister for Justice to resign, which can only have led to an increasingly tough attitude towards prison policy towards Republican prisoners being pursued. In this climate it is unsurprising that the Prisons Act 1972 was extended for a further three years in 1974, this time by a Fine Gael and Labour government. It was extended again in 1977, this time with muted opposition. During that debate, the numbers in the house were so small that a quorum was threatened to be called (Dáil Debates, vol 299, col 1189, 19 May 1977).

Hunger strikes

Hunger strikes returned to feature in prison life during the early 1970s, with fasts being conducted for up to three weeks at a time. The first such strike lasted in the Curragh for 33 days, ending on 28 July 1972, with the prisoners claiming that their demands had been met, and no comment from the government (*Irish Times*, 29 June 1972). Another hunger strike took place in September, with a number of men participating in the Curragh and in Mountjoy. This time, the prisoners argued that the government had reneged on its 'promise' to provide full political status and that the Curragh, in particular, was filthy (*Irish Press*, 9 September 1972). The government refused to give in to the pressure for further concessions and the strike was ended on 23 September 1972 with one prisoner close to death.

In November 1972 Seán MacStiofáin, the Chief of Staff of the Provisional IRA, went on a hunger and thirst strike that necessitated his removal to the Mater Hospital. Large crowds held vigils outside the hospital and even forced entry into the hospital. During this highly irregular occurrence there was shooting inside the hospital (McEvoy 2001: 79–80).

The response of the government to appeals on his behalf was clear, stating: 'hundreds of people have been killed by bombs and guns and hundreds have been maimed by bombs and guns. Many of these people were innocent women and children. Unfortunately, they had no choice between life and death' (Dáil Debates, vol 264, col 48, 28 November 1972).

Prisoner advocacy and protest

One of the striking features in any assessment of Irish prison policy during the years studied is the paucity of organisations, committees or unions established by prisoners themselves. Republican prisoners were always highly organised and capable of putting across their grievances to the prison authorities and the wider public. While these prisoners were historically internally cohesive and well disciplined, no dedicated, autonomous body had ever been founded. 'Ordinary' prisoners had certainly never formed such an organisation either.

The Portlaoise Prisoners' Union

In April 1972 a group of prisoners in Portlaoise prison established a committee that had the avowed purpose to 'work for basic human rights for all prisoners'. Three prisoners initially formulated basic demands and founded the union (*Irish Times*, 5 April 1972). This small beginning later became the Portlaoise Prisoners' Union, which led to the foundation of the Prisoners' Union. This body produced a regular periodical, the *Jail Journal*, for over four years, which contained articles written by serving prisoners and smuggled out, with copies being smuggled in; they also held weekly meetings in Liberty Hall, Dublin and elsewhere. It was highly critical of government policy on a variety of issues, including suicides, mental illness and conditions within prisons.

The union's immediate concerns, however, related to specific grievances about the treatment of prisoners in Portlaoise prison, though it is possible to view the union as part of a more general trend of protest and agitating groups developing in Ireland.

There is no evidence of the Department of Justice taking the concerns of the union seriously, however, except to dispute its claims. Allegations were made that it was government policy to 'crush' the union (O'Brien, *Irish Times*, 22 November 1973) and to cast it as a front for Sinn Féin. The Department refused to meet the group. The stated policy of the government was to refuse to recognise its existence in official discourse. 'There is no prisoners' union,' said Garret Fitzgerald, on behalf of Minister Cooney in response to Noel Lemass, T.D., arguing further that such a group sought only to intimidate other prisoners and disrupt the prison system (Dáil Debates, vol 266, question 3, 14 June 1973).

Other prisoners' rights groups

In 1973, the Prisoners' Rights Organisation was established. In the same year a Prison Study Committee, consisting initially of two law students, two trade unionists, a solicitor and a founder member of the Portlaoise Prisoners' Union, was set up. It held a press conference criticising educational facilities and calling for an independent parole board as well as new visiting committees. The members of what then became the Prison Study Group included Fr John Murphy, a representative of the Association of Irish Priests, and Garrett Sheehan, then a solicitor, among others. A grant from the Department of Psychiatry, University College Dublin was obtained to carry out the study. The report of its conference and its advertisement for a research assistant were kept on file by the Department (JUS 2002/2/211).

In addition to this, a highly organised, active and vocal group of supporters of Republican prisoners was also proving a headache for the authorities. Confrontations between these supporters, in particular the northern based People's Democracy (Arthur 1974), and the army were frequent and often tense. This group also staged a number of 'lightning strikes' whereby they would be bussed from Portlaoise prison to the Curragh and back (*Irish Times*, 3 July 1972).

Saoirse, a group set up by Official Sinn Féin, also worked for the improvement of conditions for 'political prisoners', writing to the International Red Cross, which declared it was giving its 'full attention' to the conditions in the Curragh (*Irish Times*, 27 September 1972). Both wings of Sinn Féin, the Republican Publicity Bureau and others were very active in presenting the grievances of the prisoners in tandem with their general political demands.

Protest groups and their effect on the Department of Justice

There is no indication that the Department of Justice took the demands of the Prisoners' Union or individual prisoners seriously or viewed them as having a constructive contribution to make to the formation of prison policy.

These groups were not considered worthy stakeholders, or 'acceptable' protagonists, to use Ryan's term (Ryan 1978). As such, they did not have an impact on prison policy in terms of having an input in official discussions about policy or creating close links with officials. Quite the contrary reaction ensued, with all interested parties, whether associated with Republicans or not, such as the Prison Study Group, finding the Department very unreceptive to their efforts at research and investigation. In its report *An Examination of the Penal System* the group lamented that fact that 'our main problem was the fact that the Minister for Justice and his Department did not cooperate in any way with our efforts', and that several letters sent to the Department were not acknowledged. The group was not allowed to interview chaplains, governors or prison doctors nor to visit the prisons (Prison Study Group 1973).

The main effects of the efforts at agitation on behalf of prisoners during these years served to prompt suspicion, fear and hostility rather than cooperation, understanding or sympathy among policy-makers. The Prison Study Group described itself as a 'voluntary, non-political study group' with its purpose being to study 'the factual situation, not to agitate for prison reform' (Prison Study Group 1973: 3).

Moreover, the political context did not augur well for a favourable reception to such protests. The North appeared on the brink of Civil War, a bombing campaign by Republicans had begun, Bloody Sunday and the protests thereby prompted were fresh in the memory and a tragedy of violence and destruction that would blight the island for decades to come was well under way.

Added to this cocktail, threats were made against the Minister for Justice and his officials by those connected to Republican organisations. MacStiofáin warned the Minister for Justice that 'there are some hostile warders in Mountjoy who will be in serious trouble if they are not transferred to a section away from the Republican prisoners' (*Irish Times*, 20 March 1972). The Andersonstown (Belfast) Provisional Sinn Féin Comhairle Ceantair (district executive) warned the Dublin government that if it did not release Republican prisoners from the Curragh camp, 'we will take them out' (*Irish Times*, 6 July 1972). The homes of Dublin Fianna Fáil TDs were picketed by members of Provisional Sinn Féin (*Irish Times*, 14 July 1972). Peter Berry's house became the target of picketers and protesters by members of Official Sinn Féin on the eve of the arms trial and he was under considerable personal pressure, being told that there were plans for his kidnap (Berry 1980).

In addition, archival material now demonstrates that the Prisons Act 1972 was extended on two further occasions not for the original reason that time was needed to repair the damage to Mountjoy arising out of the riot, but on the basis that military custody was needed to contain members of the Prisoners'

Union. The official thinking was that these prisoners could be housed along with members of the socialist Republican group Saor Éire who would not object to their accommodation together, unlike the Provisional IRA. The Department of Justice was clearly very concerned about the potential of the union to disrupt the prison system and, indeed, to encourage other prisoners to protest. It is intriguing that it was concern about this group of ordinary prisoners that led to the maintenance of military custody, showing that the Department was not afraid to use such responses to prisoners it considered to be disruptive (JUS 2008/156/2).

The changed policy 'style' was also reflected in the portrayal of the work of prison officers. While just a year previously advertisements had been taken out to recruit prison officers who wished to get involved in 'rehabilitation' work, in 1972 advertisements sought to recruit 100 temporary warders to further secure the prison system (*Sunday Independent*, 19 November 1972). There were no references to rehabilitation, but merely a statement of the physical requirements for the job, the salary and, ominously, the prospects of 'permanent employment'.

Secrecy and suspicion in the Department of Justice

The attitude of officials within the Department of Justice towards dealing with the media and 'interested outsiders' appears to have changed significantly during these years. Officials commenced close surveillance of criticism of the prison system. A file was opened in the Department that collated all cuttings from the newspapers that made reference or were relevant to prison security (JUS 2006/145/51). Another file, marked 'secret', was kept dealing solely with potential threats to the Minister for Justice and every item of negative commentary on his actions that was carried in the media was retained (JUS 2002/2/66).

The effects of such insularity continued for several years and resulted in difficulties being experienced by outside parties gaining information about the prison system, as noted above. The benign practice of allowing university students to visit the Dublin prisons began to receive closer scrutiny, though it did continue. Then Reid Professor of Criminal Law, Criminology and Penology and later President Mary McAleese sought to bring a group of law students at Trinity College Dublin to visit Mountjoy. An unattributed note on file states: 'can you find out if this request is genuine. Background information would help' (JUS 2002/2/23). Visits were, however, permitted.

In 1974 Minister Cooney responded to criticism of the Department, stating that 'there is nothing secret about our prisons', arguing that his officers must work in 'anonimity' (*sic*) because of public pressure (JUS 2002/2/210). The Prison Study Group had a different perspective, arguing that the Department had a 'kind of siege mentality in which all outside bodies, including study groups are regarded with suspicion', a characterisation that seems to be fair.

To counter these suggestions, Minister Cooney arranged for the representatives of four national newspapers and a small number of others to 'tour' the prisons, though the individuals were not allowed to speak to prisoners (Dáil Debates, vol 269, col 388, 22 November 1973). In addition, internal inquiries into prison disturbances, including an investigation conducted by a judge of the High Court, Finlay J, were not made public and calls to hold an independent inquiry into prison conditions were refused. A letter to the Minister for Justice from Amnesty International in 1977 expressing concern at the treatment of prisoners in Portlaoise was described as being 'influenced by propaganda documents' (Dáil Debates, vol 299, vol 443, 10 May 1977). A similar lack of openness was prevalent among the subsequent Fianna Fáil administration, when Gerry Collins stated in the Dáil that no public inquiry into prison conditions would take place (Dáil Debates, vol 302, col 1194, 13 December 1977). A request from the Irish Council for Civil Liberties to hold an inquiry was also rejected in 1978 (Dáil Debates, vol 306, col 14, 2 May 1978). A report commissioned by the Department on the prison service was conducted by the Institute of Public Administration, but it was not published either (Dáil Debates, vol 316, col 1834, 15 November 1979).

Crisis management

Security matters and lack of planning

In the particular circumstances of the early 1970s, the Department of Justice was forced to act reactively to the unfolding, volatile events, and furthermore to do so in a state of uncertainty and some fear. Crisis management became the order of the day. Such a state of affairs was entirely inimical to the formulation of long-term policy of any description.

Peter Berry's diaries from the period relate the manner in which security matters had become pervasive, suffusing the entire workings of the Department, with some matter of concern, many born out of the events of the arms crisis, arising almost daily from mid-1969. As Secretary, Berry's work at this time appears to have been almost entirely devoted to these issues (Berry 1980). It can only be speculated how many other officials were similarly mired in this work.

The Prison Rules 1947 were to be revised, but the government blamed the pressure of circumstances for the delay in doing so (Dáil Debates, vol 280, 30 April 1975). The pressure on resources occasioned by the need for extra security at Portlaoise was also blamed for the eventual postponement of the planned women's prison. More generally, as had happened so often in the past, the vast majority of debate about the prison system centred on the detention of Republican prisoners.

However, while the impact of Republican violence and the difficulties posed thereby within the prison system were two key factors, the overall increases in crime, committal and prisoner population rates were also of enormous significance in creating this climate of crisis. In this respect, the Department of Justice's own lack of planning for increases in prisoner numbers was also responsible for the challenges posed in the early 1970s.

Deflecting energy and resources away from penal planning and practices

The combined effects of these two sources of pressure on departmental officials operated to defer other plans. One clear piece of evidence in this regard concerns particular proposals being explored by the Department of Justice at the end of the 1960s. A Prisons Consolidation Bill was being considered by the Department of Justice in 1969 (OAG 2000/22/7093), having first been suggested in Charles Haughey's Programme of Law Reform in 1962. The work had reached the stage where the civil servants had drawn up a list of policy decisions that would have to be taken before this 'Comprehensive Prisons Bill', as it was being termed, could be drafted. One idea canvassed was whether provision should be made to reduce terms of imprisonment served for defaulting on fines when part payment of the fine had been made.

Such was the state of advancement that Roger Hayes declared in September 1969 that 'practically all the preliminary work on the Bill has now been completed by Mr J. J. McCarthy and Mr Toal, and I expect to be able to submit the full Scheme of the Bill in the next couple of months' (JUS 2004/32/104). This never occurred. No more discussion of these plans has been discovered and it can be speculated that this work was also deprioritised in the more difficult times that followed. Certainly no attempt at consolidation of the relevant legislation has been made to date.

As well as this, the annual reports for the prison system were published more infrequently during the 1970s, apparently because staff could not be 'diverted' to statistical work given the heavy demands placed on them during those years (Dáil Debates, vol 265, col 92, 28 March 1975).

Irish prison policy during the 1970s

Rehabilitation and repeating history

During the 1970s, Ireland had gone from being a three-prison state to having a series of institutions comprising Mountjoy (male and female), the training unit, Portlaoise, which became and remains the main prison housing prisoners posing the highest security risk, Limerick (male and female), Cork, the Curragh military camp, and Arbour Hill, for long-term prisoners. Plans had been made for a female institution at Kilbarrack, Dublin and a male prison at Dunsink, County Waterford, but these did not come to pass. At the very end of the 1970s, a site was purchased at Clondalkin, Dublin, which would eventually become Wheatfield prison (Dáil Debates, vol 317, col 1883, 13 December 1979). Shanganagh Castle, Loughan House and later Shelton Abbey were three entirely new types of institution with undoubted rehabilitationist aims.

The rehabilitative efforts in many of these institutions remained limited and the implementation of new programmes, facilities or resources was scant and patchy. At the same time, while their results may have been less clear-cut, rehabilitation had achieved the declared status of a guiding principle of prison policy for penal administrators. Even in the midst of the turmoil of 1972, the corrective training unit remained the 'highest priority project' for the Department, above extensions to Portlaoise (JUS 2002/2/66). Successive ministers declared their commitment to rehabilitation and their desire to do more in that regard. Gerry Collins, for example, in 1978 declared that in the area of rehabilitation 'much more can and should be done and my ambition is to try to do as much as I can' (Dáil Debates, vol 303, col 1114, 14 February 1978).

There was, moreover, no sense either that prison conditions for non-subversive prisoners should be made deliberately harsh or that retributivist impulses were motivating policy-makers. Ireland remained, in truth, largely immune from events that were beginning to shake the criminological world elsewhere (Kilcommins *et al.* 2004: 72).

Irish prison policy in this period was therefore a somewhat complex matrix. Rehabilitation was officially sanctioned through the Prisons Act 1970, but the Prisons Act 1972 introduced an entirely different set of assumptions, logics and objectives. The objectives of security and the preservation of the state were also to be fulfilled through the prison system.

Rehabilitation and security – a symbiotic relationship?

In many respects, these sets of sensibilities and logics, those of rehabilitation and security, operated in largely separate spheres and were two essentially distinct policy styles. However, it is fair to infer that the outbreak of Republican violence had an impact on the rehabilitationary elements of Irish prison policy, stalling progress and deflecting attention.

It would be quite neat and seductive, however, to conclude that the advent of the Troubles destroyed the potential for a system that was heading inexorably towards 'progress'. It is also tempting to assert that given the signs of the 1960s and early 1970s only time was required to allow an entirely altered prison system to be created and that, therefore, as the Department of Justice was indicating, IRA prisoners were those 'responsible' for the problems in the prison system. Perhaps Irish prison policy was on the cusp of momentous developments, only to be stalled by the outbreak of violence?

However, the interaction and mutual shaping between the rehabilitative and security policies and methods of these years is not one to be easily or glibly read or decoded. It is clear that the outbreak of the Troubles did have a very definite impact upon the work and the mentality of the Department of Justice. It felt itself under direct attack, was administering a now highly volatile and unpredictable set of institutions and prisoners, and dealing with threats to its personnel and, in its view, to the very security of the state. Long-term planning and dispassionate assessment of regimes, programmes and alternatives which would have been necessitated by the implementation of the objectives and practices of 'penal-welfarism' were affected by the climate of crisis most immediately obvious in

1972. In this new context for prison policy, lurching from one serious incident to another became the defining feature of penal administration.

However, even without the impact of the Troubles, it is unlikely that rehabilitation would have reached a state where it guided all actions, infused all practices and transformed the Irish penal system. First, the foundations had not yet solidified in Ireland and its tenets were underdeveloped by the time the Troubles came to create a new set of challenges for Irish penal administrators. These delicate roots were inherently vulnerable to the buffeting winds of the Troubles, and the Troubles in turn provided administrators with a ready excuse to account for the lack of progress in penal reform. The lack of action in the latter part of the 1960s and the early 1970s must also be reckoned with in assessing how prison policy would have developed in the years ahead had the Troubles not muddied the penological waters.

While this is so, it remains true to say that there remained an official commitment to rehabilitationism and that it was regularly and recurrently cited as the aim of the prison system. In the midst of the turmoil facing the Irish prison system, it is therefore 'interesting', as Kilcommins puts it (Kilcommins *et al.* 2004: 72), that efforts in a rehabilitative vein did in fact continue. Rottman also considers the 1970s to be the decade in which the prison system entered 'the modern era' (Rottman 1986: 106). It is all the more interesting given that there was no underpinning criminological academy or research base in the country to supply supporting evidence or, indeed, to criticise.

On the surface, this mixture of positions is somewhat puzzling. The particular developments within the prison system of the early 1970s, due to the particular changes in the North, rising crime rates in the South and the enduring legacy of the early 1960s, explain these apparent contradictions to some extent. Pragmatic matters of crisis management drove much in penal policy. The apparent flux in prison policy, however, also reflected a mixture of policy positions in a variety of other areas.

Ireland in the 1970s: the Troubles, social expansion, and other 'troubles' ahead

The Troubles: policy responses and deflecting attention

The Northern 'problem' dominated the first years of the decade, with a continuing rumble of influence over the following years. It permeated much of Irish life, affecting the criminal justice system, policing (Walsh 1998: 262), broadcasting (Cathcart and Muldoon 2003) and international relations (Whyte 2003c), though Mulcahy (2002) points out that the effect on crime levels in the Republic was relatively minor.

Reaction to these unfolding developments began to dominate political attention (O'Donnell 2007). As Whyte avers, 'Northern Ireland overshadowed the work of the government and required the investment of considerable resources' (Whyte

2003c: 320). Similarly, Farrell makes the point that 'it is impossible to calculate the destabilising effects [on the political system] of an issue ... which has absorbed so much government time and energy' (Farrell 1986: 149).

The arms crisis, for example, acted to overshadow all other political events during 1970, dominating political debate and monopolising political attention. Other issues, such as reform in social or penal policy, were dwarfed in comparison.

Irish social policy – innovation and continuing modernisation

As the 1970s continued, however, politics in Ireland assumed more of the 'business as usual' (Lee 1989: 461) approach. The 1970s produced several important innovations in Irish welfare reform and equality rights, while the liberalisation experienced in Irish culture was also maintained. The special position of the Catholic Church enshrined in the Constitution was, for example, removed after a referendum in 1973 (Whyte 2003c). The greater openness to ideas from abroad, a desire to integrate into the international economy, pursue free market policies and encourage prosperity also led to the country's accession to the then European Economic Community in 1973.

During this decade, a gradual solidification of the Irish welfare state occurred. In 1972, the Minister for Finance George Colley announced a budget that was the first to plan for a current account budget deficit in order to fulfil the needs, and expectations, of social spending, indicating its view that expansion of the economy was the responsibility of the state (Ó Gráda 1997: 69). The general election of 1973 saw the opposition parties – Fine Gael and Labour – putting forward a 14-point programme to transform Ireland into a 'modern, progressive society, based on social justice' (Whyte 2003c). Fianna Fáil, which went on to lose the election, promised to increase social welfare spending and children's allowances. The budget introduced by the new coalition government in that year has been described as 'the greatest social welfare budget of all time' (Whyte 2003c: 345).

Several innovations were introduced during the decade (Kennedy *et al.* 1988). These included a 'deserted wives' allowance', which came into being in 1970, an unmarried mothers' social welfare allowance in 1973 and an allowance for the wives of prisoners in 1974. The pension age was reduced from 70 to 66 over the years 1973–77, invalidity and retirement pensions were operational from 1970, and an adult dependent allowance for those in receipt of the non-contributory old age pension appeared in 1974. In an attempt to make some provision for older women who qualified neither for social insurance nor assistance, the single woman's allowance commenced in 1974.

As well as social welfare changes, the Health Act 1970 restructured the administration of the health system and in 1972 a 'choice of doctor' scheme was introduced for patients holding medical cards (that is, those on lower incomes and in receipt of free medical care). This was conceived of as an egalitarian measure as previously such patients had been required to attend doctors with a public practice only, giving rise to the accusation of pauperisation (Curry 2003: 148).

Reflecting a greater tendency towards the use of insurance-based social welfare schemes, and adding a further layer into the mix of Irish social provision, compulsory social insurance was extended to all employees of insurable age in 1974; and maternity and disability benefits were introduced in the same year (Carey 2007: 220).

Overall, public expenditure on social welfare increased during the 1970s, reflecting an increase in the numbers receiving such benefits and an increase in the coverage and variety of benefits available (Kennedy 1997; Sexton 2003). As Cousins notes, 'the expansionary approach to social welfare policy continued into the late 1970s' (Cousins 2005: 31). Carey further considers the 1970s to be 'the key decade for social security development' (Carey 2007: 218). Prior opposition to state intervention in these areas was largely forgotten and a commitment to social provision and improved social services remained throughout Irish social policy during the 1970s and was not reversed or truncated.

Within prison policy, a similar picture was present. During that decade, rehabilitationary techniques were still widely considered to be legitimate and, indeed, valuable. Prison policy-makers and administrators remained committed, at least officially, to the precepts of rehabilitation and took steps to implement them during the 1970s; much later than their counterparts in Britain and the USA, for example.

Contradictions in social and economic policy – the nature of Irish politics?

Though the social policy developments of the 1960s and early 1970s were significant and more sustained and radical than anything that had occurred previously, it would nonetheless be misleading to attribute them as involving a fundamental restructuring of Irish social provision or political alignments. A hegemonic commitment to the 'welfare state' or to grand concepts of any nature was not apparent. A large amount of flexibility in ideology continued to pervade Irish politics.

Much of the expansion in social protection during the 1970s came about as a result of electoral politics and 'lavish promises' made for short-term political gain (Lee 1989: 490), rather than an embedded philosophical commitment to welfarism. Reckless public spending was a characteristic of the 1970s, with the 1977 general election involving parties trying to outbid each other in their appeals to the electorate. Lee's assessment of the Fine Gael Minister for Finance, Richie Ryan, is that he presided 'over the most generous, not to say promiscuous, expansion of public expenditure in the history of the state' (Lee 1989: 479). Elections were fought on the basis of personality rather than policy, caution was no longer a feature of economic discourse and cosmetics were prioritised over serious planning (Lee 1989: 487). As will be seen in the next chapter, the licentiousness of this decade resulted in major financial crisis. In 1978 the budget deficit was expanded and borrowing rose to 13 per cent of GNP. The government gambled on growth, a gamble that proved false. In that climate, spending on penal policy could be contemplated, but spending *per se* rather than a developed commitment to strategy was perhaps another motivation.

The roots of Ireland's modernisation were, furthermore, recently apparent and not particularly deep, indicating that while the changes of the 1960s were further developed, an operating ideology was similarly absent. Many areas considered to be classic signs of a state's liberalisation were overlooked. Sexual mores, for example, were unaffected by reforming legislation comparable to that of England and Wales and some areas would not be tackled for several decades to come. A limited liberalisation of the laws on the provision of contraception occurred in 1979, having been prompted by a judicial decision on the matter (*McGee v. Attorney General* [1974] IR 284), while the possibility of introducing divorce was also investigated (Keogh 2005: 368); the final legalisation of contraception occurred in 1992, and divorce was permitted after a referendum in 1998.

The issue of discriminatory policies and practices against women came under greater scrutiny, but many of the reforms introduced were prompted largely by the requirements of EEC membership and judicial activism. The industrial and reformatory school sector was not abolished for some years, juvenile justice generally remained unaffected by legislative intervention until 2001 and the criminal justice system continued to employ nineteenth-century views of mental illness until 2006. While the principle of community care was accepted in 1966, 'progress was slow' in its implementation (Bergin and Clarke 2005: 26). Many areas of social provision remained subject to criticism on the grounds of their inadequacy and selectivity (O'Connell and Rottman 1992).

Overall, while there were definite moves towards improved social protection, there remained a limited level of coherence in the philosophy behind such activity. Farrell notes that the changing discourse that occurred in the 1960s and 1970s 'signified only that politicians were using different straws from which to make the bricks they hurled at each other, rather than that Irish parties had developed fundamentally different attitudes to subjects around which many Western European party systems had traditionally revolved' (Farrell 1986: 144).

The governments of the 1970s continued to reflect the heterogeneity of Irish electoral support and much activity was based on pragmatic and party political considerations (Gallagher 1982). The 1977 election also saw the Fianna Fáil party use the soundbites 'What law? What order?' as part of its attacks on the incumbent government. While this was the first time such sentiments had been expressed in electoral times since the 1930s, there was no rush to legislate by the new Minister, Gerry Collins, and this platform was another example of the sweeping statements made by Fianna Fáil in the run-up to the election of 1977.

Without a sustained philosophical or indeed electoral driving force behind them, the fact that the changes in prison policy were somewhat eclectic and relatively limited is less surprising.

At the same time, the 1970s also brought significant challenges for the state's economic policy. The economic growth of the early 1960s faded. Unemployment began to rise and industrial unrest became a feature (Whitaker 1986). The Public Capital programme was cut back significantly in 1970 and 1971 and borrowing by government shot up, instigating a 'cavalier' (Lee 1989: 465) approach to financial planning based on electoral interests and 'give away budgets' which eventually led to very serious exchequer deficits, made worse by the impact of the international oil crisis in 1973. These financial developments pointed to a more turbulent time for Ireland in the future.

Whyte avers that 'in the Republic, the best word to describe the years 1968–72 is "chequered". If there were no longer the intractable difficulties of the years 1949–57, neither was there the boom atmosphere of the succeeding period. Elements of gloom and optimism coexisted' (Whyte 2003c: 317). This statement would also serve as an admirable synopsis of prison policy at the end of 1979.

Prison policy during the 1970s: the genesis of crisis?

The early 1970s marked a break from the past in Irish prison policy and initiated a new phase of its development. This was particularly apparent in the emergence of 'crisis management' to deal with overcrowding within the prisons, which had not been a feature at least since the Civil War period. However, the break with the past was less patent in other areas. The ideas of the 1960s still had currency within policy-making circles and were further strengthened by the maintenance of broader liberalising tendencies in governance and an expansionary social policy.

Complementing this, however, even greater levels of political populism, opportunism and pragmatism seemed to be taking root in Irish party politics, suggesting that the incoherent and insubstantial character of Irish penal philosophies, which had become particularly evident in the early 1970s, was likely to continue. Such flexibility in ideology meant prison policy in Ireland was particularly open to the buffeting of political winds and pragmatic considerations. The manifestations of this and the altered socio-political and cultural backgrounds present in later decades will be assessed in later chapters, but they owe their roots, in part, to the particular nature of Irish prison policy as it stood at the end of the 1970s.

the crisis in numbers through the provision of small amounts of accommodation where possible and allowing the early release of large numbers of prisoners. These micro-level actions were the most prominent ones within prison policy of the 1980s. Larger scale policy ideas were not present. There was one significant initiative, the introduction of the Criminal Justice (Community Service) Act 1984. This allowed judges to sentence a person to community service where they might otherwise have imposed a custodial sanction. A progressive measure, its introduction was in truth prompted by the simple fact that the prisons could no longer accept the numbers being sent to them.

By the same token, it was again a feature of the decade that policy-makers, whatever they might actually do about conditions, did not speak the language of punitivism or evidence a desire to make conditions deliberately poor. They seemed simply unable to see beyond the next few days or weeks. Concern about crime continued to rise, but this was rarely linked to a position that more prison spaces would solve the problem. At the same time, the Department of Justice, perhaps not quite ready to move away from its stance during the late 1970s with the Northern Troubles still raging, continued to be an insular and defensive place. In terms of the formation of penal policy the Department remained the most influential force, but with its attentions engaged on managing daily events long-term strategising was not engaged in to any large degree.

This chapter analyses the developments of the period and places them in the context of the Ireland of the 1980s. As noted previously, this decade is the first in which widespread access to archival material is not present, being after the 30-year rule for the transfer of documents to the National Archives. Many other archives have similar temporal limitations, such as the Fine Gael archive, which deals with the period up to 1972. This undoubtedly limits the ability to tell the story of prison policy during these years. Further study in years to come will reveal much more, but for the moment a picture of prison policy as driven by crisis emerges clearly.

A prison system in crisis

Pressure on space

The prison system was mired in very significant difficulties during the 1980s. The rising numbers of prisoners that had commenced during the 1970s continued. This was on the back of large increases in officially recorded crime. It became painfully obvious that the existing prison stock, already significantly expanded, could not cope with this pressure on numbers. In 1980 Mountjoy male prison, with 448 cells, held a daily average of 422 prisoners, rising to 442 in 1982 (Dáil Debates, vol 338, col 1250, 8 February 1983). Cork prison, with 41 cells at that stage, held 49 prisoners in 1980 and 61 in 1982.

A very short-termist and pragmatic approach to policy-making developed in this environment. One of the mechanisms used to relieve pressure was temporary release. Such release, for the majority unsupervised and without prior planning

7

THE 1980s
Crises and committees

Introduction

Prison policy during the 1980s presents a rather bleak picture. While the concerns around 'subversive' prisoners faded from view somewhat, prison numbers continued to rise, with year-on-year increases becoming significant. In addition, disquiet about drug use within prisons and the presence of prisoners with the HIV virus led to a climate of increased anxiety and fear within penal administration. Conditions in the prisons became severely overcrowded and as the decade went on an increased number of deaths in custody occurred. The material provision of accommodation was poor, and to cope with the large increases in population doubling up in cells became prevalent and the use of unsupervised temporary release, termed 'shedding', became widespread. This was the subject of vociferous criticism.

The backdrop to this was the yet again financially precarious position of the state. Penal expansion could no longer be contemplated on any large scale. The plan for an entirely new prison, Wheatfield in Clondalkin, Dublin, was heralded as a major solution to the crisis. However, financial considerations meant that its completion was seriously delayed and the prison opened only at the end of the decade. Even with the provision of extra cells, the level of overcrowding had to be coped with through what can be described as a policy of 'making do'. It seems that during this period, the by now years of crisis, overcrowding and difficult conditions had rendered prison administrators and policy-makers almost inured to their effects. Policy-makers appeared if not content then at least resigned to the fact that the crisis within the prisons would continue for some time. This was compounded by the high turnover of ministers during the early part of the decade following several changes in government during a politically turbulent period.

An 'acceptable level' of poor conditions and high numbers seemed to have been arrived at. Policy-makers struggled through the decade, attempting to deal with

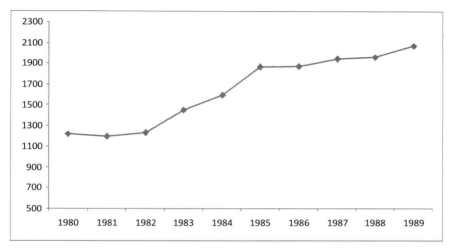

FIGURE 7.1 Average daily prison population 1980–89

or indeed notice, began to be relied on more heavily as the decade progressed. In 1980 891 prisoners were released to make way for new committals, with the figure rising to 1,298 in 1982 (Dáil Debates, vol 339, col 373, 8 February 1983). In 1984 900 prisoners were granted temporary release from Mountjoy alone (Dáil Debates, vol 361, col 248, 23 October 1985). The Department of Justice's Prisons Division would have been involved in the making of decisions regarding release and the numbers involved must have resulted in significant pressure on staff time.

The impression is given of the Department struggling to cope with immediate concerns and having to undertake a paper exercise each day of deciding who would be released. Naturally, such an environment was not conducive to strategic thinking. Though ministers insisted that the decision to place somebody on temporary release was taken on the basis of a likelihood of reoffending and being a danger to the public (Dáil Debates, vol 341, col 711, 15 March 1983), it seems highly unlikely that individual assessments could have been anything other than cursory and based on offence profile alone.

Another approach was to utilise the intriguingly named 'home leave' system in 1983. This was framed as an alternative to the unsupervised temporary release known as shedding, but in reality it involved prisoners serving sentences for minor offences being able to remain out of prison once they signed on periodically at a local Garda station. Statutory remission levels were also exceeded in order to reduce prison numbers day by day.

The Criminal Justice (Community Service) Act 1984

This pressure on space gave rise to a very pragmatic reason to introduce alternatives to custody. In June 1981 the government introduced a White Paper on Community Service. Fine Gael, *via* Alan Shatter TD, in opposition in June 1982, introduced a Private Member's Bill to introduce community service that was very quickly followed by a government bill along similar lines. Community service orders (CSOs) were introduced in England and Wales in 1972 and the Irish legislation owes a clear debt to the original Act there.

However, it is clear that the push to legislate was driven by the difficulties in accommodation then extant in Irish prisons. Introducing the bill again in 1983, Minister Noonan framed its introduction in the context of accommodation pressures, arguing that it should 'at least help' to contain an increase in the numbers likely to be committed to custody (Dáil Debates, vol 341, col 1330, 20 April 1983). A Fianna Fáil amendment to allow CSOs to be introduced even if a prison sentence was not considered appropriate by a judge was resisted on the basis that the sanction must be an alternative to custody.

Poor industrial relations

Another feature of the difficulties in Irish prison policy during the 1980s is that of poor industrial relations between successive governments and the Prison Officers Association. This group, which acted as a form of trade union and advocacy group on behalf of prison officers, became increasingly vocal and took strident action in order to secure improved conditions for its members. There were rows about overtime and threats of walk-outs by prison staff became frequent (Dáil Debates, vol 327, col 40, 24 February 1981).

It is also the case that the prison service had taken in a very large number of new recruits during the 1970s and 1980s and that the ratio of officers to prisoners was extremely high. The nature of many of the buildings and the security concerns arising out of increased prisoner numbers probably accounted for much of this increase. During the 1980s it appears that there was a great deal of frustration and some suspicion of the gradual increase of 'professionals' entering the prison, who were seen to undermine their authority (McGowan 1980: 557). All in all, it is clear that industrial relations during these years were poor, prompting suggestions from a number of bodies that the prison service be run by a statutory agency independent of the Department of Justice (CIPS 1985; CSW 1983).

Political turbulence

Another factor in the creation of a climate of apparent paralysis within prison policy-making was the absence of ministerial leadership during the early 1980s. As is recounted in further detail below, the frequent changes of government during this time meant that the Justice portfolio changed hands rapidly. A Fine Gael Minister, Jim Mitchell, was in charge from 30 June 1981 to 9 March 1982, while a Fianna Fáil Minister, Seán Doherty, held office from 9 March 1982 until 14 December 1982. A period of relative stability followed when Michael Noonan of Fine Gael, who was later to lead the party, was Minister until 14 February

1986. Such frenetic political activity did not give much of an opportunity for Ministers to put their individual stamp on prison policy, nor indeed to even get to grips with their portfolio. None appeared to have been particularly involved in penal affairs prior to their accession to ministerial office. In addition, the political intrigues of the period probably meant that interest in the broader political machinations and jostling for position took priority over the day-to-day affairs of running the Department. In such circumstances, departmental control can only have become more prominent. It is also likely that such frequent changes in personnel contributed to the delay in bringing forth the community service legislation.

Drugs

A further major pressure point within the prison system during the 1980s was the increasing concern about drug use within institutions. As has been seen, the first reference to concern about drugs in the Irish prison system occurred a decade previously. However, little in the way of concrete action to address the issue of any kind was forthcoming. During the 1980s the issue achieved more and more prominence, reflecting a broader concern about the use of drugs, particularly heroin, in Dublin's inner city in particular. A Special Governmental Task Force on Drug Abuse was established in 1983. In 1986 it was reported that the medical officers considered there to be 210 drug addicts within the prison system, though the real number was likely to be higher (Dáil Debates, vol 363, col 223, 22 January 1986).

Provision for prisoners addicted to drugs was very limited. Prisoners could be released to a residential centre for treatment, the Coolmine Centre, but the waiting list was three years in 1983, closing that avenue for prisoners (CSW 1983).

AIDS

The spectre of AIDS during the 1980s also loomed large within the prison system. The authorities, apparently attempting to grapple with a problem about which little was known and much was feared, attempted to deal with the situation by setting up a segregation unit in Arbour Hill prison. Prisoners who were HIV positive were also held in Mountjoy, with 45 male and 10 female such prisoners resident there in 1988 (Dáil Debates, vol 384, col 74, 10 November 1988), apparently in the Base. It seems that these prisoners were being held in a unit that had been intended for the transfer of prisoners from the Curragh.

Disturbances and escapes

During this undoubtedly bleak decade within the prison system there were also a significant number of disturbances within the penal estate. The security focus and the policies pursued as regards subversive prisoners appeared to have met with some success as there were far fewer disturbances of that nature than in the previous decade, though there was an attempted break-out in Portlaoise in 1985 (Dáil Debates, vol 362, col 342, 27 November 1985). However, among the 'ordinary' prison population the number of incidents was increasing.

In 1983 there was a disturbance in Mountjoy prison and a senior counsel was engaged to investigate the matter, though the report seems never to have been published (Dáil Debates, vol 354, col 790, 11 December 1984). Shortly after its opening there was what was described as a 'mutiny' on Spike Island and some prisoners were involved in disturbances resulting in the burning down of some accommodation. Not long after, it was reported that three prisoners had beaten other prisoners in Arbour Hill on the basis that the latter were serving sentences for sex offences. In that same prison 24 prisoners housed in the segregation unit for prisoners with HIV attempted to escape, managing to break through the ceiling onto the roof (Dáil Debates, vol 364, vol 1692, 12 March 1986). In 1986 there was a controversial incident in Mountjoy women's prison when male prison officers were reported to have been deployed in order to restore order (Dáil Debates, vol 398, col 827, 3 May 1980).

Escapes were a source of embarrassment to the government. In 1981 a prisoner escaped from Mountjoy after removing a panel from his cell door and escaping through a window, while another left Cork prison through the removal of a cell window and a window bar (Dáil Debates, vol 326, col 2164, 19 February 1981). These escapes were not made publicly known until questions were asked about them in the Dáil.

Prison conditions

There can be no doubt that the pressures on accommodation, staff, the old nature of buildings, the increasing numbers of prisoners with drug addictions and the general turmoil within the most overcrowded prisons led to very difficult conditions within individual prisons. Doing time in such circumstances can only have been arduous.

The reports of the visiting committees during the 1980s give some indication of the reality of the lived experience of incarceration in Ireland during this time. As described elsewhere (Rogan 2009b), visiting committees in Ireland (known as independent monitoring boards in England and Wales) have rarely acted as a force for change in Irish prison policy, with the information provided in their reports being limited and criticism restrained. However, there was a major exception in this regard with the Mountjoy Visiting Committee of the late 1980s.

As with so many aspects of Irish prison policy, it was probably the presence of an individual personality, in the form of Dermot Kinlen, a judge of the High Court and later the first Inspector of Prisons in Ireland, on the committee that led to such a change. That committee told in its reports of poor hygiene, serious overcrowding and particularly poor conditions within the women's prison (*Report of the Mountjoy Prison Visiting Committee*, 1989).

Deaths in custody

During the 1980s deaths in custody occurred more frequently than previously. There were four deaths in four months in Mountjoy in 1986 (Dáil Debates, vol 363, col 35, 22 January 1986) and nine deaths over a three-year period ending in 1988 (Dáil Debates, vol 382, col 1631, 23 June 1988).

As remains the case for the vast majority of deaths in prison custody today, the investigations into these deaths took the form of an internal inquiry and an inquest. A public inquiry was considered by the Minister Gerard Collins in 1988 to be likely to serve 'no useful purpose' (Dáil Debates, vol 385, col 1621, 14 December 1988). One jury at an inquest into such a death added a rider that improved methods of communication should be provided in Mountjoy in order to enable prisoners to be able to attract attention more easily (Dáil Debates, vol 387, col 36, 22 February 1989). Another inquest found that a prison officer on duty in Mountjoy had responsibility for 120 cells with no system of alerting attention other than banging on the door or walls. The removal of bars from windows was also recommended. In Arbour Hill it was found that of 140 prisoners 100 were on a special observation list (Dáil Debates, vol 387, col 1366, 22 February 1989). No systemic investigation of this matter of growing concern took place, however, until the following decade.

Lack of official information and research

It is perhaps unsurprising that dealing with all these matters and a Prisons Division having to decide from day to day who would be released from custody to make way for new committals meant that the collation of statistics was not a high priority for the Department. No annual reports on the prison system were published for the years 1985 or 1986 until 1987 and the 1987 report was published at the end of 1988.

Though perhaps understandable, this situation meant that any formation of prison policy was inevitably based in a vacuum. Officials had snapshots of the average daily prison population, but the emphasis was on overall figures rather than a detailed breakdown of the type of sentences for which people were imprisoned, for example. Trends in particular areas went unnoticed and a context in which to take a more dispassionate look at the penal system was not present.

Moreover, research was not conducted by the Department of Justice into the prison system and the criminological knowledge-base in the country remained very limited indeed. The material on the prison population showed, however, that Irish prisoners were largely from urban areas, a high proportion had not lived with both their natural parents during their childhood, almost a quarter had been in an industrial school or reformatory, 65 per cent had left school before the age of 14 and came from an average family of 8, with the national average being 3.45 children per family (Department of Justice 1980).

The panacea of penal expansion

Though it must have been obvious to ministers and civil servants that the possibility of securing significant capital investment in the prison system was very low, the provision of extra accommodation was mooted as a viable solution to the crisis of numbers on a regular basis. Cork prison was earmarked for expansion in the early 1980s and was allowed to take remands as well as sentenced prisoners and Loughan House was to be used to house adult male offenders. These plans would increase accommodation only modestly, however, but were a convenient answer when challenged about responses to the prison crisis. Plans to establish a new women's prison were deferred, as was provision for a male juvenile prison in Cork with 180 spaces, and the development of the planned high security adult male prison with 120 places at Portlaoise was postponed.

Penal expansion was more readily contemplated by the Fianna Fáil government of the earlier period. It provided £17.6 million in 1982 for prison building, which was then slashed by the Fine Gael administration. It is likely that the fiscal abandon of the late 1970s, which permeated into the early 1980s, was a major influence on the provision of such expenditure. Penal expansion was also welcomed by Fianna Fáil when in opposition (Dáil Debates, vol 341, col 1339, 20 April 1983).

Wheatfield

The most significant plan to create additional space was in the form of a new prison in County Dublin. This was Wheatfeld prison, an institution that took an inordinate amount of time to complete. Initial development began in 1980, but progress stalled, apparently due to financial problems. The Fine Gael administration did not refer to Wheatfield in any great depth, perhaps afraid to do so lest it might be forced to spend more money on the project, until 1983 when an increased capital budget meant that the building of Wheatfield could restart. Wheatfield came to be considered as the great hope of Irish penal administration, which would relieve pressure on accommodation. Originally it appears that Wheatfield had been planned to replace St Patrick's Institution for young males and also to provide accommodation for female prisoners, but this plan was abandoned sometime in the 1980s and it was eventually used for adult males.

In 1985 the government acquired Fort Mitchel, an old army barracks on Spike Island in Cork harbour, in a rapid reaction to concerns about 'joyriding'. The island had been used as a prison periodically since the eighteenth century, and also as a military base. Within a fortnight of the announcement, prisoners were transferred there. Initially it was purportedly run as an open centre for prisoners serving short sentences or those who were coming to the end of a longer sentence. Additional prisoners were sent there during 1985 in order to relieve pressure on the older institutions during the difficult summer months.

In the same year as the opening of Fort Mitchel it was decided to increase the planned provision of spaces in Wheatfield, from 150 up to 320 places. In 1985 it was further planned to add another 144 spaces for women (Dáil Debates, vol 359, col 107, 30 May 1985). More money appeared to become available for the prison system during this year as a contract for the building of a more modest 50-cell unit in Cork was concluded in that year (Dáil Debates, vol 362, col 16, 27 November 1985). Also in that year, Portlaoise prison was renovated with the aim of providing an extra 30 spaces. In 1986 the old officers' quarters at Mountjoy female prison was converted into multiple occupancy cells (Dáil Debates, vol 372, col 1795, 13 May 1987).

Immediate measures were also taken. The education units at Cork and Arbour Hill were 'relocated' to temporary, prefabricated, accommodation to increase cell capacity (Dáil Debates, vol 359, col 601, 6 June 1985). Accommodation or 'quarters' for single prison officers in Portlaoise were transformed into custodial accommodation. The Minister considered that it could be used to house 'alcoholic' or low risk women prisoners. Evidently little thought was being put into the needs of either group and no research was conducted or referred to upon which such decisions were made. In the event the accommodation was used, as might have been predicted, to house the burgeoning numbers of adult male offenders. These were simply short-term, stop-gap remedies.

Similarly, female prisoners in Limerick were required to relocate to Mountjoy women's prison in order to make way for male prisoners (Dáil Debates, vol 370, col 121, 17 December 1986). Previously the exercise area for female prisoners in Limerick was reduced in order to provide additional workshops and indoor recreational facilities for male prisoners (Dáil Debates, vol 339, col 442, 2 February 1983).

The prison system had to muddle along without the long-heralded Wheatfield, with that prison opening eventually in 1989.

Putting up a good front

Another distinctive feature of the discourse around prisons during these years is that of denial by policy-makers about the crisis within the prison system. It is as if those in charge did not want to admit to the level of difficulty, and that if they continued to maintain things were normal, this rhetoric would suffice to placate others and perhaps convince themselves. In 1983, for example, the Independent T.D. Tony Gregory asked the Minister for Justice whether increasing remission to 50 per cent – the level in Northern Ireland – was being considered given the high reliance on temporary release. Minister Noonan, in reply, considered that an increase to remission was not necessary, on the basis that *inter alia* prisoners were being released at the halfway stage of their sentence or even earlier anyway, and that the system in the Republic was a liberal one, which did not require change (Dáil Debates, vol 341, col 711, 15 March 1983). This statement cements the picture of prison policy in these years as one where if there was no official or statutory change, the problem had not been officially recognised, but pragmatic approaches which amounted to the same thing were tolerated.

'Getting by': pragmatic prison policy

While penal expansion was one of the strategies mooted as a way of dealing with the problems of space, very little could be done about this in practice given the perilous state of the public finances. The governments of the day during the early 1980s were careful not to promise large-scale prison building and it is likely that the Department of Finance was a very loud critic of any plans that might have been mooted. The fact that the coffers of the state were largely empty had a major chilling effect on any plans to increase prison places. Concern about crime simply couldn't afford to be translated into a larger prison system. Minister Noonan admitted that financial pressure was the reason for the slowing of development in 1983 when he said: 'the need for economy in public expenditure required that a costly programme such as the prison capital programme be re-examined and priorities within it established' (Dáil Debates, vol 340, col 920, 23 February 1983).

The prison system also had to continue to use outdated stock, such as Mountjoy. Its decommissioning was far from being contemplated as an imminent possibility, with refurbishment works planned to continue throughout the 1980s and into the early 1990s (Dáil Debates, vol 342, col 292, 11 May 1983). Dundalk jail, which had not been used as a prison for several decades, was examined to see if it was possible to reopen it. Its dilapidated state and use of parts of it for other purposes militated against its introduction (Dáil Debates, vol 344, col 64, 7 July 1983).

It was also decided, again apparently without a great deal of consideration, that a planned unit for the grounds of the central mental hospital, then being built, would be transferred on completion for the use of the Department of Justice as prison accommodation for prisoners with HIV/AIDS and drug problems (Dáil Debates, vol 364, col 637, 27 February 1986). This never happened, for reasons that are unclear. The Department of Justice was also considering the acquisition of a property owned by the Christian Brothers in the James' Street area of Dublin (Dáil Debates, vol 357, col 1434, 23 April 1985). It is hard to believe that custodial accommodation of the nature required by a prison system could be provided by such accommodation, but the impression is given of a Department almost desperate to get some extra space. Again, this development came to nothing. In this area, prison policy appeared to be occurring more in official statements and on paper than in practice.

Penal expansion was conducted in a piecemeal, almost derisory fashion, adding a few cells here and there. However, one move to increase prison capacity received little attention when compared to the impact it would have on the prison system. In 1983 the Minister for Justice signed a statutory instrument that removed the provision in the Prison Rules 1947 requiring prisoners to be kept in single cells. This immediately increased the available capacity significantly. It had a number of effects, the first being that the prisons looked less overcrowded on paper than they were in reality. More serious, however, was the effect on prison life and the increasing use of multiple occupancy as a permanent response to pressures on space, something that has never been reversed (O'Donnell 2008).

It was admitted by the then Fianna Fáil Minister for Justice in 1987 that prisoners were occupying bedding on the floor of Mountjoy as well as in the TV room in B Base and on 'secure areas leading from the landings' (Dáil Debates, vol 373, col 925, 9 June 1987). In November 1987 203 single cells were being used to accommodate two prisoners (Dáil Debates, vol 274, col 2637, 5 November 1987).

This sense of 'making do' in prison policy is evident in Minister Noonan's statement that without extra money and with Wheatfield not likely to be completed for a number of years, he was left with a situation where 'with existing accommodation and any new temporary accommodation I could acquire, I had to provide accommodation for a number which had increased from approximately 1,200 to 1,940 [in 1985]' (Dáil Debates, vol 359, col 670, 6 June 1985).

Crime and cost: concern in political debate

Irish political discourse remained relatively untroubled about crime and its solution until the 1980s in large part. As has been seen, while concern about crime and its growth had begun to emerge in the late 1960s and 1970s, this did not translate into calls for 'crackdowns' or, indeed, a linking of the growth in crime to 'soft' penal measures. While it is true that during the 1980s there were no significant or serious attempts to politicise penal policy in the sense of a rush to take more hard-line positions, the growing crime rate was nonetheless mentioned frequently within political debate. Mostly, however, this concern was linked to the social causes of increased crime, with unemployment, running at very high levels in the country, and particularly youth unemployment, seen as part of the reason driving such growth (Dáil Debates, vol 341, col 1340, 20 April 1983). Fine Gael's Michael Keating welcomed the introduction of community service as a progressive measure and warned: 'if we were to play to the gallery much more repressive, superficial and emotive measures might be introduced … It is not a case of bigger doors and more locks and more prisons' (Dáil Debates, vol 341, col 1352, 20 April 1983). In introducing further legislation, the Criminal Justice Bill 1983, the Minister considered: 'it is clear that poverty, unemployment and poor social conditions generally are factors that play an important part [in the commission of crime]' (Dáil Debates, vol 345, col 250, 2 November 1983).

Crime was linked clearly to the social and economic problems bedevilling Ireland in the 1980s. However, there was a pragmatic approach taken here also. It was recognised that solving those difficulties was arduous and looked unlikely to be carried out in any short time. It was easier to focus on deterrence and detection.

These twin rationales were put forward as the basis for the introduction of a very significant piece of legislation, the Criminal Justice Act 1984. It was originally introduced in bill form under Fianna Fáil and eventually passed into law under Fine Gael. This wide-ranging Act allowed for the detention of suspects upon arrest by the Gardaí for the first time outside of the commission of subversion-related offences. Such was the concern for civil liberties, however, that a corollary to the Act was the introduction of regulations for the treatment of persons in custody (the Custody Regulations). The Act also provided for the imposition of consecutive sentences for offences committed while on bail as well as a number of changes to criminal procedure including permitting a trier of fact to draw inferences from an accused's person's silence.

In the course of the debates on this significant piece of legislation, which represented the first major increase in Garda powers, there was little by the way of discussion of the role prison had to play in the fight against crime. What was said about prison was the need to ensure that adequate prison places would be provided to enable the Act to work, but the argument that more prison places would automatically reduce crime was not evident (Dáil Debates, vol 345, col 1296, 2 November 1983).

There is no doubt, however, that concern about crime was present in Ireland in a way that had not been experienced previously. TDs in the Dublin area began to declare that they were attending public meetings on crime at least once a week (Dáil Debates, vol 341, col 1465, 20 April 1983). A Select Committee on Crime, Lawlessness and Vandalism was established by the Oireachtas, which reported in 1984. It did not have a great deal to say about prisons, however, and *inter alia* recommended the decriminalisation of certain offences under the antiquarian Vagrancy Acts.

Prison space was not a matter from which significant political capital would be made, not yet at any rate. In 1985 the Minister for Justice warned: 'I would not like it to be thought that the problem faced by society in dealing with criminals can or should be solved solely by reference to the provision of more custodial places' (Dáil Debates, vol 362, col 349, 27 November 1985). The concern surrounding the prison system focused on space and cost. Neither could such problem be remedied easily. It was decided in 1983 to ask an outside body to provide some solutions, though as it will be seen it was also hoped that it would not provide them too soon. The Fine Gael government established a Committee of Inquiry into the Penal System in 1983.

The Whitaker Committee

It should have been clear to the government of the day that the prison system needed urgent attention and that there was every danger that a committee could take years to report or provide solutions. It is also difficult to understand why the Department of Justice could not have been tasked with the responsibility of solving the problems within the prison system, rather than an outside body that did not have anything approaching the same level of expertise. This is even more baffling when the Department of Justice during the late 1970s and early 1980s was clearly not particularly open or comfortable with external assessment or indeed interference with its work. Without access to the archival material, the reaction of the Department of Justice to the establishment of the committee may only be speculated upon.

A flowering of interest in prison conditions

The 1980s was a time when there was a increased interest in prison conditions. In 1983 the Council for Social Welfare, a committee of the Catholic Bishops' Conference, published a report entitled *The Prison System*. This was the result, it seems, of the visit of Pope John Paul II to Ireland in 1979 when he asked the bishops to pay particular attention to the position of prisoners. This group, perhaps given its origins, did not have the same problems at the Prisoners' Rights Organisation in the 1970s in terms of securing access, and was granted access to all prisons and spoke to officials of the Department, whose 'openness and forward-thinking approach' impressed them (CSW 1983: 1.14).

The MacBride Commission had also reported by this time. This body was headed by Seán MacBride who had been a prisoner during the Civil War period, whose mother was the penal reform activist Maud Gonne MacBride, and who had been counsel for the family of Seán McCaughey at the inquest into his death in 1947 which led to the introduction of the Prison Rules 1947. MacBride was by now a former Minister for Foreign Affairs, a founding member of Amnesty International, a winner of the Nobel Peace Prize and the Lenin Peace Prize and member of a variety of human rights organisations around the world. Other members of the commission were Michael D. Higgins, then a member of Seanad Éireann, and Mary McAleese, later President of Ireland. The secretary to the commission was Fr Micheál MacGréil, a Jesuit priest and author of a ground-breaking work on prejudice and tolerance in Ireland.

Despite such a glittering array of members, the MacBride Commission found it difficult to obtain cooperation from the Department of Justice. Its recommendations were broadly in keeping with those of others interested in penal reform during the 1980s.

While the interest in prison conditions and crime occurring during the 1980s were important factors, and the reports of the Council for Social Welfare – and, later, the overlooked report of the Irish Commission for Justice and Peace, the Irish Council of Churches Working Party on Prisons and the Council for Social Welfare (ICJP 1986) – it can be argued that perhaps the most compelling rationale for the establishment of the Whitaker Committee was the fact that it had the potential to deflect concern and criticism about crime and penal policy from the government and such matters on the basis of the need to wait for the Committee to report. The response of the government to the report's publication lends further credence to this contention.

The establishment of the Committee

The relative hierarchy of reasons is difficult to ascertain. Fr Peter McVerry, who was part of the Committee, says that Michael Noonan established it 'in good faith, desiring to improve the conditions for prisoners and to bring penal policy into the 20th century' (Whitaker 2007). While this may be so, the report was published in a climate where few of its recommendations would have political appeal, requiring investment and imagination when all that could be seen was a need for more space.

It appears that the decision to set up such a committee was taken by the Fine Gael government rather rapidly, in a further indication of the pressurised nature of policy-making during these years. The Taoiseach, Garret Fitzgerald, asked Dr T. K. Whitaker to chair the Committee. It is likely that the impeccable record of Dr Whitaker in public service made him an obvious candidate for the role, though Whitaker was himself surprised at the appointment (Whitaker 2007). The eventual composition of the Committee was a broad-based one, with Fr Peter McVerry, a Jesuit priest with a reformist mindset, also being appointed, along with Dr David Rottman of the Economic and Social Research Institute, Séamus Henchy, judge of the Supreme Court, and representatives of the trade union movement and business. The secretary to the Committee was Frank Dunne, then a principal officer in the Department of Justice.

Through Frank Dunne, the Committee's visits to prisons were organised. They also visited prisons in Scotland and Denmark and examined a wide variety of issues, including alternatives to imprisonment, prison officer rostering, alternatives to custody and prison conditions. The nature of the Committee's remit was wide. Despite this, it provided a very comprehensive and lengthy report in 1985. It is likely that such a rapid publication was not envisaged by the government.

The Whitaker Committee recommendations

The recommendations of the Whitaker Committee have been referred to time and again by those advocating penal reform in Ireland. It criticised the lack of statistical information on Irish crime and punishment, it recommended the development of alternatives to custody, considering imprisonment a largely futile exercise, it suggested changes to industrial relations practices within the prisons and it advocated improved educational and work training, being particularly critical of the conditions for female prisoners. Indeed, the inclusion of photographs of the female prison and the visual representation of the primitive facilities for women in Mountjoy shows that the Committee was intent on bringing those conditions to the fore.

The Committee also criticised the high level of short sentences imposed and considered that imprisonment should be a sanction of last resort (CIPS 1985). Improved reintegration and after-care supports were also called for. The committee also showed that conditions in Irish prisons were outdated, with 'appalling' washing and toilet facilities, and that Mountjoy was so unsuitable that its replacement must be a matter of priority. The Whitaker Report is of a strongly welfarist nature, emphasising the need for rehabilitation, the social context of offending, seeking a humane and less restrictive penal regime.

One of the most eye-catching recommendations was a cap on prison spaces. The Committee suggested that the prison population should be capped at 1,500 places. The Committee further advocated a long-term approach to planning, a valuable but unlikely to be implemented proposal in the context of mid-1980s Ireland. Analysing the need for space, the Committee found that the prison system as it then stood was 500 places 'short'. However, it did not advocate continued increases in prison space to cope with this matter. Instead, it suggested that a reduction in committals, shorter sentences and shorter periods in custody could reduce the population by the 500 necessary and the extra spaces at Wheatfield could be used to cater for immediate extra needs.

Reaction to the Whitaker Report

The views of the Department of Justice about Whitaker are difficult to discern. The Department had not shown itself to be particularly receptive to new ideas or any suggestions from outside bodies. It is perhaps the case that officials saw the Whitaker Committee as an attack on their work or a recognition or admission that their administration of the prison system had been problematic. In a Department as defensive as that of Justice, it is unlikely that such critique and recommendations would have been received with favour.

The Minister's reaction is similarly difficult to gauge. There is little in Dáil debate to hint at his views. He did indicate that it may propose solutions that would not be a 'quick-fix' but that would be more effective, and he hoped that its publication would lead to an informed debate on penal affairs (Dáil Debates, vol 359, col 606, 6 June 1985). Michael Noonan was in office for several months after the publication of the Whitaker Report but none of its recommendations was implemented during that time. This was a very different reaction when compared to the Inter-Departmental Committee of the 1960s. It is likely that whatever might have been the instigating factors at work in the commissioning of the report, its publication in the context of 1985 was somewhat politically inconvenient.

The reaction of the press to Whitaker was also somewhat mixed. The *Irish Times* welcomed it, but the *Irish Independent*, a far more widely read publication, considered that 'sparks would fly' at the suggestions that a milder regime for prisoners should be encouraged and that the public might consider community service 'a very soft reply' (*Irish Independent*, 9 August 1985).

Response of the policy-makers

Instead of applying the approach advocated by Whitaker, the policy-makers of the 1980s continued the approach of continuing to expand the prison system. It had been clear that this was the preferred option since the late 1970s and into the 1980s, but that capital funding had been the main stumbling block. While the Whitaker Committee had been conducting its investigations, the prison population continued its apparently inexorable rise. This was not a context in which a Minister, perhaps responding to a Department of Justice that did not appreciate the recommendations of the Whitaker Committee, was likely to implement its longer-term proposals.

The Minister could have used the crisis as a 'policy window' in which to effect long-lasting change. Indeed, the fact that proposals were presented to him essentially on a plate would have been administratively convenient and easier to justify when a committee of such calibre and broad spectrum of opinions had proposed them. Instead, however, it appears that the very immediate and practical pressures on space resulted in the continuation of the short-term perspective on policy. Fianna Fáil's pressure for more places and its record as having allocated more money than Fine Gael to increasing prison places must also have been a motivating factor in the particularly electorally competitive years of the 1980s. The short-termist perspective which prioritised the provision of more accommodation was mixed with a concern that reform of the prison system might be viewed badly in the context of rising crime rates.

Such pressure was also part of the rationale behind the rapid introduction of the use of Fort Mitchel on Spike Island. During the mid-1980s there was considered to be an 'emergency' situation arising out of high levels of car thefts in the Dublin area (Dáil Debates, vol 359, col 670, 6 June 1985). The furore this created in the media highlighted the lack of prison accommodation and whatever qualms there were about fiscal rectitude were put aside in light of the need to be perceived as responding to the problem of 'joyriding' (McVerry 2002).

While the Fine Gael administration was largely silent on the question of the Whitaker Committee's recommendations, Fianna Fáil Minister Gerry Collins in 1987 did not have much of substance to say about them either. Collins declared that he was considering the recommendations and that the report was a 'very valuable document' but nothing more specific was said (Dáil Debates, vol 373, col 1793, 12 June 1987).

An embryonic politicisation of crime?

It is of note that Minister Gerry Collins, in his first speech on the Department of Justice Estimates in 1987, did not commence his duties by laying out his vision for a vastly expanded prison system. Indeed, his speech bore a great degree of similarity to those of his predecessor when it came to the prison system, indicating the likelihood that the civil servants were propagating the messages on the prison system. Collins emphasised the need for non-custodial sanctions and the importance of the probation and welfare service in community projects for young people 'at risk'.

This quite balanced and muted tone is interesting given that in the previous two years Collins' counterparts in Fianna Fáil had launched something of an attack on the Fine Gael ministers responsible for the prison system, Michael Noonan and, briefly, Alan Dukes. The prison system was undoubtedly an easy target given the level of overcrowding, the frequency of resource to temporary release and the disturbances within and concern about the prison system. The first concerted effort to make such an attack is evident in 1985 when a motion was put before the Dáil condemning 'the government for their failure to provide adequate and secure prison accommodation to meet the present needs' (Dáil Debates, vol 359, col 1110, 11 June 1985). This took place a few months after a series of attacks on elderly persons in rural areas, which gave rise to significant concern and led to the establishment of a Garda task force involving checkpoints and calls for intervention by the army (Dáil Debates, vol 356, col 1995, 12 March 1985).

During the debate on the motion there is a mix of positions evident that displays the ideological flux on crime matters prevalent during these years. What was perceived as a breakdown in law and order was decried, but at the same time it was felt that another major source of contention, unemployment, was a significant source of crime and that young people were rebelling against a system that denied them a job and that 'imprisonment is no substitute for our failure to order a fair and just society' (Dáil Debates, vol 359, col 1111, 11 June 1985). Most interesting is the contribution of Bertie Ahern, who linked the lack of investment in prison-building to increased crime and lawlessness. However, almost in the same breath, crime was linked to unemployment, and the diminution in educational facilities within prisons was criticised.

In 1986 similar sentiments were expressed in a motion of confidence in the government when Charles Haughey, by now leader of Fianna Fáil, stated, responding to a Cabinet reshuffle, that Michael Noonan's 'position at Justice with anarchy reigning in the prisons, low Garda morale and crime of all kinds at unprecedented levels; was becoming untenable' (Dáil Debates, vol 363, col 1145, 20 February 1986).

It is likely that these statements were as much driven by the scent of a general election as anything else. As will be seen below, Ireland in the 1980s was a place in which electoral competition was intense and it is perhaps most surprising that relatively little political capital was made out of a prison system in such grave difficulty. The context in which prison policy was formed was similarly difficult.

Ireland during the 1980s

Political actions in the late 1970s in Ireland left the country with a number of hangovers. After the 1977 election the Fianna Fáil government pursued an approach of increasing the budget deficits and increasing public borrowing. Growth was predicted to be high, but failed to live up to expectations. After the second oil crisis in 1978 trade decreased but in Ireland wages continued to increase. It seems that the lavish promises of the 1977 election had created a climate in which both the government and individuals could not come to grips with the fiscal reality. Public expenditure exceeded public income significantly by the end of the 1970s and personal borrowing was also high. Lee describes 1979 as 'truly bruising on the financial front' in which net foreign debt jumped from £297m at the end of 1978 to £1,089m in 1979 (Lee 1989: 500). Unemployment, a true scourge of the decade, grew significantly. By 1981 unemployment ran at 147,000 people, hitting 250,000 later in the decade.

Within the party of government there was a major internal row occurring between two rivals for the leadership after Jack Lynch announced his intention to step down: George Colley and Charles Haughey. Charles Haughey triumphed and became Taoiseach at the end of 1979 (Keogh 2003). These internal divisions and tension continued throughout the 1980s.

Haughey as Taoiseach: penal reform not on the agenda

Charles Haughey had proved himself to be a reforming Minister for Justice, interested in, prepared to expend intellectual energy on and committed to changing the penal system. In the Dáil after moving from Justice he did not betray a similar level of dynamic engagement with prison issues, though in 1973 he responded to Paddy Cooney's statement that he would continue the good work of the Department in penal reform thus: 'Started by whom? By myself?' (Dáil Debates, vol 265, col 933, 10 May 1973). However, Haughey became much quieter regarding penal issues as time went on. For a start, Haughey's political career had looked over after the scandal of the arms trial and he spent a number of years on the back benches before his political rehabilitation was complete. Haughey was clearly enormously ambitious and had an eye on the position of Taoiseach. In his efforts to become leader of Fianna Fáil he did not pursue, it appears, a penal reform agenda as part of his platform.

Lee argues that Haughey's main preoccupation after he became Taoiseach was to win elections and that he was keenly aware that if he lost the election in 1981 that his political ambitions would be seriously dented. In Lee's assessment, 'winning the election had to take precedence over everything else' (Lee 1989: 500). It has also been suggested that Haughey was seeking to present a new image in the late 1970s. Though he cultivated a 'a green image', perhaps Haughey was fearful that in the context of the 1970s too strong statements on penal affairs might place him in a similar category to the Prisoners' Union and Republican prisoner support groups, entities that were maybe somewhat too sensitive for Haughey in the early days of his leadership. In addition, in those early days there was relatively little heat in the debates about crime and punishment that might prove useful or troublesome for the new Taoiseach. Haughey approached any task with zeal. In the 1960s it was Justice, in the 1980s it was leading the country. Penal reform was inevitably only a small element of that, and not of great use to his ambitions to remain as leader of Fianna Fáil and Taoiseach.

An economic crisis and three general elections

Having assumed the position of Taoiseach, Haughey was faced with an economic crisis of huge proportions. In 1980 he made his famous television appearance in which he advised the country that it was living way beyond its means and that borrowing had reached enormous proportions in order to provide public services. These concerns were likely to be of graver import to the new government in these years than penal reform.

However, graver again were the fears about losing office, and despite the recognition by Haughey of the need to restrain public spending this did not happen. Lee (1989) argues that Haughey recognised that there would be serious political consequences if he cut public spending in the order that was necessary, so taxes were raised as a less unattractive option. The budget deficits continued.

Haughey lost the general election of 1981, his vote being drained by support for prisoners in the H–Blocks in Northern Ireland. Garret Fitzgerald of Fine Gael was installed as Taoiseach. This was not to be for long, with the government falling later in 1982. The coalition had introduced an emergency budget in July, which increased taxation and included the introduction of VAT on children's clothes and footwear, which led to the defeat of the budget.

The outcome of the subsequent election was finely balanced and both parties courted the Independent TD Tony Gregory with offers of investment in his Dublin constituency. Fianna Fáil's proposals were more attractive than those of Fine Gael and Gregory supported Haughey as Taoiseach. Again, this administration was short-lived with budget cuts leading to the support of some Independents and the Workers' Party being withdrawn. This led to the third general election in 18 months and was a time of immense political turmoil.

Financial restraint

Economic matters dominated all of these elections and the same can be said for political life generally in Ireland during these years (Ferriter 2004: 694). Fianna Fáil had called for fiscal restraint, but continued initially to increase public expenditure. When it came to prisons this was similarly apparent, with Fianna Fáil able to contemplate capital spending on penal expansion far more readily than Fine Gael. Under Fine Gael administrations spending cuts and financial restraint were in evidence. In opposition, Fianna Fáil could conveniently state that it was committed to increasing spending on prisons, when in reality the capital spending programme would have had to be reduced no matter who was in power and 'deflationary medicine' was required (Ó Gráda 1997: 31).

As had been the case so often in Ireland's past, it was the issue of finances that dictated much in prison policy during these years. It is likely that penal expansion would have occurred far earlier had the economic position of the state during the 1980s not been so dire. The budget of 1987, for example, has been described as so tight that it made 'Margaret Thatcher's efforts look gentle' and capital spending was cut sharply (Haughton 2008: 23).

However, this was tinged with the beginnings of a position that prison places were part of a broader concern about increased crime. What is striking is that opinion polls from the period do not show a high level of public concern about crime, even though recorded indictable crime was increasing (Kilcommins *et al.* 2004: 133). The reasons for this increase in crime are beyond the scope of this work, but it is likely that though financial circumstances for many were poor in the 1980s the overall increased prosperity, the raised expectations of the 1970s, the rapid growth of the capital city, Dublin, unemployment and, most particularly, the increase in drug use and addiction were factors in this climate. However, crime was very far down the list of important issues in polls conducted in 1981 and 1982 (Kilcommins *et al.* 2004: 134), far lower than the issues of unemployment and prices.

During this period prison policy was in crisis, but this did not translate into significant politicisation of the issue, or linking it to crime rates. Something of a change in this picture emerges in 1985 when Fianna Fáil, possibly getting ready for the next election, began to criticise the government on its record of fighting crime and suggesting that the lack of prison places was bringing the criminal justice system into contempt. However, even in that period, crime continued to be linked to social and economic deprivation in political discourse and the resolution of these broader ills was seen to be part of the way in which the crime problem could be tackled. The concern about drugs in prisons was a mirror of the broader anxiety about the prevalence of heroin, particularly in Dublin.

Crime: a political issue

This sense that crime was becoming something of a political issue may be grounded in the highly competitive electoral atmosphere of the mid-1980s. Haughey was nominated as Taoiseach in 1987 through the casting vote of the Ceann Comhairle, the Chairman of the Dáil. In 1987 crime was considered by 11 per cent of those surveyed by the *Irish Times* to be one of the main issues that parties should be concerned about (Kilcommins *et al.* 2004: 135). Though still very low, it is likely that Fianna Fáil was leaving nothing to chance, recognising that every vote counted.

However, upon assuming power, the Fianna Fáil government did not rush out to install a punitive penal agenda or plan major penal expansion. The financial situation of the state and the attempts to rein in public expenditure, supported by Fine Gael, which agreed not to oppose economic policy, were pragmatic factors militating against such an approach, operating to curtail any tendencies to trumpet penal expansion, which would have been very expensive. Cuts were made to the health and other budgets, with hospitals being closed (O'Hearn 2003). Spending on public health was below the European average in the 1980s. During this period Ireland suffered mass emigration, had tax rates of the order of 60 per cent, devalued its currency, the punt, in 1986 and unemployment rates were very high.

Prison planning and the civil service: a failure of imagination?

Lee describes the national mood in the 1980s as one of 'dithering despair' (Lee 1989: 507), a description that might be apposite for the prison system also. One of the other striking features of Irish prison policy during these years is the shambolic nature by which planning for the increased prison population took place. The Department seemed to be on a tour of disused buildings in an attempt to increase bed capacity. The rapidly increasing prison population posed difficulties for the Department, without question, but the lack of preparedness given that the prison population had been increasing for years is hard to fathom.

There was a more generalised lack of interest in long-term planning among the government. The amazing decision to cancel the census in 1976 was taken on the grounds of expense, yet the country was undergoing enormous change. The census resumed in 1979, but the impression of an administration happy to proceed without robust statistical evidence is remarkable.

Added to this, Lee makes the assertion that the civil service generally underwent a decline in the years 1975–85, becoming cautious and conservative after a more innovative period during the 1960s. In Lee's assessment, the system of promotions that depended on length of service acted to discourage innovation on the basis that challenging the *status quo* might threaten one's chances of promotion (Lee 1989). For Lee, this meant that a disproportionate number of ideas for change came from ministers, and without active ones departments could descend into torpor.

The beginnings of social inquiry

The increasing interest in penal affairs that had commenced in the previous decade was maintained, with a series of high-profile committees and commissions turning the spotlight on prison conditions. This was part of a continuing and often difficult period when it came to matters of sexual morality, and gradual opening up of Irish social life to investigation and a broader airing of social issues (Ferriter 2004: 702). The language of social inquiry and often unsophisticated attempts to speak about the links between crime and deprivation reflected this.

However, as was demonstrated years later, much remained under the carpet. Some of the murkier aspects of 1980s Ireland included scandals involving the tapping of journalists' phones, interference by ministers in policing (Keogh 2003: 387) and the allegations of the existence of a 'heavy gang' within the Gardaí that was prepared to use 'third-degree' methods in interrogations (O'Halpin 1999a: 328).

The language of prison policy, which attempted to demonstrate that things were under control, that conditions were acceptable in the circumstances, that progress was being made, reflected a wider and similar use of language in other areas of social life. This need to 'put up a good front' and its darker relation, cover-up, were still potent forces in Ireland during the 1980s, leading to a climate of denial and also a refusal to grasp or respond to realities.

While it would be unwise to draw too many parallels with an issue of great sensitivity and complexity in Ireland, this comfortableness with maintaining one picture on the surface while permitting the existence of another was similarly demonstrated in the debates around abortion during the 1980s. A pro-life amendment to the Constitution was passed in 1983, but high numbers of women continued to go to England in particular for abortions, with the legislature apparently reconciled to this solution (Keogh 2003: 362).

Prison policy in the 1980s

Within prison policy, the continued avowed commitment to rehabilitation showed that policy-makers did not wish to demonstrate harsh attitudes towards prisoners, but little was done to put such sentiments into practice. There wasn't the stomach for punitivism, but neither was there a determined commitment to deal with poor conditions and overcrowding.

Prison policy-making in Ireland during the 1980s was driven by a constant need to react to the pressures on space and attempts to expand the system within the confines of very restrictive financial circumstances. One of the legacies of the period is an emphasis on space as the main problem within the prison system and, correspondingly, the creation of the view that the provision of space is the main solution. The effects of the reification of this perspective were enduring, as the next chapter will relate.

8

THE 1990s
The crucial decade

Introduction

The 1990s was a time of change in Irish prison policy that was matched only
by the 1960s. However, a number of different impulses were apparent. Criticism
of the prison system became intense. The content of that criticism operated
on two planes. First, there were criticisms about the conditions in the prisons
and concern that those conditions were not humane. Second, there was a very
different criticism evident. This became more intense towards the middle of the
decade and related to the continued problems with overcrowding in the system.
This critique was put vociferously by Fianna Fáil's Justice spokesman when in
opposition, John O'Donoghue, but was also evident in the contributions of the
Progressive Democrat TDs Liz O'Donnell and Michael McDowell. As had been
threatened in the previous decade, penal expansion was linked to crime rates and
in a few politically feverish years between 1994 and 1997 debate on the prison
system in Ireland was more intense and sustained than at any time previously.

During this time the expansion of the prison system was contemplated. Each
fresh policy position on crime or Dáil statement seemed to add more projected
spaces. This took place in the context of unprecedented economic growth and a
tendency to invest large sums in eye-catching capital projects. The Pandora's box
that debate about increased prison places opened could not be closed again. As
with all periods, a penal ideology is hard to establish, with a great deal of pragmatic
penal politics being evident and preparation for elections evident. The trumpeted
penal expansion seemed to stall towards the end of the decade, indicating that
once in government, Ministers for Justice have tended to follow the Department
of Justice rather than lead it.

The early 1990s: familiar problems continue

During the early 1990s what was by now an old problem, increasing prisoner numbers and resultant overcrowding, continued to bedevil the prison system. The average daily prison population continued to rise. Very large numbers were on temporary release. In 1992 there were 2,782 prisoners on what was termed 'full' temporary release, while in 1993 this figure increased to 3,563 (Dáil Debates, vol 455, col 2218, 20 September 1995). Full temporary release meant that a prisoner was not liable to be recommitted if the conditions of that release were observed. 'Renewable' temporary release, which required prisoners to have the period of release renewed at intervals, was also resorted to very frequently.

Wheatfield prison opened at the end of the 1980s, but the promise that it would relieve pressure on the system during the 1990s was not fulfilled as the 320 extra spaces it brought were inadequate to deal with the increasing numbers being sent to custody. The plans for various developments such as a prison in Cork, a high security unit at Portaoise and a new women's prison were quietly dropped. The Fianna Fáil administration of the early 1990s took no steps to reintroduce the plan to invest more in prison building that it had mooted at the beginning of the 1980s.

The policies of making do remained and these seemed to address the most immediate crises of accommodation through the use of temporary release and permanent overcrowding. Reflecting the thinking of the time, a unit for prisoners with infectious diseases was planned within the Mountjoy complex (Dáil Debates, vol 409, col 18, 6 June 1991). It was also stated that all major reconstruction work would act to provide in-cell sanitation. The Minister for Justice in 1992, Pádraig Flynn, announced the reopening of the Curragh, which would hold 40 prisoners considered to be 'disruptive', re-establishing government policy to use that institution for such a purpose (Dáil Debates, vol 419, col 734, 7 May 1992).

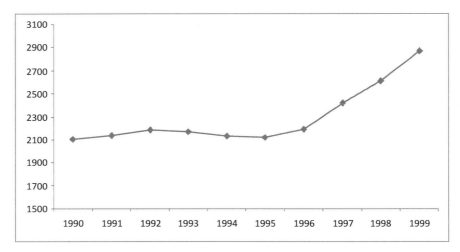

FIGURE 8.1 Average daily prison population 1990–99

Other features of the 1980s also endured. The concern about deaths in prison, and perhaps the political pressure occasioned thereby, led to the establishment of the Advisory Group on Prison Deaths. Its first report was published in 1991 and made 57 recommendations. Some related to basic improvements such as increased medical orderly cover, allowing for a 24-hour service to be provided, the removal of bars on windows, and the review of the way in which special observation lists were managed and the response time to cells. Other recommendations involved training for staff on suicide prevention mechanisms and an end to slopping out (AGPD 1991).

Getting to grips with prison policy?

After a prolonged period of delay, however, it appeared that some efforts were being made to get to grips with the problem. This sense of a Department no longer reeling from the day-to-day pressure of prison overcrowding and temporary release decisions is reflected in its work on broader prison policy. In 1992 Minister Flynn announced at the annual conference of the Prison Officers' Association that it was his 'intention to draw up a comprehensive document that will update the overall aims and objectives of the prison system and set out a strategy to meet them' (Dáil Debates, vol 419, col 735, 7 May 1992).

This announcement appeared to come somewhat out of the blue. It seems that having managed to achieve some semblance of organised chaos within penal administration, the Department of Justice wished to take stock and attempt to plan a more long-term future for the penal system. Though Flynn declared that it was his intention to draw up the document, it also seems likely that the Department of Justice had been planning this change of approach, and after the departure of Ray Burke, who had held the portfolios of both Justice and Communications for a period, had found a Minister more amenable to taking an interest in such an announcement.

Flynn assumed office in February 1992 and this announcement was made at the end of April of that year. Perhaps this was the case of another new Minister eager to show an energetic side in the early stages of a new portfolio. Again, Flynn stated: 'I believe I am the first Minister who has taken a personal interest in this for quite some time' (Dáil Debates, vol 420, col 923, 27 May 1992). A major change in sentiment appeared with Flynn stating: 'I do not intend to tinker with individual problems in a vacuum. I am preparing the groundwork for a planned and coordinated approach to getting it right on prison reform. It will not happen overnight. We are talking about developing a considered policy' (Dáil Debates, vol 420, col 923, 27 May 1992).

The Management of Offenders strategy document

This strategy document turned out to be *The Management of Offenders: A Five Year Plan*. It was published in 1994 and is associated with Máire Geoghegan-

Quinn, who was the Minister for Justice, again from the Fianna Fáil party. This document was produced in a relatively short period of time. The reason why it was introduced then is a matter of some uncertainty. The Department of Justice still had the Whitaker Report and many of its recommendations remained valid. There are a number of possibilities.

First, and pragmatically, the numbers in the prison system had continued to increase significantly after the publication of Whitaker. Second, it may be that without a sense of departmental ownership over plans and recommendations any such change was unlikely to succeed. In addition, there seems to have been a significant change in thinking and approach within the Department, and for the first time in three decades a commitment to long-term strategising was present. 1994 was also a time in which there appeared to be hopes for lasting peace in Northern Ireland and the Department was less preoccupied with subversive activity. Finally, there was probably a simple realisation that the prison system could not be allowed to continue as it had during the previous decade.

The document was seminal in the sense that it was the first deliberate official plan of any kind for the prison system, which was designed to plan for the following five years. The document was a frank one and in truth brave, given the historic aversion to penal planning. It was also filled with language that suggested a tentative, hesitant and not terribly confident approach among policy-makers.

In her introduction, Geoghegan-Quinn stated the purpose of the document was to outline the difficulties facing the prison system and to set out policies and plans for the years ahead. In addition, the document was framed as providing an indication of where the implementation of the Whitaker Report stood. It is interesting that the Minister felt the need to link the document to Whitaker. It indicates, perhaps, that the criticisms of the lack of implementation of the report had hit home within the Department and the pressure of criticism forced the first significant official statement on the status of Whitaker since its publication.

The frankness of the document is equally striking when it states that though the main problem facing the system was overcrowding, it was not the only one. Others included:

> The absence of clear aims and objectives, inadequately planned arrangements for release of offenders, excessive resort to unsupervised temporary release, various shortcomings in support services (medical, welfare, psychological, education, work/training, aftercare) and less than satisfactory arrangements for dealing with special problems such as drug abuse and the care and management of sex offenders.
>
> *(Department of Justice 1994: 7)*

Some of the most interesting recommendations include the provision of a relatively modest 210 extra prison places, including 60 in a purpose-built facility for women and, crucially, ensuring that the prison population would not drift at about the 2,200–2,300 level. Other specific measures were the provision of in-cell sanitation in Mountjoy, Portlaoise and Limerick, the establishment of a 'positive sentence management' committee in each institution, new prison rules, the creation of an Inspector of Prisons post, increased provision for the treatment of sex offenders and expanded drug-free prison unit spaces. Strategic objectives for the Department as well as local prison management were established. Interestingly, for the Department, the establishment of an adequate research resource was considered an aim (Department of Justice 1994).

Given what had gone before and the *ad hoc* and chaotic attempts to increase prison space the analysis in the plan is somewhat remarkable. As matters then stood, an increase of 825 spaces was needed to cope with present demand, whatever the future growth. However, the plan shared the doubts expressed in the Whitaker Report of the potential of imprisonment to act as a deterrent or a mechanism of reform or rehabilitation, and the plan advocated 'caution' in calling for continued expansion of the numbers held in custody as a response to the growth in crime and considered modest expansion and supervised release sensible options to ensure the number of offenders in custody is 'not allowed to expand excessively' (Department of Justice 1994). The much lower figure of 210 extra spaces was therefore arrived at, and the plan announced that approval for that number of spaces had been secured. These were planned to take the form of a new women's prison and the conversion of the former St Patrick's Hospital, Castlerea, County Roscommon in the west of Ireland.

The immediate political reaction to the document was muted, with little discussion of it taking place in the Oireachtas. This makes it all the more likely that the document was very much the product of departmental thinking, with no major impetus coming from a politician to call for its introduction. However, it does seem that Geoghegan-Quinn had a direct role in the decision to replace the very outdated stock for women prisoners.

A committee was established to advise her on the building of a new women's prison in early 1994. This committee was chaired by the Assistant Secretary of the Department of Justice with responsibility for prisons, and the chairwoman of the Council for the Status of Women and the chief executive of the Employment Equality Agency were also appointed. It is likely that the development of campaigning for women's rights had some impact on these decisions also.

Another great 'what if' for Irish prison policy is what would have happened if there had not been a political storm in the year in which *The Management of Offenders* was published. On the question of female prisoners at any rate, there seemed to be a ministerial commitment to implementing its proposals and a desire for speedy action. However, the Fianna Fáil–Labour coalition then in power came to an end after a number of scandals, including the manner of the prosecution of Fr Brendan Smyth for offences of child sexual abuse. There was no general election. Instead, the Labour Party left the coalition and formed a new government with Fine Gael and Democratic Left.

The implementation of *The Management of Offenders* fell to the new Minister for Justice, Nora Owen of the Fine Gael party. It might be considered that the common denominator of Labour, with the presence of Michael D. Higgins, who had sat on the MacBride Commission a decade previously, would have ensured that the transition to a new form of coalition would not hinder the progress of the plan's implementation. However, it seems that the plan, though probably an idea and product of the thinking of the Department of Justice, had its greatest associations with the Fianna Fáil ministers who had overseen its introduction and publication.

Máire Geoghegan-Quinn retired from politics in 1997. Pádraig Flynn left to become a European Commissioner in 1993. The Secretary General of the Department of Justice, Joseph Brosnan, left at the same time, continuing to work with Flynn. He had been in the position for just under two years, during which time *The Management of Offenders* had been drafted. The departure of them all probably acted to stall progress.

Nora Owen does not appear to have given her own views on the plan in her early days in office, although in 1995 she announced that she was proceeding with plans to provide a prison at Castlerea and a women's prison, both proposals put forward in *The Management of Offenders*.

However, it seems that internal tensions between the coalition partners and the recurring theme of finances were creating hurdles for the implementation of these plans. It is clear that there was a marked reluctance to proceed with the building of Castlerea after the change in the composition of the government. A perimeter wall had already been built but in 1995 Owen affirmed that she had established an interdepartmental committee to examine the Castlerea project and that she was also considering the additional use of non-custodial sanctions to deal with the pressure on space and that the release of prisoners as part of the peace process would also free up space (Dáil Debates, vol 456, col 577, 3 October 1995). The building of Castlerea had been officially deferred. It seemed that, as O'Donnell and O'Sullivan put it, *The Management of Offenders* had been 'shelved' (O'Donnell and O'Sullivan 2001: 31).

Political focus and debate on prison issues

Without access to the records of Cabinet discussions it is difficult to substantiate the claims of the opposition, and specifically Fianna Fáil's new spokesman on Justice, John O'Donoghue, that the decision on Castlerea was not that of the Minister for Justice but was, in fact, a decision of the Minister for Finance, the Labour leader Ruairí Quinn, taken when Owen was not present (Dáil Debates, vol 474, col 1395, 12 February 1997). It is likely that financial pressures were involved, but it may also be the case that there were objections on the basis that penal expansion was undesirable. Kathleen Lynch, for example, emphasised rehabilitation and social issues in debates about crime (Dáil Debates, vol 474, col 261, 12 February 1997). Whatever about the truth of this, such a perception was used by the Progressive Democrats in particular to indicate that a 'left-wing' approach to crime was in the ascendancy and it was soft on crime.

The opposition became very exercised about the plans for Castlerea. Fianna Fáil, probably smarting after the departure of Labour from government, sought to expose possible cracks in the coalition. The Progressive Democrats TDs were also very critical of the decision, highlighting the continued high numbers of individuals on temporary release.

This debate generated political heat on prison issues in a way that had not been seen in Ireland before. In 1994, when Fianna Fáil was still in office, Fine Gael put a motion before the Oireachtas stating that in view of the increasing number of armed robberies, crimes committed on bail and the 'revolving door' system that 'passes for a penal system' (Dáil Debates, vol 443, col 186, 24 May 1994), the government should restore law and order. While this language was dramatic, almost in the same breath the TD putting down the motion, Gay Mitchell, stated that the party's members did not consider themselves part of the 'hang 'em and flog 'em' brigade and that increasing prison spaces was not necessarily the answer (Dáil Debates, vol 443, col 196, 24 May 1994).

Notably, in the same year the Progressive Democrats also focused attention on the prison system. The Progressive Democrats had been founded during the 1980s by Dessie O'Malley who had been expelled from the Fianna Fáil party and a number of others, including Michael McDowell, then a barrister and later Attorney General and later again Minister for Justice. Known for their policies of low taxation and economic and social liberalism (Collins 2005) it appears that individual members of the party, particularly O'Donnell and McDowell, had personal interests in the criminal justice system and a strident manner of advocating reform.

In 1994 O'Donnell introduced a private member's bill called the Criminal Justice Bill. She argued: 'My generation grew up with a liberal approach to crime. However, as one encounters crime, those liberal views are quickly diminished' (Dáil Debates, vol 443, col 1946, 15 June 1994). In particular, change to the law on bail so that individuals could be refused bail if they were considered likely to commit an offence on bail was proposed. As well as this, a wide variety of archaic procedural issues such as guilty but insane verdicts were put forward. It is likely that McDowell, who appears to have had a crusading attitude to law and court reform, was very closely involved in the drafting of the bill. On the question of prisons, concern was expressed about the presence of persons with psychiatric illnesses in prison and the 'scandal' of housing remand prisoners with convicted prisoners. Increased prison spaces were also advocated, though no specific details were given.

However, it was after the entry of Nora Owen into the position of Minister for Justice that the greatest political attention on the prison system developed. The discourse about the prison system now revolved almost exclusively around space. It had done so for many years, but the tone and persistence of the opposition in its critique of the government were notable. The temporary release system was criticised with one Fianna Fáil T.D. describing the prison system has having a greater turnover than Dunnes Stores, a high-profile chain of shops (Dáil Debates, vol 459, col 1812, 29 November 1995).

Attacks on elderly people also gave rise to calls for increased prison spaces on the basis that without them individuals would be more likely to commit crime (Dáil Debates, vol 459, col 1309, 12 December 1995). The Minister did not respond in kind, instead appearing to favour an approach of consultation and commissioning reports on crime. This kind of deliberative response was probably a tactical error in the face of the intensity of criticism she was experiencing as it allowed the opposition to cast her as dithering and unresponsive.

While prison policy was attacked regularly, it is true to say that a great deal of the critique was aimed squarely and directly at the Minister and her competence. She was cast as indecisive, described as the Minister for committees or charters (Dáil Debates, vol 452, col, 1457, 3 May 1995).

Electoral politics, concern about conditions and penal expansion

The influence of John O'Donoghue

John O'Donoghue, Fianna Fáil's spokesperson for Justice, was the author of statements about crime and punishment that had never been seen before and, largely, have not been seen since in Ireland. Much of what was said glossed over the nuance and complexity of the crime issue in Ireland and the analysis of prison places cannot be said to have been grounded in in-depth study of punishment or indeed prison population projections. But the criticism of the lack of space in the prison system and the direct links with what was portrayed as an out-of-control crime problem was relentless and put in colourful language, with a tone that seems inexhaustible in its outrage.

Proposing changes to the bail laws, a perennial source of political heat, he described an Ireland that since 1994 had been 'all but devastated by wave after wave of remorseless crime' (Dáil Debates, vol 452, col 653, 3 May 1995), with depravity 'commonplace' in a 'tide of criminal terror' that had 'turned many of our streets into fearsome incubators of evil'. The choice of time-frame was deliberate given the recent departure of Fianna Fáil from office.

Numerous questions were tabled by O'Donoghue and O'Donnell about early release, particularly early release for prisoners who had been convicted of armed robbery and burglary (Dáil Debates, vol 460, col 135, 23 January 1996). The prison system was an easy target given the high numbers on temporary release and the overcrowded prison system.

It also appeared that each time a high-profile crime occurred in Ireland it was discussed in the Dáil and was portrayed as yet another example of an ineffectual government and, particularly, Minister.

The demands of the Progressive Democrats

Though John O'Donoghue has stolen the criminological headlines for his positions on crime and punishment, he was not alone in focusing on crime and punishment in 1995–96. The Progressive Democrats were similarly persistent when it came to these issues. However, their stance was somewhat more considered and had greater depth. While there were calls to curtail the right to silence and plans to increase prison numbers, there were also demands to establish a statutory prison service. Michael McDowell again seemed particularly interested in this issue, and that of the creation of a prison inspectorate as well as an independent review body for sentences. It is clear that McDowell regarded much in the prison system as unaccountable (Dáil Debates, vol 430, col 1714, 13 May 1993).

In addition, the issue of criminal justice was positioned by the Progressive Democrats as one of political ideology. Making regular attacks on 'left-wing' ideas and a 'left-wing administration', Michael McDowell in particular analysed the prison issue in these terms. Liz O'Donnell also criticised a lack of prison building as being an example of a 'woolly-minded preoccupation that all criminals are ultimately victims' (Dáil Debates, vol 474, col 1092, 11 February 1997).

However, McDowell also showed an understanding and level of analysis of the prison system without parallel in the Oireachtas at the time. His concerns about drug use, about remission and space were all prescient in light of the fact that he was later to become Minister for Justice and in a position to put his obviously many and strongly held views into practice. Another idea was to use public-private partnerships, though that term was not used at the time, whereby private entities would build prisons and the state would then lease them back. Into this mix was the desire to rid the prison system of 'Victorian hell-holes' and to replace them with modern establishments (Dáil Debates, vol 474, col 1101, 11 February 1997).

The events of summer 1996

The pressure on the Minister for Justice regarding the prison system must have become almost intolerable in the aftermath of the killings of Veronica Guerin, an investigative journalist who explored the drug trade in Ireland, and Detective Garda Jerry McCabe. The level of outrage about these crimes in the media and within the houses of the Oireachtas was intense and has been well documented elsewhere (Kilcommins et al. 2004; O'Donnell and O'Sullivan 2003). It has been described as a 'textbook case of moral panic' (Kilcommins et al. 2004: 137). This took place, furthermore, in an environment that was increasingly interested in prison affairs, resulting in a documentary about Mountjoy being broadcast on RTÉ. Media interest in crime was also at a very high level (O'Brien 2007).

It is certainly the case that these deaths catalysed legislative action on crime. However, such concern and a raised political temperature had been apparent ever since the Rainbow Coalition government had entered power. The debates around these crimes did not come out of the blue; it is more accurate to say that the tensions and outrage of the previous 18 months crystallised around these events. Suddenly, all the bills that Fianna Fáil had proposed, including plans to introduce a system of civil forfeiture for the proceeds of crime and changes to the bail laws, took on a renewed impetus. In addition, expanded powers of detention of suspects in cases of drug trafficking and related offences were introduced in the Criminal Justice (Drug Trafficking) Act 1996.

Veronica Guerin was shot dead in June 1996. By July the government announced an 'accelerated prison building programme'. The fiscal restraint and the opposition to prison building gave way in the face of such intense political and media pressure. Given the nature of the criticism of the Minister for Justice, the government could not afford to be seen to have no response to these crises or to prevaricate.

The building of Castlerea was back on. It is also of note that the construction of Castlerea prison was tied very closely to concerns that the government had been neglecting rural development after the 'Save the West' campaign was inaugurated in the same year. A total of 68 places were planned for the Curragh prison, an expansion of Limerick was envisaged and, most strikingly, a tender was issued for the building of a remand centre that was to become Cloverhill prison. It would take the inevitably increased numbers of people refused bail by the courts after the planned changes to the bail laws came into effect. It was now planned to increase prison spaces, not by 210 as envisaged by *The Management of Offenders*, but by 800.

Further controversy and criticism

Another departmental discussion document, *Tackling Crime*, appeared in 1997. While this highlighted matters such as community prevention, it also dropped any reference to a limit on the number of prison spaces considered necessary and stated that an extra 840 cells were required. Kilcommins *et al.* indicate that a Cabinet Minister at the time described this new figure as having been come up with 'on the back of the envelope' (Kilcommins *et al.* 2004: 238).

It can only have been so. Another remarkable feature of Irish prison policy during the 1990s is that no annual reports on the prison system for the years 1994 to 1998 were published until 1999. This is extraordinary given that fundamentally important decisions about prison policy were made during these years. The absence of the collection of this data has been attributed to pressure on staff time (Dáil Debates, vol 511, col 472, 23 November 1999). This relatively benign phrase indicates a deeper malaise within the Department of Justice during this period.

There was a further political controversy when it emerged that a judge had been delisted from the Special Criminal Court but had not been informed of this decision and so continued to preside over cases in that court. This meant that a number of those convicted by courts on which he sat had to be released. An investigation into the incident revealed that there had been a serious breakdown of communications within the Department and that clerical processes left much to be desired. The pressures on staff and poor organisational structures came in for criticism in that report (Dáil Debates, vol 471, col 1575, 21 November 1996).

There can have been little time for prison population projections and the documents that did emerge, such as *Tackling Crime*, are perhaps remarkable for their approach in such circumstances. These criticisms would have also made the case for a body other than the Department of Justice to run the prison system more pressing.

The outcome of 1996 was a distinctive change in discourse about penal affairs, which was now shared by government and opposition. While there were immediate consequences in terms of planned prison building, what was probably more consequential in the long term was the now unquestioned public position among the majority of penal policy-makers that increased prison spaces offered a solution to the problems of crime and that to resist penal expansion was politically risky. Minister Owen, who had previously spoken of alternatives to crime as a response to pressures on accommodation, was now talking about prison building as a way of dealing with crime (Dáil Debates, vol 470, col 122, 15 October 1996). In 1997 she stated: 'the record of this Government will show that we have launched upon the greatest prison building programme since the foundation of the State' (Dáil Debates, vol 474, col 1106, 11 February 1997).

In February 1997 the Progressive Democrats upped the stakes again when the party introduced a Prisons Bill which proposed, *inter alia*, to increase the number of prison places by 50 per cent and to set up a review group of sentences to make decisions on temporary release.

Further weight was added to Minister Owen's woes when prison officers were taken hostage in Mountjoy in 1997. After that, the Prison Officers' Association lobbied for a secure unit, which was agreed, but in fact never used as intended (O'Donnell 2005: 101–2). All of this political pressure, however, acted to ensure that there could be no further opportunities given to the opposition to argue that the Minister was not in charge of the prison system.

The general election of 1997

The events of 1996 were all the more intense given that a general election was approaching. The 1997 election saw the issue of law and order being employed in a way that it had not been since 1932. It was unlikely that John O'Donoghue would fail to capitalise on the progress he had made when it looked like he had Minister Owen on the run, and he linked prison building, and the lack thereof, to his view that the Rainbow Coalition would lose the election. He stated in the Dáil that the epitaph of the coalition would be 'By a Lonely Prison Wall', in reference to the famous ballad, 'The Fields of Athenry', and argued that the cancellation of Castlerea prison sealed the government's political fate as it had led to 1995 becoming 'the year of the criminal' (Dáil Debates, vol 474, col 1112, 12 February 1997).

O'Donoghue hammered home his points, which revolved around prison space. Ivor Callely, another Fianna Fáil T.D., took a related but different approach. Callely had asked a series of questions of the Minister for Justice regarding the provision of facilities and items such as magazines to prisoners. This was a prelude to his attacks on the government for providing 'recreational facilities ... to prisoners but not to law abiding citizens'. Swimming lessons, outdoor pursuits and telephone calls were indications of something 'seriously wrong with our prison system' (Dáil Debates, vol 475, col 76, 18 February 1997).

Though Fianna Fáil and the Progressive Democrats could be expected to fight the election on, among other things, law and order, in fact all the political parties dedicated significant amounts of space in their manifestos to these matters (Marsh and Sinnott 1999), reflecting the fact that politicians during these years felt that they could not afford to avoid the issue. Fianna Fáil spoke of 'zero tolerance' in striking terms. In one piece of electoral literature, under a picture of leader Bertie Ahern, considered to be a major electoral asset, ran the statement: 'Crime is out of control in our towns, cities and countryside. Innocent citizens are being assaulted, their homes and property vandalised and burgled. Children are being corrupted by drugs and pornography ... Fianna Fáil has led the fight against crime from the opposition benches.'

Part of the strategy proposed was to 'immediately set about' providing 2,000 extra prison places, plus whatever many more were needed to ensure people served their sentence fully.

An opinion poll in March 1997 found that 41 per cent of those surveyed considered that crime and law and order should be one of the main issues on which the parties fought the election (cited in Kilcommins et al. 2004 136). It is therefore remarkable that crime seems to have had a comparatively negligible effect on the result. Fianna Fáil secured enough seats to enter coalition with the Progressive Democrats but Fianna Fáil gained less than 1 per cent of an increase in its vote and the Progressive Democrats lost several TDs, including Michael McDowell, indicating that for his constituents at least law and order was not a vote-getter.

Indeed, the results of the 1997 election show that crime had a very circumscribed effect on voter's choices. Its main impact was to reduce substantially the relative odds of voting Labour in comparison to voting Fianna Fáil, but affected none of the other parties. The issues that had the most significant bearing on the election were Northern Ireland, honesty in politics, taxation and a dash of left–right ideology (Marsh and Sinnott 1999).

The sense that the public were not as inflamed about crime as their politicians is further enhanced by the low turnout for the constitutional referendum to amend the laws on bail in 1996 (Kilcommins et al. 2004: 138). It may be that the 1997 general election was a classic case of politicians leading public opinion while proclaiming to follow it.

This being so, the new parties of government, Fianna Fáil and the Progressive Democrats, negotiated a programme for government called *An Action Programme for the New Millennium*. This document continued with the language of zero tolerance but appeared to owe a significant debt to the UK's New Labour approach of the time, stating that crime would be tackled through tough measures but also addressing the factors that contributed to crime, economic deprivation and social exclusion.

With regard to crime the key priorities were deemed to be an increase in the strength of the Gardaí, an independent prisons authority and inspectorate, along with an extra 1,000 prison places in the first two years of government.

The new government's plans for expansion

The effect of the referendum on bail

Given the centrality of bail and its perceived deficits in the mid-1990s it is important to give a brief analysis of how this issue came to be intertwined with prison policy and the call for increased prison spaces. The history of attempts to alter the bail laws would reward sustained assessment in their own right.

It would be wholly incorrect to say that the bail laws were the subject of criticism and plans for change for the first time in 1996. As has already been seen, as far back as 1967 the then Fianna Fáil government wanted to bring in legislation to overrule the *O'Callaghan* decision which prevented the possible commission of an offence while on bail as a ground for refusing bail. The issue cropped up during the 1970s and 1980s, and both Fianna Fáil and Fine Gael Justice Ministers expressed the desire to do what the referendum of 1996 allowed and there were proposals to introduce legislation to that effect. It is clear that it was the advice and trenchant objection of successive Attorneys General (the most senior law officer in the state) to any such proposals that ensured that such a change did not happen earlier in Irish history (JUS 2008/156/9).

The eventual clearing of the way for such a change in the law had a major impact on the need for custodial accommodation. A remand prison became immediately necessary and high numbers of remand prisoners continue to be a feature of the Irish prison population today.

Minister O'Donoghue

From the manner of his contributions in the Dáil it might have been expected that the new Justice Minister John O'Donoghue would rush to sanction several hundred new prison places and that tenders would be published for a rash of penal construction. This did not happen. Almost six months after his accession to office O'Donoghue announced again the construction of a special unit in Portlaoise designed to deal with 'disruptive' prisoners (Dáil Debates, vol 484, col 116, 3 December 1997) but no similar units were planned.

A year after entering office the Minister was asked to account for the progress made on providing the promised extra prison places. His response was to declare himself pleased that the commitment would be met and cited the building of Castlerea, the remand prison at Cloverhill, the new female prison at Mountjoy and the construction of an extra 400 places at Portlaoise, which eventually was named the Midlands prison. This was calculated to a total amount of 1,092 prison places. However, what was not admitted, nor was it picked up on in any meaningful way by the opposition, was that all of these projects, with the exception of the Portlaoise plan, had been sanctioned by previous administrations. The impression was that there would be an extra 1,000 places on top of those already planned, not the conclusion of existing plans.

In addition, statements by John O'Donoghue while Minister were generally of a very different character from those while in opposition. It seems reasonable to suggest that on assuming ministerial office his officials put something of a dampener on the Minister's tendencies, or else that the practical difficulties of managing the prison system became more apparent and the problems were viewed as being more complex than they had been presented previously. In 1999 Minister O'Donoghue was asked about his efforts to reduce reoffending. His response referred to work and training programmes, treatment for drug addicts, therapeutic interventions for those convicted of sexual crime and alternatives to violence projects (Dáil Debates, vol 499, col 1504, 4 February 1999). This statement, in the form of a written answer to a parliamentary question, is likely to have been written entirely by Department of Justice officials.

2,000 extra places?

The plan for an increase to 515 spaces at the Midlands prison was the only project that O'Donoghue could claim as his own initiative. This is not to underplay the significant expansion of the prison system that it entailed, but it was still much less than that promised. The Minister's promises came back to haunt him to some degree in that there was pressure to ensure that the remand prison at Cloverhill was opened as quickly as possible to fulfil part of the planned increase in prison capacity. The prison was officially opened on 1 June 1999 but a variety of construction problems and security concerns meant that there were only 74 prisoners detained in it by the following February (Dáil Debates, vol 514, col 777, 15 February 2000). Indeed, the commencement of the Bail Act 1997 which followed the referendum on bail was delayed pending the opening of Cloverhill as the prison system would otherwise be placed under even graver pressure.

There were some uncomfortable reminders for the Minister about these promises, with Brendan Howlin of the Labour Party moving a motion of no confidence in him and arguing that the prison-building programme was the 'last residue of his discredited zero tolerance philosophy' (Dáil Debates, vol 511, col 532, 23 November 1999).

On the basis of these calculations, the government's promise to add an additional 1,000 places to the prison system may have been eye-catching, but it involved a large degree of taking the credit for plans already in place and counting prison openings as additional places it had provided. The Dóchas Centre, a prison for women beside Mountjoy, opened in 1999 but had been planned for a number of years before that. The Midlands prison was not opened until 2000, meaning that the plan for 1,000 prison spaces in two years had failed.

Space as the only consideration

The dominance of the discussion about space in the prison system had another effect on prison policy. As well as establishing a pattern that space was the pre-eminent consideration in prison policy, it also acted to deflect attention and resources from other penal issues that could have been remedied quite quickly. The Prison Rules of 1947, for instance, were still in place and out of date but another decade was to pass before new ones were finally brought into law, even though fresh rules had been drafted in 1994. The inspectorate of prisons, also planned for in the 1990s, did not receive an official appointment until 2002. Most particularly, the poor prison conditions that had, by now, been a feature of the Irish prison system for two decades, remained and were documented in numerous reports, in particular of the Mountjoy Prison Visiting Committee and the Committee for the Prevention of Torture after its visits in 1994 and 1998.

Prison policy at the beginning of the Celtic Tiger era

Ireland during the 1990s was beginning to experience profound change. The decade heralded a time of economic growth that has come to be known as the 'Celtic Tiger era' in reference to the tiger economies of Asia. The reasons for this growth are varied and have been attributed to the policies of spending cutbacks in the 1980s, wage restraint, increased competitiveness, the participation of women in the workforce and significant levels of foreign direct investment from US multinationals in particular (Ó Gráda 1997). Access to the European single market was also a factor. Whatever the reasons, the consequences are, at this remove, breathtaking.

GNP rose rapidly between 1995 and 2000, increasing by 11 per cent in one year (O'Hearn 2003). Public debt fell significantly. Ireland, for so long a poor country, was now experiencing prosperity, and gloom gave way to self-confidence 'bordering on euphoria' (Ó Gráda 1997: 33). Unemployment dropped dramatically (Haughton 2008). Life expectancy and standards of living increased. Absolute poverty declined, but income inequality remained stubbornly persistent. Economic policies of low taxation prevailed, though public spending, fuelled by the huge increases in revenue coming into the Exchequer, did go up. Spending on health and social welfare increased, but large numbers of Irish residents continued to subscribe to private healthcare schemes.

Another radical change was a demographic one. Immigration was a novel feature of Irish life and the numbers entering the country to apply for asylum in the early 1990s overwhelmed the limited administrative resources to deal with their claims. Other migrants were needed to provide the labour necessary to keep pace with demand.

The rate of social and economic change was profound. It is tempting to read prison policy as a cipher for these changes, to consider penal expansion as a way in which the rapidly changing state acted out its insecurities about the new

Ireland being created – an increasingly prosperous, urban and secularised nation, one that was harsh to those who had failed in an environment where success seemed to be easier than before. Such explanations are alluring, but are likely to be overstated. First, Ireland of the 1990s was a confident rather than insecure nation. Second, though there was a flare of ideological division in Irish politics during the 1990s, particularly when it came to taxation, the main political parties continued to dominate and the by now clichéd pragmatism in politics (after all, increased prosperity was unlikely to lead to electoral failure) was not replaced. The lack of a lasting ideological agenda when it came to crime is reflected in the dissipation of public concern after 1997 (Kilcommins *et al.* 2004: 139).

However, above all of these there are more practical and perhaps prosaic explanations for the character of Irish prison policy during the 1990s, which lie in the process of policy formation. First, there was an undeniable pressure on space and the political failures to deal with this in previous decades left an administrative and policy headache for the governments of the 1990s. This was added to by increasing numbers of individuals being convicted of drug offences and sexual offences, again two hangovers from the previous decade if not decades, for which those in the 1990s had to pick up the tab. Continued prevarication could not continue.

Second, signs of a considered response indicated that the Department of Justice had a plan that did not foresee significant penal expansion. However, those plans were undone by 'events', in this case the fall of the Fianna Fáil–Labour coalition and a period of opposition for Fianna Fáil along with the Progressive Democrats (PDs). The prison system and its history of problems was a major possible source of embarrassment and controversy for a Minister for Justice and this was exploited at every possible opportunity by opposition spokespeople seeking electoral success, though from the PDs there was also an indication of a concern about prison conditions. Financial restraint was less necessary in the late 1990s than at any other time in the state's history and prison building could be contemplated. Once promises were made, rowing back on them would be difficult, especially when the stakes regarding public safety had been presented as being so high. However, departmental impulses acted to neutralise the possible effects of political hyperbole and the bulwark of departmental caution and inertia acted to slow any further expansionary tendencies. The relationship between Minister and Department was once again influential on the creation of penal change.

John O'Donoghue, in his resignation speech from the position of Ceann Comhairle in 2009, reflected on very different circumstances thus: 'transient political benefit will never be a compensation for long-term political damage' (*Irish Times*, 13 October 2009). Inadvertently, the man most associated with penal change during the 1990s had perhaps written its most apposite epitaph.

9

PRISON POLICY SINCE 2000 AND BEYOND

Introduction

As prison policy moved into a new millennium, penal expansion became a clear aim. This was perhaps an inevitable consequence of the rhetoric and promises of the mid to late 1990s and it is likely that a concern to 'save face' by ensuring that those planned spaces were delivered drove this approach to some degree. In addition, the continued simple pressure on accommodation and the increasing numbers within the prison system created its own internal drivers.

Initially, it seemed that 700 or so places were being planned for, which would also account for a new prison for young people. However, a radical increase was envisaged during the decade. The name Thornton Hall has come to symbolise prison policy during this decade. This, the name of a site in north County Dublin on which a 2,200-space prison was planned to be built, has developed a variety of meanings.

To the Irish Prison Service and Department of Justice it is a solution, a way to ensure that all of the difficulties about space would be eradicated for the foreseeable future. To some of its critics it was too large, too far away from centres of population and represented a worrying trend towards planned penal expansion on a large scale. More recently, it has been cast as a 'penal white elephant' (*Irish Times*, 27 July 2010). After a long period of uncertainty, in July 2010 it was announced that Thornton Hall would be built, though with 400 rather than 2,200 places, which would accommodate 700 prisoners.

This was the first time that doubling up became part of official policy rather than being cast as an unfortunate consequence of overcrowded prisons. After a period when it didn't seem to matter, cost reappeared as a critical driving force in penal planning. This was very much in keeping with the development of Ireland generally during these years, which went from a thrusting, high-spending place to one where the financial future looked much less certain and economic woes returned to dominate political and social life.

As had happened on occasions in the past, another significant influence on the penal scene in this decade was Michael McDowell, who became Minister for Justice in 2002 and whose legacy looms large across the criminal justice system.

This chapter assesses some of the key developments in this decade and notes a number of areas of concern within Irish prison policy.

Continued plans for penal expansion

John O'Donoghue continued as Minister for Justice throughout the life of the Fianna Fáil-Progressive Democrat coalition, until the election of 2002. Having cast the prison building that had occurred or was continuing as the fulfilment of the promise to add 1,000 prison places before 1999, further expansion was also contemplated. Despite the addition of extra space, most prisons were still operating at or close to their bed capacity (which was calculated on the basis of multiple occupancy in single cells) and well above their original design capacity, with Mountjoy and Cork particularly bad in this regard. In mid-2000 O'Donoghue announced that he had received government approval for 700 extra spaces, which would 'transform the Irish prison system beyond all recognition' (Dáil Debates, vol 520, col 846, 1 June 2000). However, nothing else was done for some time.

The somewhat frenetic tone of criminal justice debates also seemed to recede. The much trumpeted, and ridiculed, zero tolerance plans were no longer as visible as previously and the content of them underwent a radical shift. O'Donoghue was at pains to point out that zero tolerance meant tackling the roots of crime as much as cracking down.

However, what remained constant was the contention that increased prison space was a firm plank of the government's approach to crime. This unsophisticated connection between crime rates and prison building was used regularly as an indication of the success of zero tolerance. There was something of a return to the heated days of 1997 during another election year of 2002. In this case, the opposition attacked the government on its track record in the area of crime.

This tendency to react to political crises by making announcements about increased penal capacity was again witnessed during 2002. In that year two Gardaí were killed after their car was in collision with a car that had been stolen by teenage joyriders. The government announced that a new institution would be opened to deal with this crisis, but it was never so used (O'Donnell 2005).

The McDowell factor

It is clear that much in Irish prison and criminal justice policy during the 2000s was driven by the efforts of the Minister for Justice during the period 2002–07. Michael McDowell, re-elected in 2002, had already enjoyed considerable success by the time he came to be appointed as Minister, having served as Attorney

General and enjoying a busy practice at the Bar as well as previous terms in the Dáil. His contributions during those previous terms indicated that he had his own vision for penal change, as well as the energy, ambition and capacity to do so. It was a matter of chance and his varying electoral fortunes that meant that he did not assume office earlier and what might have happened had he been Minister in the 1990s can now only be guessed at.

McDowell's energy and verve bears comparison with the work of Charles Haughey during the 1960s. Though the foci and principles were different, the similarity in terms of commitment, a desire to cut through bureaucratic constraints and a personal zeal is striking. This energetic Minister published 35 bills during his time in office (five years) and 25 of these were passed, representing a quarter of the legislative programme for the whole government (Collins 2005). Though Justice would be likely to produce a large volume of legislation, this is nonetheless striking. McDowell was responsible for introducing legislation for the reform of An Garda Síochána, changes to asylum and refugee law, citizenship, defamation, and the introduction of anti-social behaviour orders. In addition, through two mammoth Criminal Justice Acts of 2006 and 2007 sweeping change took place in criminal procedure, sentencing, insanity verdicts, post-release monitoring, the laws of evidence and bail. There can be no doubt that this was a Minister on top of his brief, with a clear plan for change and the dedication and commitment to implement it – and quickly.

McDowell's tenure when it came to prison policy adhered quite closely to the concerns he had expressed while on the back benches. This was a somewhat curious mix, but also reflected the political philosophy of his party, the Progressive Democrats, more broadly. First, there was an evident desire to eradicate what McDowell regularly described as the Victorian conditions in the state's prisons. There was also a commitment to accountability, with the establishment of an inspector of prisons taking place, though other such mechanisms did not follow. In addition, there was a resolute determination to tackle the high cost of overtime among prison officers, which he clearly believed to be a scandal. This concern with the taxpayer and reducing cost was also, paradoxically, a driver in the legacy for which McDowell is most remembered in the world of penal policy – Thornton Hall.

Thornton Hall

The plan to build a new prison with space for around 2,200 prisoners on a greenfield site outside Dublin was taken in 2004. While Thornton Hall has achieved the most prominence, at the same time it was announced that a new prison in the southern region of the country, to be called Kilworth, was to be built as well. Criticisms of the plan to build Thornton Hall in particular were varied and fierce. Its cost and the procurement procedures were politically the most contentious, with allegations made that the site purchased was overpriced (Dáil Debates, vol 606, col 960, 29 September 2005).

The justifications for Thornton Hall were put stridently by the Minister for Justice who appeared to be fighting an essentially one-man campaign on behalf of the proposals in the Oireachtas. Policy-makers had long declared that extra space was necessary in the prison system, but the ambitious plans of McDowell had not previously been seen. It is likely that the impetus for change on this scale came squarely from the Minister and he was able to secure a commitment to funding in a more economically prosperous Ireland. The institutional memory of the days of overcrowding and the 'revolving door', the name given to the phenomenon of large numbers of people on temporary release, would also have ensured that McDowell had a sympathetic hearing. His civil servants, many of whom would have lived through those days, could not have been averse to the ideas proposed either. This was a way of 'future-proofing' the Irish prison system.

There was an ideological position apparent also, though not in the way one might expect when it comes to plans for huge penal expansion. This ideology was one of financial restraint. Though this seems bizarre given the massive costs involved in the construction of such a prison, the logic behind the change was that, eventually, the costs of a prison constructed on that scale would be lower than for the existing prisons and would enable other institutions to be closed, thus consolidating staff and resources.

It cannot be said with any certainty that a punitive agenda was behind the decision to establish Thornton Hall or Kilworth. While penal expansion was undoubtedly involved on a very large scale, the driving forces were those outlined above. Space, which had become the lightning rod for the problems in the prison system, was seen as the solution and it seems that there was a view that once the issue of space was solved then other matters, such as rehabilitative services, could be dealt with. This led to Thornton Hall being cast as a way of ensuring that the 'bad old days' would never be returned to. However, it also meant that the presence of a plan for Thornton Hall led to a sense in which immediate concerns became less pressing and that criticisms of conditions in the prisons that continued to be used could be deflected by reference to the hope that was Thornton.

There is also little sense in which Michael McDowell, unlike his predecessor, wished to make significant political capital out of his planned penal expansion. Again, this seems strange given the possible fanfare that could be made regarding the albeit dubious claims about fighting crime. The Programme for Government agreed between the coalition parties made no reference to any figure at all regarding increased prison spaces, with the parties perhaps somewhat reticent to provide such an easy and eye-catching target for criticism if the figure had not been fulfilled. Nothing of the order of what transpired seemed to be envisaged in that statement. In addition, the programme also indicated that the high levels of illiteracy among prisoners would be tackled and that skills training courses would be provided to enhance the employment prospects for prisoners after release.

Statements from Michael McDowell during his time in office give the impression of a man in a hurry, with a clear view of what needed to be done, a fear of returning to the past and absolute conviction about the rightness of his actions.

Prison conditions

Almost as frequently as McDowell referred to his determination to ensure that the days of high usage of temporary release were over did he refer to the question of prison conditions. In 2003 he declared his intention to replace all traditional padded cells, which were extremely outdated, with new safety observation cells (Dáil Debates, vol 562, col 439, 25 February 2003). He linked his plans for making efficiencies in spending on prisons to a desire to improve conditions, arguing:

> I refuse, point blank, to allow a situation to continue where the capital budgets needed to ensure that our Prison Service will be properly developed ... and will not be a model in which Victorian practices such as slopping out are the norm, are cannibalised to pay stratospheric overtime costs ... I am not prepared to allow the *status quo* to remain in place ... I will not be deflected from my goal.
>
> *(Dáil Debates, vol 572, col 940, 15 October 2003)*

He described decreasing overtime costs and increasing rehabilitative practices as 'two sides of the same coin' and that anyone advocating longer sentences should 'walk the walk' and visit a prison (Dáil Debates, vol 572, col 940, 15 October 2003).

This language was also used to justify the decision to build an entirely new prison rather than refurbish Mountjoy. The question of what to do about Mountjoy had been troublesome for years and McDowell's solution was to abandon it entirely. The criticisms of the conditions from international human rights organisations such as the Council of Europe's Committee for the Prevention of Torture as well as the Inspector of Prisons were cited as supporting evidence for the decision. Interestingly, the need to fulfil 'legal requirements', presumably a fear of prison litigation about the conditions, was also described as an impetus for change (Dáil Debates, vol 596, col 1127, 1 February 2005). McDowell said: 'I am determined to improve facilities for prisoners and to do away with the practice of slopping out' (Dáil Debates, vol 597, col 1620, 16 February 2005).

McDowell was also motivated by the fact that it would become more difficult to throw drugs over the walls of a prison at Thornton Hall than it was in a city centre location (Dáil Debates, vol 600, col 36, 12 April 2005) and that more modern technologies would reduce costs, presumably referring to the possibility of eliminating the use of staff time for gate duties. Cost, it seems, was a critical factor in the development of the prison plans (Brangan 2009).

Temporary release

Another significant motivation for McDowell was to reform the temporary release system. As a backbencher he had been vociferous in his criticism of what he considered to be a system in chaos, where large numbers were not serving the sentence imposed on them by the courts because of a lack of accommodation. It is clear that McDowell was unshakeable in his belief that this was a scandal that needed immediate change. The previous government had given sanction for a new bill to deal with temporary release and it was McDowell who saw it into law in an early exercise of his powers. His tendency to increase the accountability of decisions made in prison was likely to have impelled him to press on with this change, which led to the introduction of what became the Criminal Justice (Temporary Release of Prisoners) Act 2003. It was also necessary after the establishment of the Parole Board in 2001, which examined long-term sentences to see if the individual was suitable for release. The 2003 Act was designed to provide a clearer legislative basis on which temporary release could be granted and so amend the original Criminal Justice Act 1960.

The 2003 Act set out criteria upon which temporary release could be granted. It did not take the opportunity to ban temporary release for prisoners or to restrict its operation from entire categories of prisoners. Instead, temporary release was restated as being of importance to reintegration and sentence planning (Dáil Debates, vol 557, col 1563, 21 November 2002).

The main perceived concern regarding temporary release was the fear that it would be relied upon to the extent it had been in the 1980s. In his speeches, McDowell returned to the theme of eradicating the revolving door again and again. His skills of oratory in the Dáil contained indications of this on several occasions. In 2003, for example, he stated that 'a fundamental part of our approach to crime – in stark contrast to that of our predecessors – is to ensure that there is sufficient custodial accommodation available' (Dáil Debates, vol 562, cols 102–4, 25 February 2003). He considered himself to be 'solving that problem which is the legacy of many years of failure to solve it … I know where I am going on this issue' (Dáil Debates, vol 574, cols 1025–6, 18 November 2003) and that there would be 'no return to the revolving door' (Dáil Debates, vol 624, col 1234, 3 October 2006).

Finance: a different kind of concern

In the history of prison policy financial considerations and, most usually, pressures have acted to drive that policy in particular directions, either towards caution and lack of innovation or to 'making do' approaches. In Ireland during these years money was no longer a matter of major concern and there was the ability to invest in significant capital projects such as the two proposed prisons. However, it is a paradox that it was actually the prospect of reducing financial outlays that seemed to exercise the Minister most.

Overtime and the Prison Officers' Association

Outside of the Dáil the Minister had written in strident language about the levels of overtime payment made to prison officers. In the *Sunday Independent* (20 December 1998) he wrote that prison officers were 'holding the State to ransom', referring to a 'Golden Goose culture' in relation to overtime which was 'a huge scandal'. It seems that as Minister, McDowell embarked on an almost personal quest to change this culture. He described the cost of the prison service while in office as 'unsustainable' (Dáil Debates, vol 572, col 926, 15 October 2003) and embarked on negotiations with the Prison Officers' Association. He also stated 'the current pattern of cannibalising the State's budget for capital development in prisons to pay for massively excessive overtime is unsustainable and will not continue' (Dáil Debates, vol 572, col 927, 15 October 2003).

It seems that it was as part of these negotiations that the spectre of prison privatisation was raised. Privatisation was easy to associate with the economic liberal agenda of the Progressive Democrats. However, it is more likely that the prospect of privatisation was not unwelcome as a levering tool with the Prison Officers' Association. A Prisons Act 2007 allowed for the contracting out of prisoner escort and transfer services, but privatisation of prisons has never been introduced. Instead, the privatisation model was used to build prisons, employing the public-private partnership model which had become popular within government. McDowell considered it a 'dereliction' of his 'duty to the taxpayer' not to address the question of privatising out such services (Dáil Debates, vol 572, col 928, 15 October 2003).

Prison closure?

Given the plans to invest in capital projects for the prison system on an enormous scale, it again seems contradictory that it was also simultaneously planned to reduce the existing capacity of the prison system by closing two institutions. The first was Shanganagh Castle and the other was Fort Mitchel on Spike Island. On the surface this expansion and contraction of the prison system is hard to explain. However, the reasons for this mixture of policy positions becomes clearer when placed in the context of the dispute with the Prison Officers' Association and the desire to reduce the financial cost of the prison system.

The decision to close Shanganagh was stated to be based on the fact that it was becoming increasingly difficult to find suitable prisoners between the ages of 16 and 21 eligible for an open centre and the low numbers and high cost were argued to warrant its closure (Dáil Debates, vol 558, col 1482, 4 December 2002). It was alleged, however, that Shanganagh was being deliberately 'run down'. Shanganagh Castle stood on 24 acres and was a valuable site.

Evidently, financial and operational considerations were influential in the decision and it was felt that the small number of prisoners could be transferred to St Patrick's Institution and staff could be sent to other locations and, perhaps most importantly, the site could be sold and the proceeds reinvested in other development. The Minister stated: 'I intend to close the centre in order to contribute to the control of costs in the prison service, to make more effective use of prison service staffing ... and to release funds ... for more productive prison related purposes' (Dáil Debates, vol 558, col 1483, 4 December 2002).

Fort Mitchel was also closed. This decision was based very pointedly in the continuing dispute with the Prison Officers' Association regarding the reduction in overtime. McDowell described a government decision at the end of 2003 to 'mothball' Fort Mitchel and transfer the open centres such as Loughan House and Shelton Abbey to independently managed post-release centres in the event that negotiations with prison staff were unsuccessful (Dáil Debates, vol 580, col 748, 18 February 2004). These stakes were quite high as the prospect of job losses, relocation and the eradication of some of the nicer institutions in which to work would not have been met with favour. While a compromise was reached, Fort Mitchel remained closed.

Cost-cutting was also declared as the reason why Minister McDowell took the decision to appoint members to visiting committees in their home county or neighbouring county, reducing the expenses claimed thereby significantly (Dáil Debates, vol 594, col 1128, 8 December 2004).

Changes in perspective

If the decisions to close prisons were ideological decisions, they were ones grounded in a financial ideology rather than a penal one. It is also of note that McDowell dropped all references to the zero tolerance policies of his predecessor and he also stated, 'I strongly believe that prison should be the remedy of last resort for the courts in dealing with offenders' (Dáil Debates, vol 572, col 940, 15 October 2003).

If there was one area in which a more punitive perspective was evident it was that of the length of sentences for murder. McDowell indicated that in cases of murder there would be 'no single digit sentences … except in the most extraordinary circumstances, which I cannot even envisage' (Dáil Debates, vol 562, col 104, 25 February 2003).

The rights of victims

It was perhaps outside the prison system where a more obvious ideology was in place. When it came to the rights of suspects, Minister McDowell was evidently concerned to 're-tilt' the perceived balance of rights away from suspects and towards victims. A Balance in the Criminal Law Review Group was established and its report dealt with procedural changes in significant breadth and detail. That report, however, was prefaced by a statement from its chairman, Dr Gerard Hogan SC (now judge of the High Court) which ran:

> I cannot help thinking that society must not ignore the fact that the majority of prisoners are drawn from the more disadvantaged sections of the community and that any balanced response to the problems of crime must also have regard to this factor … some at least of the prison community can justly say that they too are also in some sense the victims of society.
>
> *(Hogan 2007: 4)*

An Inspector of Prisons

Though the 2000s are most notable for the promised penal expansion, there are a number of other features of the decade in the area of prison policy. One of the most significant changes, in keeping with Minister McDowell's declared commitment to increased accountability, was the introduction of the Office of Inspector of Prisons. This was created in 2002 and was put on a statutory footing in 2007. In a neat twist of history, Dermot Kinlen, who had sat on the Mountjoy Visiting Committee, which had made some of the most serious criticisms of the prison system ever committed to print, was appointed and he served in office until his death, whereupon Judge Michael Reilly, former district court judge, took over. Both incumbents produced reports that spoke of very poor material conditions, the effects of overcrowding, tension and a lack of educational, training and health facilities.

Projects to help prisoners

In addition, in the early part of the decade the CONNECT project, which was designed to increase the employability of prisoners on release, was given funding in a national development plan, having been run since 1998 (Dáil Debates, vol 520, col 650, 31 May 2000). However, the funding for that project was cut and it did not continue later in the decade.

That said, other initiatives were introduced, such as the Building Better Lives project which sought through a variety of therapeutic mechanisms to deal with the causes of sexual offending and to address such behaviour in preparation for release. This plan commenced in 2009. There were also long-announced plans to develop a system of 'positive' or 'integrated' sentence management for all prisoners, though the numbers subject to such initiatives were small. The majority of prisoners living in overcrowded conditions could not be said to be having their sentences planned in any meaningful way.

The Prisons Act 2007

It is fitting that a Minister with such an active legislative programme introduced a Prisons Act, in 2007. That Act in many respects symbolised the mixture of positions under McDowell's leadership. The Act provided for the privatisation of prison escorts, a cost-cutting measure, provisions for the construction and extension of prisons and the establishment of the Office of the Inspector of Prisons on a statutory footing. It also contained the authority to draft new prison rules. It is also appropriate that it was McDowell who finally grasped the nettle on an issue that had been put on the long finger for several years. The Prison Rules 2007 were the result.

The Irish Prison Service

A significant change into the 2000s occurred in the organisational structure of the management of prisons. This was the introduction of the Irish Prison Service, a statutory agency responsible for the management and operational aspects of the prison system, with the Department of Justice maintaining control over policy direction. This had been planned for several years and was probably the result of the investigations into the running of the Department of Justice and other civil service entities that took place in that decade. It is arguable that the creation of the Irish Prison Service has had some effects on the creation of policy. A body that is attempting to manage space and operations on a daily basis is likely to see space as being the most prominent concern in the formation of prison policy and that impetus can be fed back into the policy-making process.

Prison policy after McDowell

In 2007 another general election was called. This saw a third term in government for Fianna Fáil commence. However, the Progressive Democrats were essentially wiped out. For all his activity, Michael McDowell failed to be re-elected in his constituency and immediately resigned from politics.

Without Michael McDowell, it might be expected that the drive would have ebbed out of prison policy as it had done after the departure of Haughey. This is largely true and the planned completion date for Thornton Hall has been put back on numerous occasions. The plan for a prison at Kilworth seems to have been deferred for the present, though it has not been officially discontinued (Dáil Debates, written answers, 1 June 2010). The reasons for the delayed development at Thornton Hall are perhaps emblematic of the changes being experienced in contemporary Ireland. The successful consortium for the tender for the project is no longer able to carry it out for financial reasons and the project stalled as a result. Again, it is perhaps symbolic that the project will now be built using Exchequer funding rather than through a public-private partnership (*Irish Times*, 27 July 2010).

Recently it has been announced that the prison will now be built in phases, with the first phase to consist of a 400-cell prison to accommodate 700 prisoners. This decision seems remarkable given that doubling up, illegal until the early 1980s, is now a part of planned penal policy instead of being an unfortunate by-product of overcrowding. The current Minister, Dermot Ahern, indicated his view that one cell per prisoner was 'a bit much', despite having previously stated that in Thornton 'prisoners will be held in individual cells meeting the requirements of the 21st century' (Dáil Debates, vol 655, col 478, 27 May 2008). More troublesome again is the confirmation that Mountjoy prison will not be closed when Thornton Hall is built, but will be phased out 'if possible'. The hope that Thornton Hall would lead to improved conditions and the final closure of Mountjoy has proven groundless.

Michael McDowell's aim to end overcrowding and high reliance on temporary release has also been unfulfilled. At present, the Irish prison system contains more people than it has ever done since the days of the Civil War, standing at around 4,317 prisoners. Mountjoy and Cork prisons along with the Dóchas Centre continue to be severely overcrowded and the material conditions are very poor (IPRT 2010). Temporary release has become a common feature of Irish prison administration once again. Around 1,000 prisoners are being dealt with in this way. Committals have risen, with an increase of 1,000 between 2008 and 2009 (*Irish Independent*, 26 July 2010). Crisis is a word frequently associated with the prison system once more and *ad hoc* increases in prison space have returned, with short-term plans to extend Wheatfield and the Midlands prison (Dáil Debates, written answers, 7 July 2010).

The prison system in the late 2000s

The late 2000s bears more than a passing resemblance to the 1980s with high numbers, pressure on space, increased reliance on temporary release and a plan for a new prison that will 'solve everything'. Making do and realising that outdated accommodation will be in service for some time yet are also similar features.

Michael McDowell didn't have the chance to ensure that his plans would come to fruition under his leadership. However, his actions have left a lasting legacy in a number of ways. First, Thornton Hall has become a decision that a government does not seem to be able to roll back on. Second, the very presence of a site in the ownership of the state provides its own incentive to build. Third, the plan of Thornton Hall has had an important effect on the discourse around prisons and prison policy in Ireland. Criticism of current practices and poor conditions can be deflected by the answer that Thornton Hall is coming, that it will eradicate overcrowding, eliminate poor conditions and solve all these concerns.

This focus on space and increased capacity has had a further legacy, one that is perhaps more invisible but more important than the creation of further prison places. This operates at the level of deflecting attention away from other aspects of prison policy. So much of the debate on Irish prisons has concentrated on space, but there are many other issues that receive significantly less attention but are no less important or indeed pressing.

The improved accountability structures introduced by Michael McDowell did not extend to creating an independent and effective prisoner complaints mechanism nor was there significant reform to the visiting committee structure, which remains rooted in the Act of 1925. There is no prisons ombudsman in Ireland; deaths in prison custody are not investigated by such a dedicated or specialised body, being instead investigated internally or by *ad hoc* commissions. There is very limited public scrutiny over the process of investigation (Rogan 2009b). There continues to be no provision to expunge a conviction in Ireland.

The usual problems that have been a feature of Irish prison life for decades now also remain. Overcrowding has brought inevitable tension, and pressure on material conditions which are largely antiquated. Mountjoy prison regularly contains over 700 prisoners, though the Inspector of Prisons has said that it should contain 540 at the most. The conditions have been characterised by him as constituting inhuman and degrading treatment (*Annual Report of the Inspector of Prisons*, 2008). Violence within prisons is a cause of concern and the effect on regimes besides is serious (CPT 2006). Slopping out is the norm for 30 per cent of the prison population.

In addition, the Irish prison population is characterised by high numbers of people committed for short sentences, largely for non-violent property crime (*Annual Report on Prisons*, 2008) and it is only recently that imprisonment for fine defaulters has been made more difficult through the Fines Act 2010. In 2008 62 per cent of committals were for six months or less. The prison population contains high numbers of persons awaiting deportation along with a very significant remand population. There is still an underuse of alternatives to custody and significant scope to increase their use. Imprisonment rates remain low by international standards, but are rising.

Irish prisoners are characterised by socio-economic deprivation, poor literacy, drug addiction (O'Mahony 1997) and mental health problems, being drawn from some of the most deprived parts of Ireland (O'Donnell *et al*. 2008).

Another less immediately obvious but very major problem is the absence of data on Irish prisons. The introduction of a Prisoner Record Information System has opened up research possibilities that were previously impossible (O'Donnell *et al*. 2008). However, when it comes to breakdowns of the specific type of offences people are imprisoned for, the courts they are coming from, their health and socio-economic indicators, details are not easily to be found and require significant effort to collate. The absence of linked data across the criminal justice system, such as the courts, Gardaí, probation and prisons, is another major impediment to our understanding of trends in the prison population. The effect this has on official penal planning can only be guessed at. Increasing prison capacity is unlikely to address any of these problems.

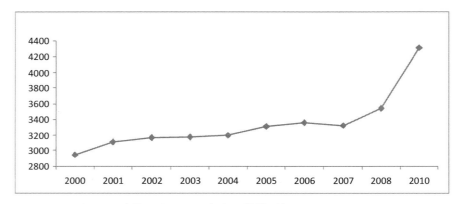

FIGURE 9.1 Average daily prison population 2000–10

Prison policy at the end of the Celtic Tiger era

As with previous periods in Irish penal history the story of Irish prison policy is rather prosaic. There have been undoubted shifts in Irish society and a nation that became so prosperous so rapidly is now coming to terms with a transition to a much more financially precarious position, high levels of government debt, cuts in public spending, rising unemployment, a return to emigration and a generally more uncertain future. There is also no doubt that the financial largesse being dispensed during the boom years created a climate in which a project the size of Thornton Hall could be considered. However, it was the continuing effects of overcrowding, a reliance on temporary release, a memory of the 'bad old days' and an activist Minister bent on changing the future of the Irish prison system that resulted in the greatest penal change occurring. Coupled with this, a lack of imagination to 'do' punishment differently, or to see beyond considerations of space, has endured and has given rise to a sense that increasing prison populations are inevitable and penal expansion required. It also means that Irish prison policy is especially vulnerable to the effects of the particular predilections and vision of Ministers and civil servants. In addition, action that revolves around space means that other aspects of penal change happen much less quickly, with the 60-year wait for the development of new prison rules and the lack of a consolidated Prisons Act being two cases in point. O'Donnell describes this vividly as constituting a 'poverty of thought' in penal planning (O'Donnell 2005: 102).

What does this say, then, about the formation of prison policy in Ireland? Clearly individual ministers and civil servants have a key role to play and have a particularly influential position. These actors seem to take steps without a great deal of reference to empirical evidence, prison projections or criminological research, which continues to be underdeveloped. However, this situation is changing as a growing band of researchers begins to investigate the field, along with the Irish Penal Reform Trust, established in 1994, which has developed into the leading penal reform organisation in the country. Political crises and concern about crime has an effect on policy (O'Donnell 2004a), but particularly active ministers can have a more profound long-term effect (Rogan 2009a). Both phenomena have tended to overcome the more usual setting of inertia in prison policy and have results that outlive them. Perhaps the continuation of this tendency is the only thing that can be predicted with any certainty for the future of the Irish prison system.

10

CONCLUSION
Unravelling the nature of Irish prison policy

Introduction

This work has investigated the practice and nature of Irish prison policy since 1922. It has examined the various events that comprised that policy, the sources of influence and potential influence on that policy and the socio-political and cultural contexts in which such policy was made and was also shaped by. The form of policy analysis employed allowed the conflict and nuance of the years under assessment to be revealed, but some more general conclusions can also be drawn about the period studied. From a distillation of these assessments, three hallmarks or motifs of the period can be identified, under the broad rubrics of political imprisonment, penal-welfarism and politics.

Political imprisonment

Underlying the entire half-century after Independence in particular, but present until the 1990s, the theme of 'political imprisonment' recurred perennially. The need to secure order and defeating periodic – most usually Republican – threats were played out across Irish prison policy at a variety of times. Ongoing concerns about the state's sovereignty prompted a usually hard-line position being adopted towards considered to be endangering it.

The imprisonment of Republicans also instigated what was often the only interest in the penal system from the public. Republican detainees were the sole focus of support and provided the few alternative sources of ideas or potential influence upon policy-makers. In the aftermath of the death of Seán McCaughey in 1946, this interest did lead to concrete change in Irish prison policy.

While suppressing disorder of this nature was a central objective in Irish prison policy in its own right, the achievement of this aim had some ramifications for 'ordinary' prison policy. This was particularly acute during the Civil War period, the Emergency and in the early 1970s, with the Mountjoy riot standing as a classic example of 'events' forcing political hands (Downes and Morgan 2007). The attentions and concerns of the Department of Justice in the Republic in the 1920s, 1930s, during the Emergency and the early part of the 1970s were also turned, almost exclusively, towards the very pressing problems faced by a prison system dealing with subversive threats to the state.

While security matters left little room for other activities, plans or reflections on behalf of prison policy-makers, during the period 1922–58 especially there were long periods of relative calm in which little was done with the ordinary prison system. As such, the presence of subversion cannot be considered the only reason why interest in the prison was so low, and changes were so few and far between. Stagnation and caution were key features of Irish prison policy as well.

A different picture emerges during the period 1958–72. The early 1960s particularly remained untroubled by security concerns. Interest in the more usual business of prisons began to become more prevalent. Much of this activity was directed towards creating a prison system that was rehabilitationist in aim.

Had the prison system retained the 'quiet' of the 1960s, the trajectory of subsequent prison policy thereafter might have been somewhat different. However, a number of factors indicate that the 'progressive' future for the prison system was not simply blown off course by the outbreak of the Troubles. By 1972 the Irish prison system was already displaying signs of pressure more generally and the rise in committals of ordinary prisoners was a very significant development. The confluence of these factors prompted a 'policy' that could be described as one of crisis-management or reaction, as opposed to long-term dispassionate planning or the creation of policy based on a bedrock of principle and evidence.

Irish prison policy

1922–58: stagnation

Irish prison policy was remarkably homogeneous and uniform for three and a half decades after Independence. As O'Donnell argues, 'the early years of the Irish state, after its foundation in 1922, were characterised by a parsimonious approach to imprisonment and a low level of interest in penal affairs' (O'Donnell 2004a: 253).

Prison policy in these years was, in the main, driven by a near obsession with financial cut-backs, retrenchment of the system and minimal intervention by the state. There were few innovations propagated and little by way of change and the picture of prison policy was essentially one of stasis. Prison closures were the main events punctuating an otherwise unaltered penal landscape. No documents laying out the official 'vision' for imprisonment in Ireland were produced; no reports were commissioned by the government; no statement of policy of any description ensued.

Closure of prisons was a matter of practicality rather than ideology and the sentiments uttered were far easier to say than to implement. However, the fact that there was an element of benevolence in discourse surrounding prisoners should not be taken for granted. Policy-makers during this period displayed a much more stringent approach to prisoners exhibiting signs of 'political' dissent and penal administrators were evidently capable of implementing a harsh regime. A kind of benevolent neglect is perhaps the most accurate assessment of the period.

The reasons for this level of neglect and stasis are manifold. With the exception of the Emergency years, until the mid-1960s the crime rate in Ireland was remarkably low and committals to prison under sentence declined. Other factors were also influential. The first of these is what can be described as the 'Cinderella factor' or the marginality (O'Donnell 2004a) of Irish prison policy within public administration. Prison policy, except at times of political instability associated with outbreaks of Republican violence, was far down the agenda of successive administrations.

There were, moreover, few other sources of ideas or influence on the prison policy-making process, with the academic community and the media largely silent on prison matters. Except for Fr Flanagan's visit, members of the Catholic Church appear to have had comparatively little to say regarding prison policy. While an organisation with such an enormous role throughout the Irish social fabric might have been expected to become involved in debates over prison policy, this does not seem to have occurred. Instead, the Catholic Church focused its attentions on a variety of institutions in its own care that were responsible for social control. It may also be the case that protesting over prison conditions may have led to some unwanted and awkward questions being posed about the institutions within its own charge. Other religious denominations appear to have been mainly silent on the matter, with nothing like the Quaker presence, so influential elsewhere, occurring here.

The socio-political and cultural climate of the time was not one conducive to radical shifts in direction or restructuring social policy. This was both a practical and philosophical influence on the nature of the state's prison policy during these years, removing the potential for an ideological impulse to instigate change.

Many areas of social provision exhibit similar trajectories to that of prison policy, with education and health policy also considered to be very slow to modernise (Robins 1960; Sheehan 1979). The development of social welfare in Ireland was slow and almost niggardly, with all administrations being somewhat restrained in their efforts to provide greater provision in this area. As Fanning notes, 'Ireland … did not experience a "big bang" welfare resettlement after the Second World War' (Fanning 2003: 6). Nor had the Civil War radically reshaped Irish social relations. Three parties, Fianna Fáil, Fine Gael and Labour dominated the political scene, with the ideological differences between each often difficult enough to spot.

Those who would stand to benefit most from any forthcoming social reforms were those who were forced to emigrate in the 1950s in particular. This 'safety valve' affected the prison system in that it kept numbers artificially low, but also allowed the social system and the country to continue without a crush of young unemployed males to overwhelm the system, thereby removing the need to extend social solidarity to all members of Irish society, or at least obviating the embarrassment occasioned by the display of its absence. It also depleted the state of some of those who may have questioned the direction of Irish politics more generally, removing many sources of potential dissent and progressive ideas. This was compounded by the fact that the number of people seeking entry to the state at other times was very limited. Ireland would not become home to significant numbers of individuals fleeing oppressive regimes and their accompanying penal practices. No thinkers with the experience of Sir Leon Radzinowicz, for example, would receive the chance to reframe Irish penal thinking. As a result of this stagnation and inertia, the features of the prison system that had been inherited on Independence remained for decades.

The lack of change evident in Irish prison policy may be somewhat frustrating and the pace of change in the Irish prison system was often painfully slow. This stagnation could, however, also be read as 'stability'. The fact that Ireland became a stable, democratic state after significant political turmoil is something that could not be taken for granted, particularly when compared to the fates of other states emerging out of civil war.

1958–72: from stagnation to 'solo runs' and social change

1958 marks something of a break with the past, with the years 1960–64 and 1970 being most notable in terms of penal developments.

One of the most significant features of the early 1960s is the fact that prison policy began to be moved in a clearer direction for the first time in the history of the state. It was not until Michael McDowell became Minister for Justice in 2002 that a similar level of energy was expended. Kilcommins *et al.* (2004) posit that contemporary Irish prison policy, in keeping with other elements of public administration, is characterised by flexibility in ideology and an absence of bureaucratic expertise or long-term perspectives on the desired purpose for the prison system. As such, they suggest that there are few mechanisms present whereby any agenda, punitive or otherwise, can be implemented.

It is true that one of the main factors behind the change in approach evident in the 1960s is strongly tied to the personnel involved in the crucial period of the 1960s. While individual ministers and civil servants were crucial in putting forward a reform agenda, the wider social, political, economic and cultural contexts ensured that the changes they advocated were not considered controversial and were, generally, implemented without criticism.

While the role of individual ministers and civil servants was particularly crucial during the 1960s, the direction that policy-makers felt was desirable was one rooted in the changing socio-political climate of Ireland during the 1960s.

The Lemass era (1959 to 1966) is much lauded as one when change took place across the economic, social and cultural landscape of Ireland. The introduction of systemised planning for the economy in particular with the Whitaker Programme for Economic Development, greater investment in social infrastructure and greater emphasis on long-term strategising across the public sector are all key features of these years.

This notion of refashioning archaic structures and an impatience with what were perceived to be old-fashioned attachments permeated the political, social and cultural spheres. 'Change' *per se* was one of the central driving forces in Irish political culture, economics, social practice and policy during this period and its penal culture was similarly affected. This commitment to 'change' was perhaps stronger than a commitment to any particular form of change. No entrenched ideology, such as penal-welfarism or the use of prison as a coercive tool for the majority of offenders, was driving developments. Instead, a less pronounced desire to be seen as socially progressive and interested in developments from abroad motivated policy-makers. Advancement, rather than the detail of its direction, was their main concern.

Ireland and penal-welfarism

Penal-welfarism did not become significantly apparent or embedded in Irish penal policy, though it made some incursions in the 1960s and early 1970s, ironically at a time when countries in which it had achieved greater dominance, such as the USA and UK, had begun to recognise problems with such an approach and were turning away from it.

The point is well made by Kilcommins *et al.* (2004) that the form of penal-welfarism that existed in Ireland did so through a variety of sites other than the prison. This analysis can be extended to include the function of 'control' which was maintained through these institutions, many of them extra-judicial.

Ireland's relationship with the 'welfare' side of penal-welfarism during the period under assessment is influenced by a number of factors. The social, economic and cultural assumptions identified by Garland as giving rise to the implementation of penal-welfarist philosophies and practices in Britain after 1895 and particularly after World War Two were not present in Ireland to the same degree and those that are comparable did not appear until much later than their emergence in Britain.

In terms of finances, assumptions about the proper role of the state in the provision of social care and cross-class solidarity were all inhibitors to the establishment of similar movements here.

A further bedrock of penal-welfarism as identified by both Loader and Ryan, that of an intellectual base for its tenets, was missing in Ireland. There was effectively no research into prison matters until the 1960s and no academic criminological community to speak of. More generally, sociological inquiry in

Ireland was distinctly underdeveloped until the 1960s, and its contacts with public policy-makers were effectively non-existent.

Loader (2006) identifies a particular class of administrator in the British Home Office which considered it its duty to insulate the prison system from what was considered to be the ignorant and potentially punitive politicians and public during the formative years of what Loader describes as 'liberalism' in British prison policy. Until the 1960s there was no similar group in Ireland, with the evidence tending to suggest that the Prisons Division of the Department of Justice was small, somewhat forgotten about and concerned with internal regulation and economy. Its staff members were also far from envisaging themselves as part of a grand project to effect widespread change in the prison system. Nor was there a strong relationship fostered with researchers.

The conditions for the establishment of penal-welfarism were more favourable in the 1960s, when the economic climate was less inimical and a social reform agenda more apparent. Moreover, the Inter-Departmental Committee of 1962 and supportive civil servants and ministers can be conceived of as comparable to the 'liberal elites' identified by Loader and Ryan. This group was remarkably small, being civil-service-centric and with limited connections to academia or other sectors outside public administration. The changes propagated in the 1960s were led from within government. The views of 'the public' and their reaction to initiatives were apparently never considered.

Penal developments in Ireland largely follow tendencies in social policy, with the period prior to 1958 being one of limited penal-welfarist style action, but following years brought about changes with a greater flavour of that philosophy. However, the limited nature of these developments and the apparent contradictions in the content of Irish prison policy indicate that the reasons for change in that policy during the 1960s and early 1970s are more complex.

While significant underlying social change was at work in Ireland during this period, with elements of this altered framework becoming apparent in the prison system also, these impulses were joined by another factor that was decisive to the manner of development exhibited by Irish prison policy during the 1960s and early 1970s. This was the 'policy' dimension, involving the role of politics, the nature of Irish social and economic provision, and political agency.

Politics and welfare policy

Carey, in her history of the provision of social security in Ireland (Carey 2007), reiterates that the task of identifying or characterising the contemporary Irish welfare state has proven problematic, holding that Ireland has proven difficult to compare to other countries across a whole range of indices, including politics, sociology and economics and noting the importance of the 'agrarian' nature of Irish society in its development.

The notion of Irish 'exceptionalism' is perhaps another way of describing the vital role of political agency and pragmatism in the creation of policy generally in the state. Carey argues that political choice was crucial in the trajectory of the Irish welfare state, having a very direct impact on developments therein. Electoral interests, the impact of individual politicians and mediating or reacting to past policy choices all operated to lend a distinctly 'Irish' character to social security in Ireland.

Kilcommins makes a similar point to that of Carey, noting that 'attempts to both describe and define the characteristics of the Irish welfare state, particularly with relevance to arrangements in other European countries, are elusive and a contentious area of intellectual endeavour' (Kilcommins *et al.* 2004: 284).

It is, however, pertinent to point out the nature of Irish welfare provision and the characteristics of social policy provision may themselves provide explanatory potential. It is largely accepted that the Irish welfare state did not take hold until at least the 1960s, and from then on the state was considered to take on the primary role in social provision. However, within this picture a large element of nuance was present, and there was no evident commitment to an ingrained 'philosophy' of welfare. There has been a large degree or flexibility of fluidity in Irish social and economic provision (Fanning 2003), with much of its development exhibiting an *ad hoc* quality (Curry 2003). This peculiarity, 'particularistic approach' (Carey 2007: 224) or 'distinctiveness' (O'Connell and Rottman 1992: 230) is recognised at an official level; in 2005, the National Economic and Social Council described Ireland's arrangements for providing social protection as 'hybrid' (NESC 2005: 35). No single coherent creed or dogma can be identified to explain the Irish case.

The particular nature of Irish party politics, already noted above, is a key influence on the development of its form of welfare provision and the prison policy. While the post-Independence Cumann na nGaedheal government pursued a comparatively clear social and economic agenda, it is much more difficult to delineate the contours of later governments' philosophical positions. Within Irish politics, an unequivocal left–right social cleavage is not readily apparent (Mair and Weeks 2004). Farrell argues that, historically, 'the major parties … avoided ideological labels' (Farrell 1986: 144) and there is a striking heterogeneity in their support bases. The varying fortunes of the more ideologically driven party, the Progressive Democrats, indicates this clearly.

An oft-repeated quotation comes from Whyte, who argued that Ireland could be considered to have 'politics without social bases' (Whyte 1974), or 'non-ideological' politics (Lee 1986: 156) and exhibited neither strongly socialist nor conservative tenets (Coakley 2004a). At another level, apparent contradictions between parties that espoused Republican beliefs and expressed sympathy with IRA prisoners on the one hand (such as Fianna Fáil in the 1920s) and employed distinctly hard-line policies while in office, indicates that even among sacrosanct ideals a large degree of pragmatism was in evidence.

One of the key reasons given for this state of affairs is the 'persistently dominant position of Fianna Fáil' (Mair and Weeks 2004: 144), which held power for the bulk of the period under view and has a widespread appeal across classes and a pragmatic approach towards political philosophies. The centrist nature of Irish party politics has had an effect such that parties try to keep everybody happy. Indeed, the current government is perhaps the supreme example of pragmatism triumphing over potentially incompatible principles with the coalition of Fianna Fáil and the Green Party. As Mair states: 'there is simply no other country which has a party that was equivalent to Fianna Fáil' (Mair 1990: 212), though it bears some comparisons with French Gaulism and Italian Christian Democracy.

This picture is compounded by the fact that Irish politicians are extraordinarily close to their immediate electorate and act as brokers for gaining access to social benefits and facilitating rights and favours (Collins and O'Shea 2003). Such activity appeals across party political lines.

This pragmatic nature of Irish political 'ideology' has made it difficult to pinpoint overall trends or coherent motifs across economics and social policy. Instead, political agency, party politics and a significant amount of opportunism have operated to give such policies, and their constituent elements, their particular complexion. This means that policy developments in a variety of areas cannot be considered manifestations of a particular political philosophy. Instead, a confluence of individual and particularistic factors must be appraised.

Characterising Irish prison policy requires a similar recognition of the role of these factors, including the pivotal role of individual ministers and civil servants. The timing of Haughey's arrival as well as his particular talents were, for example, most crucial in the development of Irish prison policy. The fact that Michael McDowell wasn't elected in 1997 was another aspect of chance, as was the ability of his party to lobby for two Cabinet posts in 2002.

The 1960s gave penal administrators and policy-makers opportunities – a 'policy window' of sorts – to carry forward the ideas propagated during this period. Crucially, the changing background conditions, or 'contextual features of the policy environment' (Ismaili 2006: 262) were joined and facilitated by the presence of political and civil service determination to take action.

Theoretical eclecticism – Ireland's modernisation

Kilcommins (2004) shows that Garland's theories in *The Culture of Control* may not be applicable to contemporary Ireland. It is also the case that Garland's model in *Punishment and Welfare* does not fully explain the developments of this period, with significant differences between the social and economic make-up of both countries apparent. It is certainly true that the 'conditions' Garland identifies for the propagation of penal–welfarism did not appear here until the mid-1960s.

However, while the growth of the Irish welfare state was accompanied by a developing emphasis on rehabilitation in the Irish prison system, the role of other factors must be acknowledged. These factors help to explain the manner in which rehabilitation was implemented and its endurance during the 1970s.

Welfare indicators are not the only relevant parameters of investigation when exploring the development of prison policy. Close attention must be paid to local nuances and influences, the nature of party politics, the impact of individual politicians and civil servants and unforeseen events that bring about change. As has been said of investigations of social security arrangements, 'the Irish case points to the value of theoretical eclecticism' (Carey 2007: 233). However, this point can be applied to all penal systems and this level of investigation may demonstrate that individual reforming ministers or civil servants can have effects that have long-lasting and profound consequences for prison policy. There has, however, been no comparable impact by the houses of the Oireachtas.

It is more accurate to view Irish prison policy during the 1960s and early 1970s less in terms of penal-welfarism and its comparison with Britain, and more in terms of the overall 'modernisation' of the Irish state during these years.

Such a characterisation of the period also helps to explain why the impact of penal-welfarism on Irish prison policy was so confined, late and comparatively brief. Part of the reason lay in the fact that much of the endeavour in prison policy was associated with a combination of personalities operational during the 1960s and early 1970s. When these individuals moved on, the surge of developments petered out. Moreover, while there was an undoubted drive for social reform in Ireland during the 1960s, this was less vigorous in the later part of the decade. As this work has shown, these local factors were also determinative of policy in later years.

Policy analysis and the sociology of punishment

This political landscape has been responsible for much of the nature of Irish prison policy. Lacking an obvious large support base, penal reform is an issue that politicians are unlikely to get particularly exercised about. More cynically, political posturing on crime may have a broader appeal, and evidence of that around election time in Ireland is present, as was seen most vividly in 1997. However, the sentiments expressed about prisons and the perennial need to 'get tough' does not translate, largely, into a penal agenda when in government.

There are advantages to this as it means that Ireland has escaped policies that seek to increase prison populations to very high levels. However, it also means that drifting along is another recurrent feature of Irish prison policy, with reform slow and piecemeal as well as being dependent on particularly active or interested ministers or a dyad of minister and civil servant. It leads to a situation where policy is often created by accident rather than design. Political crises and highly emotional moments such as high-profile crimes can force politicians out of penal inertia. These *ad hoc* and hard to predict decisions have contributed to the character of Irish prison policy. However, the degree to which there remains a commitment to introducing rehabilitative programmes, however token, and the absence of political determination, for example to reintroduce the death penalty or to abolish temporary release, should not be underestimated.

There is perhaps another element to this story that has been underexplored and dimly grasped at. As recent painful reports on the abuse of children and the extent of the incarceration of Irish people in a variety of coercive institutions outside of prison have shown, there is a huge capacity for denial within Irish society. Many were able to espouse the language of forgiveness, compassion and care, but in so many instances this was not practised towards those detained in industrial and reformatory schools, mental institutions and Magdalene homes.

It could be described as lip-service, or hypocrisy, but there is a sense in which Irish society does not desire harsh treatment and would not want to be seen as deliberately punitive. However, these words do not translate into action towards a more punitive approach or to a more liberalising one either.

In light of the above, this work demonstrates the importance of engagement with the insights provided by policy analysis as carried out in criminological scholarship. Such an approach has, it is hoped, ensured that due consideration has been given to the role, thoughts and intentions of political actors and others with an influence on the policy-making process. It has exposed the 'messiness' of that process and the pragmatic and political imperatives behind change, or – sometimes – the lack thereof. This seems to be particularly appropriate for the Irish case. It is also submitted, however, that all analyses of penal change would do well to engage in explorations of the policy process in order to test, refine and modify the theoretical models produced.

A multi-disciplinary approach and the consideration of a wide range of parameters by which penal culture can be investigated are particularly revealing endeavours. It is submitted that the fusion of the two types of analysis – policy and cultural – provides the fullest and most compelling account and explanation of prison policy's nature and development. As well as being careful about importing policy, it is important to tread carefully when importing theory. Local conditions continue to have a major influence on the direction of penal change. Developing an understanding of the policy-making process and the politics of penal change will assist us to understand the nature of that change more clearly.

APPENDIX

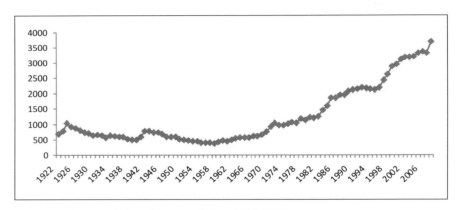

FIGURE 1 Average daily prison population 1922–2008

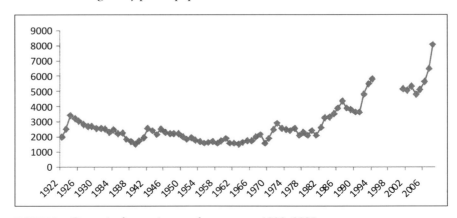

FIGURE 2 Committals to prison under sentence 1922–2008

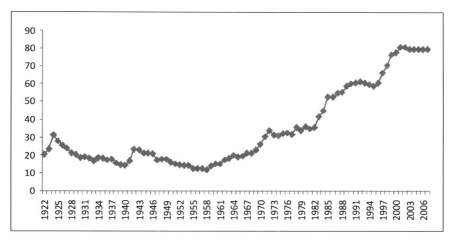

FIGURE 3   Average daily prison population per 100,000 population 1922–2008

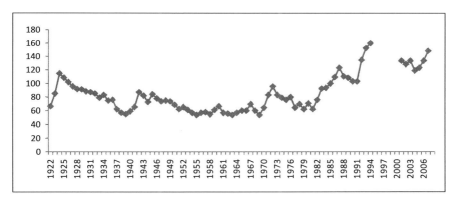

FIGURE 4   Committals to prison under sentence per 100,000 population 1922–2008

Note to Figures 2 and 4

The official annual figures for the years 1995 and 2000 do not provide a breakdown of the number of committals under sentence. Only the total number of committals for these years (including remand prisoners and those detained under immigration laws) is provided. These figures for the relevant years are:

1995	9,928
1996	10,355
1997	11,429
1998	11,307
1999	10,834
2000	11,626

The number of sentenced committals cannot be determined. However, some indication of the possible figures is derived from an analysis of other years. In 1994 out of a total of 12,091 committals, 6,866 were under sentence. In 2001 there were 5,160 committals under sentence out of a total of 12,127 committals.

BIBLIOGRAPHY

Primary sources

Archives

National Archives of Ireland
    Department of An Taoiseach files (TAO)
    Department of Justice files (JUS)
    Office of the Attorney General files (OAG)
Dublin Diocesan Archives (DDA)
University College Dublin Archives (UCDA)
Kilmainham Jail Archives
The Irish Film Archive
The Irish Military Archive
Radio Telefís Éireann Archive
National Library of Ireland Archives (NLI)
Trinity College Dublin Manuscripts Collection (TCD MS)

Oireachtas Debates

Dáil Debates
Seanad Debates

Official publications

Annual Reports on Prisons 1922–2008
Reports of the Visiting Committees 1925–2008
Reports of the Inspector of Prisons 2002–2009
Reports of the Curragh Visiting Committee 1972–83
Committee of Inquiry into the Penal System (1985) *Report of the Inquiry into the Penal System*. Dublin: Stationery Office.
Department of Justice (1994) *The Management of Offenders: A Five Year Plan*. Dublin: Department of Justice.

Newspapers

The Irish Times
The Irish Independent
The Sunday Independent
The Evening Herald
The Irish Press
The Sunday Press
The Nation
Éire
The Irish Farmers' Journal
The United Irishman

References

AGPD (1991) *Report of the Advisory Group on Prison Deaths*. Dublin: Stationery Office.

Allen, G. (1999) *The Garda Síochána: Policing Independent Ireland, 1922–82*. Dublin: Gill and Macmillan.

Anttila, I. (1974) 'The foundation of cooperation in European criminological research: Sir Leon Radzinowicz and the Criminological Scientific Council at the Council of Europe', in R. G. Hood and Sir L. Radzinowicz (eds) *Crime, Criminology and Public Policy: Essays in Honour of Sir Leon Radzinowicz*. London: Heinemann Educational.

Arnold, B. (2001) *Jack Lynch: Hero in Crisis*. Dublin: Merlin.

Arthur, P. (1974) *The People's Democracy, 1968–1973*. Belfast: Blackstaff Press.

Barker, V. (2006) 'Deliberating crime and punishment: a way out of get tough justice?', *Criminal Justice*, 5(1): 37–44.

Barrington, R. (1987) *Health, Medicine and Politics in Ireland, 1900–1970*. Dublin: Institute of Public Administration.

Barrington, T. J. (1967) 'Public administration 1926–1939', in F. MacManus (ed.) *The Years of the Great Test*. Cork: Mercier Press.

Barrington, T. J. (1980) *Irish Administrative System*. Dublin: Institute of Public Administration.

Barrington, T. J. (1982) *Whatever Happened to Irish Government?* Dublin: Institute of Public Administration.

Bazelon, D. L. (1966) 'Justice stumbles on science', *Irish Jurist*: 273–84.

Beckett, K. L. and Western, B. (2001) 'Governing social marginality', in D. Garland (ed.) *Mass Imprisonment: Social Causes and Consequences*. London: Sage.

Behan, B. (1956) *The Quare Fellow: A Comedy-Drama*. London: Methuen.

Behan, B. (1990) *Borstal Boy*. London: Arrow.

Bell, J. B. (1998) *The Secret Army: The IRA*, revised 3rd edn. Dublin: Poolbeg.

Bergin, M. and Clarke, J. (2005) 'Mental health in the community', in S. Quin and B. Redmond (eds) *Mental Health and Social Policy in Ireland*. Dublin: University College Dublin Press.

Berry, P. (1980) *Diaries*. In *Magill*.

Bew, P. (2007) *Ireland: The Politics of Enmity 1789–2006*. Oxford: Oxford University Press.

Bew, P. and Patterson, H. (1982) *Seán Lemass and the Making of Modern Ireland, 1945–66*. Dublin: Gill and Macmillan.

Bottoms, A. E. (1995) 'The philosophy and politics of punishment and sentencing', in C. M.V. Clarkson and R. Morgan (eds) *The Politics of Sentencing Reform*. Oxford: Oxford University Press.

Bowman, J. (1982) *De Valera and the Ulster Question, 1917–1973*. Oxford: Clarendon Press.

Bradley, J. (1988) 'Economic planning: lessons of the past and future prospects', *Administration*, 36(1): 51–66.

Brangan, L. (2009) 'Thornton Hall: a policy analysis: uncaring or unthinking?', in *Social Sciences*. Dublin: Dublin Institute of Technology.

Breen, R. (1990) *Understanding Contemporary Ireland: State, Class and Development in the Republic of Ireland*. Dublin: Gill and Macmillan.

Brewer, J. D., Lockhart, W. and Rodgers, P. (1997) *Crime in Ireland, 1945–95: 'Here be Dragons'*. Oxford: Clarendon Press.

Brown, T. (1981) *Ireland: A Social and Cultural History, 1922–1985*. London: Fontana.

Browne, N. (1986) *Against the Tide*. Dublin: Gill and Macmillan.

Buckley, M. (1938) *The Jangle of the Keys*. Dublin: J. Duffy and Company

Campbell, C. (1994) *Emergency Law in Ireland, 1918–25*. Oxford: Oxford University Press.

Carey, S. (2007) *Social Security in Ireland, 1939–1952: The Limits to Solidarity*. Dublin: Irish Academic Press.

Carey, T. (2000) *Mountjoy: The Story of a Prison*. Cork: Collins Press.

Carrabine, E. (2004) *Power, Discourse and Resistance: A Genealogy of the Strangeways Prison Riot*. Aldershot: Ashgate.

Cathcart, R. and Muldoon, M. (2003) 'The mass media in twentieth century Ireland', in J. R. Hill (ed.) *A New History of Ireland, Vol. VII: Ireland, 1921–84*. Oxford: Oxford University Press.

Cavadino, M. and Dignan, J. (2007) *The Penal System: An Introduction*, 4th edn. London: Sage.

Chubb, B. (1982) *The Government and Politics of Ireland*, 2nd edn. London: Longman.

CIPS (1985) *Report of the Committee of Inquiry into the Penal System*. Dublin: Stationery Office.

Clarke, K. and Litton, H. (1991) *Revolutionary Woman: Kathleen Clarke 1878–1972*. Dublin: O'Brien Press.

Coakley, J. (2004a) 'Society and political culture', in J. Coakley and M. Gallagher (eds) *Politics in the Republic of Ireland*, 4th edn. London: Routledge in association with PSAI Press.

Coakley, J. (2004b) 'The foundations of statehood', in J. Coakley and M. Gallagher (eds) *Politics in the Republic of Ireland*, 4th edn. London: Routledge in association with PSAI Press.

Coakley, J. and Gallagher, M. (2010) *Politics in the Republic of Ireland*, 5th edn. Oxford: Routledge.

Cohen, S. (1985) *Visions of Social Control: Crime, Punishment and Classification*. Cambridge: Polity Press.

Collins, N. and O'Shea, M. (2003) 'Clientilism: facilitating rights and favours', in M. Adshead and M. Millar (eds) *Public Administration and Public Policy in Ireland: Theory and Methods*. London: Routledge.

Collins, S. (2005) *Breaking the Mould: How the PDs Changed Irish Politics*. Dublin: Gill and Macmillan.

Connolly, E. (2004) 'The government and governmental system', in J. Coakley and M. Gallagher (eds) *Politics in the Republic of Ireland*, 4th edn. London: Routledge in association with PSAI Press.

Convey, M. A. (1994) *Keeping the Faith in a Changing Society: Religious Practice and Belief in Ireland in the Light of Vatican II*. Dublin: Columba Press.

Coogan, T. P. (1966) *Ireland Since the Rising*. London: Pall Mall Publications.

Coogan, T. P. (1995) *The IRA*. London: Harper Collins.

Coolahan, J. (1981) *Irish Education: Its History and Structure*. Dublin: Institute of Public Administration.

Coolahan, J. (2003) 'Higher education in Ireland 1908–84', in J. R. Hill (ed.) *A New History of Ireland, Vol. VII: Ireland, 1921–84*. Oxford: Oxford University Press.

Cope, S. (2001) 'Analysing criminal justice policy-making: towards a policy networks approach?', in M. Ryan, S. P. Savage and D. Wall (eds) *Policy Networks in Criminal Justice*. Basingstoke: Palgrave.

Cousins, M. (1997) 'Ireland's place in the worlds of welfare capitalism', *Journal of European Social Policy*, 7(3): 223–35.

Cousins, M. (2002) *The Birth of Social Welfare in Ireland, 1922–1952*. Dublin: Four Courts.

Cousins, M. (2005) *Explaining the Irish Welfare State: An Historical, Comparative and Political Analysis*. Lewiston: Edwin Mellen Press.

Cowan, P. (1960) *Dungeons Deep: A Monograph on Prisons, Borstals, Reformatories, and Industrial Schools, in the Republic of Ireland and some Reflections on Crime and Punishment and Matters Relating Thereto*. Dublin: Marian Printing.

CPT (2006) *Report to the Government of Ireland*. Strasbourg: Committee for the Prevention of Torture, Council of Europe.

CSW (1983) *The Prison System*. Dublin: Council for Social Welfare.

Culp, R. F. (2005) 'The rise and stall of prison privatization: an integration of policy analysis perspectives', *Criminal Justice Policy Review*, 16(4): 412–42.

Curry, J. (2003) *Irish Social Services*, 4th edn. Dublin: Institute of Public Administration.

Daly, S. (2007) 'Mapping civil society in the Republic of Ireland', *Community Development Journal*, 43(2): 157–76.

De Búrca, M. (2000) *The GAA: A History*, 2nd edn. Dublin: Gill and Macmillan.

Dooney, S. (1976) *The Irish Civil Service*. Dublin: Institute of Public Administration.

Downes, D. and Morgan, R. (2007) 'No turning back: the politics of law and order in the new millennium', in M. Maguire, R. Morgan and R. Reiner (eds) *The Oxford Handbook of Criminology*, 4th edn. Oxford: Oxford University Press.

Dunphy, R. (1995) *The Making of Fianna Fáil Power in Ireland, 1923–1948*. Oxford: Clarendon Press.

Durkheim, E. (1997) *The Division of Labor in Society*, 2nd edn. New York: Free Press.

Dwyer, T. R. (2005) *Haughey's Forty Years of Controversy*, 2nd edn. Cork: Mercier Press.

Elias, N. and Jephcott, E. (1994) *The Civilizing Process*. Oxford: Blackwell.

English, R. (1994) *Radicals and the Republic: Socialist Republicanism in the Irish Free State, 1925–1937*. Oxford: Clarendon Press.

English, R. (2006) *Irish Freedom: The History of Nationalism in Ireland*. London: Macmillan.

Fahy, E. (1940) 'The Prisons', *The Bell*, 1(2): 18.

Fairchild, E., Webb, V. J. and Sciences Academy of Criminal Justice (1985) *The Politics of Crime and Criminal Justice*. Beverly Hills: Sage.

Fanning, B. (2003) 'The construction of Irish social policy', in B. Fanning and T. McNamara (eds) *Ireland Develops: Administration and Social Policy, 1953–2003*. Dublin: Institute of Public Administration.

Fanning, R. (1978) *The Irish Department of Finance, 1922–58*. Dublin: Institute of Public Administration.

Fanning, R. (1983) *Independent Ireland*. Dublin: Helicon.

Farrell, B. (1970) 'Labour and the Irish political party system: a suggested approach to analysis', *Economic and Social Review*, 1(4): 477–502.

Farrell, B. (1971) *Chairman or Chief? The Role of Taoiseach in Irish Government*. Dublin: Gill and Macmillan.

Farrell, B. (1986) 'Politics and change', in K. A. Kennedy (ed.) *Ireland in Transition*. Cork: Mercier Press.

Feilzer, M.Y. (2007) 'Criminologists making news? Providing factual information on crime and criminal justice through a weekly newspaper column', *Crime, Media, Culture*, 3(3): 285–304.

Ferriter, D. (2004) *The Transformation of Ireland, 1900–2000*. London: Profile.

Finance, Department of (1958) *Programme for Economic Expansion*. Dublin: Stationery Office.

Finlay, I. (1966) *The Civil Service*. Dublin: Institute of Public Administration.

Foster, R. F. (1990) *Modern Ireland 1600–1972*. London: Penguin.

Foster, R. F. (2007) *Luck and the Irish: A Brief History of Change, 1970–2000*. London: Allen Lane.

Foucault, M. (1977) *Discipline and Punish: The Birth of the Prison*. London: Penguin.

Gallagher, M. (1982) *The Irish Labour Party in Transition: 1957–82*. Manchester: Manchester University Press.

Gallagher, M. (2004) 'Parliament', in J. Coakley and M. Gallagher (eds) *Politics in the Republic of Ireland*, 4th edn. London: Routledge in association with PSAI Press.

Garland, D. (1985) *Punishment and Welfare: A History of Penal Strategies*. Aldershot: Gower.

Garland, D. (1990) *Punishment and Modern Society*. Oxford: Oxford University Press.

Garland, D. (2001) *The Culture of Control: Crime and Social Order in Late Modernity*. Oxford: Oxford University Press.

Garland, D. (2002) 'The cultural uses of capital punishment', *Punishment and Society*, 4(4): 459–88.

Garland, D. (2005a) 'Capital punishment and American culture', *Punishment and Society*, 7(4): 347–76.

Garland, D. (2005b) 'Penal excess and surplus meaning: public torture lynchings in 20th century America', *Law and Society Review*, 19(4): 793–834.

Garland, D. (2006) 'Concepts of culture in the sociology of punishment', *Theoretical Criminology*, 10(4): 419–47.

Garvin, T. (1996) *1922: The Birth of Irish Democracy*. Dublin: Gill and Macmillan.

Girvin, B. (2003) 'The Republicanisation of Irish society: 1932–1948', in J. R. Hill (ed.) *A New History of Ireland, Vol. VII: Ireland, 1921–84*. Oxford: Oxford University Press.

Girvin, B. (2006) *The Emergency: Neutral Ireland, 1939–45*. London: Macmillan.

Girvin, B. and Murray, J. (2005) *The Lemass Era: Politics and Society in the Ireland of Seán Lemass*. Dublin: University College Dublin Press.

Girvin, B. and Roberts, G. (eds) (2000) *Ireland and the Second World War: Politics, Society and Remembrance*. Dublin: Four Courts Press.

Goold, B. J. (2004) *CCTV and Policing: Public Area Surveillance and Police Practices in Britain*. Oxford: Oxford University Press.

Green, D. A. (2006) 'Public opinion versus public judgment about crime: correcting the "comedy of errors"', *British Journal of Criminology*, 46: 131–54.

Greenberg, D. F. (2001) 'Novus ordo saeclorum? A commentary on Downes and Beckett and Western', in D. W. Garland (ed.) *Mass Imprisonment: Social Causes and Consequences*. London: Sage.

Groombridge, N. (2007) 'Criminologists say …: an analysis of UK national press coverage of criminology and criminologists and a contribution to the debate on "public criminology"', *Howard Journal of Criminal Justice*, 46(5): 459–75.

Hamilton, C. (2007) *The Presumption of Innocence in Irish Criminal Law: 'Whittling the Golden Thread'*. Dublin: Irish Academic Press.

Haughton, J. (2008) 'Historical background', in J. W. O'Hagan and C. Newman (eds) *The Economy of Ireland*, 8th edn. Dublin: Gill and Macmillan.

Healy, J. (1968) *The Death of an Irish Town*. Cork: Mercier Press.

Healy, J. (1978) *Nineteen Acres*. Galway: Kennys.

Hillyard, P. A. R. (1971) 'The use of judges to chair social enquiries', *Irish Jurist*, 6: 93–100.

Hogan, G. (2007) *Final Report: Balance in the Criminal Law Review Group*. Dublin: Stationery Office.

Home Office (1959) *Penal Practice in a Changing Society: Aspects of Future Development*. London: HMSO.

Hood, R. (1987) 'Some reflections on the role of criminology in public policy', *Criminal Law Review*: 527.

Hood, R., Zedner, L. and Ashworth, A. (eds) (2003) *The Criminological Foundations of Penal Policy: Essays in Honour of Roger Hood*. Oxford: Oxford University Press.

Hopkinson, M. (2003) 'Civil War and aftermath 1922–24', in J. R. Hill (ed.) *A New History of Ireland, Vol. VII: Ireland, 1921–84*. Oxford: Oxford University Press.

Horgan, J. (1997) *Seán Lemass: The Modern Patriot*. Dublin: Gill and Macmillan.

Horgan, J. (2004) *Broadcasting and Public Life: RTÉ News and Current Affairs, 1926–1997*. Dublin: Four Courts.

Hyland, A. (1997) 'Primary and second level education in the early twenty first century', in F. Ó Muircheartaigh (ed.) *Ireland in the Coming Times: Essays to Celebrate T. K. Whitaker's 80 Years*. Dublin: Institute of Public Administration.

ICJP (1986) *Response to the Report of the Committee Inquiry into the Penal System*. Dublin: Irish Commission for Justice and Peace.

IPRT (2010) *Irish Penal Reform Trust Portal – http://www.iprt.ie*. Dublin: Irish Penal Reform Trust.

Ismaili, K. (2006) 'Contextualising the criminal justice policy-making process', *Criminal Justice Policy Review*, 17(3): 255–69.

Jenkins, R. (1975) 'On being a cabinet minister', in V. Herman and J. E. Alt (eds) *Cabinet Studies: A Reader*. London: Macmillan.

Jewkes, Y. (2007) 'Prisons and the media: the shaping of public opinion and penal policy in a mediated society', in Y. Jewkes (ed.) *Handbook on Prisons*. Cullompton: Willan Publishing.

Jones, T. and Newburn, T. (2002) 'Policy convergence and crime control in the USA and UK: streams of influence and levels of impact', *Criminology and Criminal Justice*, 2: 173–203.

Jones, T. and Newburn, T. (2004) 'The convergence of US and UK crime control policy: exploring substance and process', in T. Newburn and R. Sparks (eds) *Criminal Justice and Political Cultures: National and International Dimensions of Crime Control*. Cullompton: Willan Publishing.

Jones, T. and Newburn, T. (2005a) 'Comparative criminal justice policy-making in the United States and the United Kingdom', *British Journal of Criminology*, 45: 58–80.

Jones, T. and Newburn, T. (2005b) 'Symbolic politics and penal populism: the long shadow of Willie Horton', *Crime, Media, Culture*, 1(1): 172–87.

Jones, T. and Newburn, T. (2006) 'Three strikes and you're out: exploring symbol and substance in American and British crime control politics', *British Journal of Criminology*, 46(5): 781–802.

Jones, T. and Newburn, T. (2007) *Policy Transfer and Criminal Justice: Exploring US Influence over British Crime Control Policy*. Maidenhead: Open University Press.

Jordan, A. J. (1993) *Sean MacBride: A Biography. Dublin: Blackwater Press*.

Justice, Department of (1980) *Summary of Report Prepared by the Irish National Council on Alcoholism on the Prevalence and Treatment of Problem Drinkers among Prisoners*. Dublin: Department of Justice.

Justice, Department of (1994) *The Management of Offenders: A Five Year Plan*. Dublin: Stationery Office.

Kelly, J.M. (1980) *The Irish Constitution*. Dublin: Jurist.

Kennedy, F. (1975) *Public Social Expenditure in Ireland*. Dublin: Economic and Social Research Institute.

Kennedy, F. (1997) 'The course of the Irish welfare state', in F. Ó Muircheartaigh (ed.) *Ireland in the Coming Times: Essays to Celebrate T. K. Whitaker's 80 Years*. Dublin: Institute of Public Administration.

Kennedy, K. A. (1986) *Ireland in Transition*. Cork: Mercier Press.

Kennedy, K. A., Giblin, T. and McHugh, D. (1988) *The Economic Development of Ireland in the Twentieth Century*. London: Routledge.

Keogh, D. (Dáire) (2004) 'There's no such thing as a bad boy: Fr Flanagan's visit to Ireland, 1946', *History Ireland*, 12(1): 29.

Keogh, D. (Dermot) (2003) 'Ireland 1972–84', in J. R. Hill (ed.) *A New History of Ireland, Vol. VII: Ireland, 1921–84*. Oxford: Oxford University Press.

Keogh, D. (2005) *Twentieth Century Ireland: Revolution and State Building*. Dublin: Gill and Macmillan.

Keogh, D., O'Shea, F. and Quinlan, C. (2004) *The Lost Decade: Ireland in the 1950s*. Cork: Mercier Press.

Kilcommins, S. *et al.* (2004) *Crime, Punishment and the Search for Order in Ireland.* Dublin: Institute of Public Administration.

King, J. and Jarvis, F. (1977) 'The influence of the probation and after-care service', in N. D. Walker and H. Giller (eds) *Penal Policy-making in England: Papers Presented to the Cropwood Round-Table Conference.* Cambridge: University of Cambridge, Institute of Criminology.

Kingdon, J. W. (1995) *Agendas, Alternatives, and Public Policies,* 2nd edn. New York: HarperCollins.

Labour Party (1946) *Prisons and Prisoners in Ireland: Report on Certain Aspects of Prison Conditions in Portlaoighise Prison.* Dublin: The Labour Party.

Lalor, S. (1996) 'Planning and the Civil Service 1945–1970', *Administration,* 43(4): 57–75.

Lalor, S. (2003) 'Planning and the Civil Service', in B. Fanning and T. McNamara (eds) *Ireland Develops: Administration and Social Policy, 1953–2003.* Dublin: Institute of Public Administration.

Lee, J. (1979) 'Continuity and change in Ireland 1945–70', in J. Lee (ed.) *Ireland 1945–70.* Dublin: Gill and Macmillan.

Lee, J. (1986) 'Whither Ireland? The next twenty five years!', in K. A. Kennedy (ed.) *Ireland in Transition.* Cork: Mercier Press.

Lee, J. (1989) *Ireland, 1912–1985: Politics and Society.* Cambridge: Cambridge University Press.

Lewis, D. (1997) *Hidden Agendas: Politics, Law and Disorder.* London: Hamish Hamilton.

Loader, I. (2006) 'Fall of the "Platonic Guardians" Liberalism, Criminology and Political Responses to Crime in England and Wales', *British Journal of Criminology,* 46(4): 561–586.

Loader, I. and Sparks, R. (2004) 'For an historical sociology of crime policy in England and Wales since 1968', *Critical Review of International Social and Political Philosophy,* 7: 5–32.

Longford, F. P. (Earl) and O'Neill, T. P. (1974) *Eamon de Valera.* London: Arrow.

Lyons, F. S. L. (1973) *Ireland Since the Famine.* London: Fontana.

MacBride, S. (2005) *That Day's Struggle: A Memoir, 1904–1951.* Dublin: Currach Press.

MacEoin, U. (1987) *Survivors,* 2nd edn. Dublin: Argenta.

MacSwiney-Brugha, M. (2006) *History's Daughter: A Memoir from the Only Child of Terence MacSwiney.* Dublin: O'Brien Press.

Maguire, J. (2008) *IRA Internments and the Irish Government: Subversives and the State, 1939–1962.* Dublin: Irish Academic Press.

Mahon-Smith, W. (1945) *I Did Penal Servitude.* Dublin: Metropolitan Publishing.

Mair, P. (1990) 'The Irish party system into the 1990s', in M. Gallagher and R. Sinnott (eds) *How Ireland Voted 1989.* Galway: Centre for the Study of Irish Elections, University College Galway.

Mair, P. and Weeks, L. (2004) 'The Irish party system', in J. Coakley and M. Gallagher (eds) *Politics in the Republic of Ireland,* 4th edn. London: Routledge in association with PSAI Press.

Manning, M. (1999) *James Dillon: A Biography.* Dublin: Wolfhound Press.

Manning, M. (2006) *The Blueshirts,* 3rd edn. Dublin: Gill and Macmillan.

Mansergh, M. (1985) *The Spirit of the Nation: The Speeches of Charles J. Haughey.* Cork: Mercier Press.

Marion, N. E. (2002) 'Symbolic politics in Clinton's crime control agenda', in B. A. Stolz (ed.) *Criminal Justice Policy Making: Federal Roles and Processes.* Connecticut: Praeger.

Marsh, M. and Sinnott, R. (1999) 'The behaviour of the Irish voter', in M. Marsh and P. Mitchell (eds) *How Ireland Voted 1997.* Oxford: Westview Press.

Mathiesen, T. (2000) *Prison on Trial,* 2nd edn. Winchester: Waterside.

McCarthy, C. (1973) *The Decade of Upheaval: Irish Trade Unions in the Nineteen Sixties.* Dublin: Institute of Public Administration.

McCashin, A. (2004) *Social Security in Ireland.* Dublin: Gill and Macmillan.

McConville, S. (2005) *Irish Political Prisoners, 1848–1922: Theatres of War*. London: Routledge.

McCoole, S. (1997) *Guns and Chiffon: Women Revolutionaries and Kilmainham Gaol 1916–1923*. Dublin: Stationery Office.

McCoole, S. (2003) *No Ordinary Women: Activists in the Revolutionary Years*. Dublin: O'Brien Press.

McCormack, W. J. (1999) *The Blackwell Companion to Modern Irish Culture*. Oxford: Blackwell.

McCullagh, C. (1988) 'A crisis in the penal system? The case of the Republic of Ireland', in M. Tomlinson, T. Varley and C. McCullagh (eds) *Whose Law and Order? Aspects of Crime and Social Control in Irish Society*. Dublin: Sociological Association of Ireland.

McCullagh, D. (1998) *A Makeshift Majority: The First Inter-Party Government, 1948–51*. Dublin: Institute of Public Administration.

McEvoy, K. (2001) *Paramilitary Imprisonment in Northern Ireland: Resistance, Management and Release*. Oxford: Oxford University Press.

McGowan, J. (1980) 'The role of the prison officer in the Irish Prison Service', *Administration*, 28(3): 259.

McVerry, P. (2002) 'Juvenile crime re-visited', *Studies in History*, 43.

Meenan, J. F. (1970) *The Irish Economy Since 1922*. Liverpool: Liverpool University Press.

Melossi, D. (1981) *Prison and the Factory: Origins of the Penitentiary System*. London: Macmillan.

Moloney, E. (2007) *A Secret History of the IRA*, 2nd edn. London: Penguin.

Morgan, R. (2006) 'With respect to order, the rules of the game have changed: New Labour's dominance of the "Law and Order" agenda', in T. Newburn, P. E. Rock and D. M. Downes (eds) *The Politics of Crime Control: Essays in Honour of David Downes*. Oxford: Oxford University Press.

Moriarty, M. (1977) 'The policy-making process: how it is seen from the Home Office', in N. D. Walker and H. Giller (eds) *Penal Policy-making in England: Papers Presented to the Cropwood Round-Table Conference*. Cambridge: University of Cambridge, Institute of Criminology.

Mulcahy, A. (2002) 'The impact of the Northern "Troubles" on criminal justice in the Irish republic', in P. O'Mahony (ed.) *Criminal Justice in Ireland*. Dublin: Institute of Public Administration.

Murphy, G. (2010) 'Interest groups in the policy-making process', in J. Coakley and M. Gallagher (eds) *Politics in the Republic of Ireland*, 5th edn. Oxford: Routledge.

Murphy, J. A. (1979) 'Put them out! Parties and Elections 1948–1969', in J. Lee (ed.) *Ireland 1945–70*. Dublin: Gill and Macmillan.

NESC (2005) *The Developmental Welfare State*. Dublin: National Economic and Social Council.

Newburn, T. (2003) *Crime and Criminal Justice Policy*. Harlow: Longman.

Ní Chuilleanáin, E. (2001) *'As I Was Among the Captives': Joseph Campbell's Prison Diary, 1922–1923*. Cork: Cork University Press.

Nolan, S. (1984) 'Economic growth', in J. W. O'Hagan (ed.) *The Economy of Ireland: Policy and Performance*, 4th edn. Dublin: Irish Management Institute.

Ó Drisceoil, D. (1996) *Censorship in Ireland, 1939–1945: Neutrality, Politics and Society*. Cork: Cork University Press.

Ó Drisceoil, D. (2001) *Peadar O'Donnell*. Cork: Cork University Press.

Ó Gráda, C. (1995) *Ireland: A New Economic History, 1780–1939*. Oxford: Clarendon Press.

Ó Gráda, C. (1997) *A Rocky Road: The Irish Economy Since the 1920s*. Manchester: Manchester University Press

Ó Longaigh, S. (2006) *Emergency Law in Independent Ireland, 1922–1948*. Dublin: Four Courts Press.

O'Brien, G. (1990) *The Village of Longing and Dancehall Days*. Harmondsworth: Penguin.

O'Brien, J. (2000) *The Arms Trial*. Dublin: Gill and Macmillan.

O'Brien, J. (2002) *The Modern Prince: Charles J. Haughey and the Quest for Power*. Dublin: Merlin.

O'Brien, M. (2007) 'Selling fear? The changing face of crime reporting in Ireland', in J. Horgan, B. O'Connor and H. Sheehan (eds) *Mapping Irish Media: Critical Explorations*. Dublin: University College Dublin Press.

O'Connell, P. and Rottman, D. (1992) 'The Irish welfare state in comparative perspective', in J. H. Goldthorpe and C. T. Whelan (eds) *The Development of Industrial Society in Ireland*. Oxford: Oxford University Press.

O'Connor, F. (2005) *An Only Child and My Father's Son: An Autobiography*. London: Penguin.

O'Donnell, C. (2007) *Fianna Fáil, Irish Republicanism and the Northern Ireland Troubles, 1968–2005*. Dublin: Irish Academic Press.

O'Donnell, I. (2004a) 'Imprisonment and penal policy in Ireland', *Howard Journal of Criminal Justice*, 43(3): 253.

O'Donnell, I. (2004b) 'Interpreting penal change', *Criminal Justice*, 4(2): 199–206.

O'Donnell, I. (2005) 'Crime and justice in the Republic of Ireland', *European Journal of Criminology*, 2(1): 99.

O'Donnell, I. (2008) 'Stagnation and change in Irish penal policy', *Howard Journal of Criminal Justice*, 47(2): 121–33.

O'Donnell, I. and O'Sullivan, E. (2001) *Crime Control in Ireland: The Politics of Intolerance*. Cork: Cork University Press.

O'Donnell, I. and O'Sullivan, E. (2003) 'The politics of intolerance – Irish style', *British Journal of Criminology*, 3(1): 41–62.

O'Donnell, I., Baumer, E. P. and Hughes, N. (2008) 'Recidivism in the Republic of Ireland', *Criminology and Criminal Justice*, 8(2): 123–46.

O'Donnell, P. (1965) *The Gates Flew Open*. Cork: Mercier Press.

O'Flynn, M. (1971) 'Prisoner after-care in the Irish Republic', *Irish Jurist*, 7: 1–17.

O'Halpin, E. (1999a) *Defending Ireland: The Irish State and its Enemies since 1922*. Oxford: Oxford University Press.

O'Halpin, E. (1999b) 'Policy-making', in J. Coakley and M. Gallagher (eds) *Politics in the Republic of Ireland*, 4th edn. London: Routledge.

O'Halpin, E. (2003) 'Politics and the State 1922–32', in J. R. Hill (ed.) *A New History of Ireland, Vol. VII: Ireland, 1921–84*. Oxford: Oxford University Press.

O'Hearn, D. (2003) 'Macroeconomic policy in the Celtic Tiger: a critical reassessment', in C. Coulter and S. Coleman (eds) *The End of Irish History? Critical Approaches to the Celtic Tiger*. Manchester: Manchester University Press.

O'Mahony, P. (1997) *Mountjoy Prisoners: A Sociological and Criminological Profile*. Dublin: Stationery Office.

O'Malley, E. (1978) *The Singing Flame*. Dublin: Anvil Books.

O'Malley, T. (2006) *Sentencing Law and Practice*, 2nd edn. Dublin: Thomson Round Hall.

O'Sullivan, E. and O'Donnell, I. (2007) 'Coercive confinement in the Republic of Ireland', *Punishment and Society*, 9(1): 27–48.

Oliver, W. M. and Marion, N. E. (2006) 'Budgets, institutions, and change: criminal justice policy in America: revisited', *Criminal Justice Policy Review*, 17(4): 451–67.

Osborne, R. D. (1996) *Higher Education in Ireland: North and South*. London: Jessica Kingsley.

Osborough, W. N. (1985) 'An outline history of the penal system in Ireland', in *Report of the Committee of Inquiry into the Penal System*. Dublin: Stationery Office.

Patterson, H. (1997) *The Politics of Illusion: A Political History of the IRA*. London: Serif.

Patterson, H. (2006) *Ireland since 1939: The Persistence of Conflict*. Dublin: Penguin.

Prison Study Group (1973) *An Examination of the Irish Penal System*. Dublin: Prison Study Group.

Puirséil, N. (2005) 'Political and party competition in post-war Ireland', in B. Girvin and J. Murray (eds) *The Lemass Era: Politics and Society in the Ireland of Seán Lemass*. Dublin: University College Dublin Press.

Puirséil, N. (2007) *The Irish Labour Party 1922–73*. Dublin: University College Dublin Press.

Quinlan, C. (2003) 'The women we imprison', *Irish Criminal Law Journal*, 13(1): 2–10.

Radzinowicz, Sir L. (1965) *The Need for Criminology and a Proposal for an Institute of Criminology*. London: Heinemann.

Radzinowicz, Sir L. (1999) *Adventures in Criminology*. London: Routledge.

Radzinowicz, Sir L. and Hood, R. (1979) 'The status of political prisoners in England: the struggle for recognition', *Virginia Law Review*, 65(8): 1421–81.

Rafter, K. (1996) *The Clann: The Story of Clann na Poblachta*. Cork: Mercier Press.

Robins, J. (1960) 'The Irish hospital: an outline of its origins and development', *Administration*, 2(8): 146–65.

Rock, P. (1995) 'The opening stages of criminal justice policy-making', *British Journal of Criminology*, 35: 1–16.

Rogan, M. (2009a) 'Prison policy in Ireland: a historical overview', *Prison Service Journal*, 186 (November): 3–13.

Rogan, M. (2009b) 'Visiting committees and accountability in the Irish prison system: some proposals for reform', *Dublin University Law Journal*, 31: 298–323.

Rottman, D. (1980) *Crime in the Republic of Ireland: Statistical Trends and their Interpretation*. Dublin: Economic and Social Research Institute.

Rottman, D. (1986) 'Crime and the criminal justice system', in K. A. Kennedy (ed.) *Ireland in Transition*. Cork: Mercier Press.

Rottman, D. and O'Connell, P. (1982) 'The changing social structure', *Administration*, 30: 63–88.

Rusche, G. and Kirchheimer, O. (1968) *Punishment and Social Structure*. New York: Russell and Russell.

Ruth, H. S. and Reitz, K. R. (2003) *The Challenge of Crime: Rethinking our Response*. Cambridge, MA: Harvard University Press.

Rutherford, A. (1996) *Transforming Criminal Policy: Spheres of Influence in the United States, the Netherlands and England and Wales during the 1980s*. Winchester: Waterside Press.

Ryan, M. (1978) *The Acceptable Pressure Group: Inequality in the Penal Lobby: A Case Study of the Howard League and RAP*. Farnborough: Saxon House.

Ryan, M. (1983) *The Politics of Penal Reform*. London: Longman.

Ryan, M. (1996) *Lobbying from Below: INQUEST in Defence of Civil Liberties*. London: University College London Press.

Ryan, M. (2003) *Penal Policy and Political Culture in England and Wales*. Winchester: Waterside Press.

Ryan, M. (2007) 'Book review: *Penal Populism*, John Pratt', *Punishment and Society*, 9(4): 437–9.

Sexton, J. (1986) 'Employment, unemployment and emigration', in K.A. Kennedy (ed.) *Ireland in Transition: Economic and Social Change since 1960*, Cork: Mercier.

Sexton, J. (2003) 'Emigration and immigration in the twentieth century: an overview', in J. R. Hill (ed.) *A New History of Ireland, Vol. VII: Ireland, 1921–84*. Oxford: Oxford University Press.

Sheehan, J. (1979) 'Education and society in Ireland 1945–70', in J. Lee (ed.) *Ireland 1945–70*. Dublin: Gill and Macmillan.

Skehill, C. (2003) 'Social in the Republic of Ireland: a history of the present', *Journal of Social Work*, 3(2): 141–59.

Solomon, P. (1981) 'The policy process in Canadian criminal justice: a perspective and research agenda', *Canadian Journal of Criminology*, 23: 5–25.

Spierenburg, P. (1984) *The Spectacle of Suffering*. Cambridge: Cambridge University Press.

Stolz, B. A. (2002) 'The roles of interest groups in US criminal justice policy making: who, when and how', *Criminology and Criminal Justice*, 2: 51–69.

Sweeney, G. (1993) 'Irish hunger strikes and the cult of self-sacrifice', *Journal of Contemporary History*, 28(3): 421–37.

Thomas, J. E. (1977) 'The influence of the prison service', in N. D. Walker and H. Giller (eds) *Penal Policy-making in England: Papers Presented to the Cropwood Round-Table Conference*. Cambridge: University of Cambridge, Institute of Criminology.

Timonen, V. (2002) *Irish Social Expenditure in a Comparative International Context*. Dublin: Institute of Public Administration and Combat Poverty Agency.

Tobin, F. (1984) *The Best of Decades: Ireland in the Nineteen Sixties*. Dublin: Gill and Macmillan.

Toch, H. (1994) 'Catering to the public: prison policy in the nineties', in A. Duff (ed.) *Penal Theory and Practice: Tradition and Innovation in Criminal Justice*. Manchester: Manchester University Press in association with the Fulbright Commission, London.

Tomlinson, M. (1995) 'Imprisoned Ireland', in M. Ryan, J. Sim and V. Ruggiero (eds) *Western European Penal Systems: A Critical Anatomy*. London: Sage.

Tonry, M. (2001a) 'Symbol, substance, and severity in western penal policies', *Punishment and Society*, 3(4): 517–36.

Tonry, M. (2001b) 'Unthought thoughts', *Punishment and Society*, 3(1): 167–81.

Tonry, M. (2004) *Thinking about Crime: Sense and Sensibility in American Penal Culture*. Oxford: Oxford University Press.

Tonry, M. (2007) *Crime, Punishment and Politics in a Comparative Perspective*. Chicago: University of Chicago Press.

Tovey, H. and Share, P. (2003) *A Sociology of Ireland*, 2nd edn. Dublin: Gill and Macmillan.

Walsh, B. (1979) 'Economic growth and development 1945–1970', in J. Lee (ed.) *Ireland 1945–70*. Dublin: Gill and Macmillan.

Walsh, B. (1986) 'The growth of government', in K. A. Kennedy (ed.) *Ireland in Transition*. Cork: Mercier Press.

Walsh, D. P. J. (1998) *The Irish Police: A Legal and Constitutional Perspective*. Dublin: Round Hall Sweet and Maxwell.

Ward, M. (1983) *Unmanageable Revolutionaries: Women and Irish Nationalism*. Dingle: Brandon Books.

Ward, M. (1997) *Hanna Sheehy Skeffington: A Life*. Dublin: Attic Press.

Waters, J. (1991) *Jiving at the Crossroads*. Belfast: Blackstaff Press.

Whelan, C. T., Breen, R. and Whelan, B. J. (1992) 'Industrialisation, class formation and social mobility in Ireland', in J. H. Goldthorpe and C. T. Whelan (eds) *The Development of Industrial Society in Ireland*. Oxford: Oxford University Press.

Whitaker, T. K. (1986) 'Economic development 1958–1985', in K. A. Kennedy (ed.) *Ireland in Transition*. Cork: Mercier Press.

Whitaker, T. K. (2007) 'Foreword', in IPRT (ed.) *The Whitaker Committee Report 20 Years: Lessons Learned or Lessons Forgotten*. Dublin: The Katherine Howard Foundation.

White, R. W. (2006) *Ruairí Ó Brádaigh: The Life and Politics of an Irish Revolutionary*. Bloomington: Indiana University Press.

White, T. (2001) *Investing in People: Higher Education in Ireland from 1960 to 2000*. Dublin: Institute of Public Administration.

Whyte, J. H. (1974) 'Ireland: politics without social bases', in R. Rose (ed.) *Electoral Behavior: A Comparative Handbook*. New York: Free Press.

Whyte, J. H. (1980) *Church and State in Modern Ireland, 1923–1970*. Dublin: Gill and Macmillan.

Whyte, J. H. (2003a) 'Economic crisis and political Cold War, 1949–57', in J. R. Hill (ed.) *A New History of Ireland, Vol. VII: Ireland, 1921–84*. Oxford: Oxford University Press.

Whyte, J. H. (2003b) 'Reconciliation, rights and protests 1963–71', in J. R. Hill (ed.) *A New History of Ireland, Vol. VII: Ireland, 1921–84*. Oxford: Oxford University Press.

Whyte, J. H. (2003c) 'The North erupts, and Ireland enters Europe', in J. R. Hill (ed.) *A New History of Ireland, Vol. VII: Ireland, 1921–84*. Oxford: Oxford University Press.

Wills, C. (2007) *That Neutral Island: A Cultural History of Ireland during the Second World War*. London: Faber.

Wilson, D. (2001) 'Networking and the lobby for penal reform: conflict and consensus', in M. Ryan, S. P. Savage and D. Wall (eds) *Policy Networks in Criminal Justice*. Basingstoke: Palgrave.

Windlesham, D. J. G. H. (Baron) (1987) *Responses to Crime*. Oxford: Oxford University Press.

Windlesham, D. J. G. H. (Baron) (1993) *Responses to Crime*. Oxford: Oxford University Press.

Windlesham, D. J. G. H. (Baron) (1996) *Responses to Crime*. Oxford: Oxford University Press.

Windlesham, D. J. G. H. (Baron) (2001) *Responses to Crime*. Oxford: Oxford University Press.

Wynne, S. (2001) 'Education and security – when the twain do meet!', *Journal of Community Education*, 52(1): 39–43.

Young, J. (2002a) 'A critical criminology for the twenty first century', in K. Carrington and R. Hogg (eds) *Critical Criminology: Issues, Debates, Challenges*. Cullompton: Willan Publishing.

Young, J. (2002b) 'Searching for a new criminology of everyday life: a review of "The Culture of Control"', *British Journal of Criminology*, 42: 228–61.

Zedner, L. H. (2002) 'Dangers of dystopias in penal theory', *Oxford Journal of Legal Studies*, 22(2): 341–66.

Zedner, L. H. (2003) 'Useful knowledge', in R. G. Hood, L. Zedner and A. Ashworth (eds) *The Criminological Foundations of Penal Policy: Essays in Honour of Roger Hood*. Oxford: Oxford University Press.

Zedner, L. H. (2004) *Criminal Justice*. Oxford: Oxford University Press.

INDEX